Teaching Kids to Be
Confident, Effective Communicators

Differentiated Projects to Get All Students Writing, Speaking, and Presenting

Phil Schlemmer, M.Ed., & Dori Schlemmer

free spirit
PUBLISHING®

Copyright © 2011 by Phil Schlemmer, M.Ed.

Teaching Kids to Be Confident, Effective Communicators: Differentiated Projects to Get All Students Writing, Speaking, and Presenting was originally published in 2009 as *Projects & Presentations for K–6 Students: Preparing Kids to Be Confident, Effective Communicators.*

Library of Congress Cataloging-in-Publication Data
Schlemmer, Phil.
  Teaching kids to be confident, effective communicators : differentiated projects to get all students writing, speaking, and presenting / Phil Schlemmer, Dori Schlemmer.
    p. cm.
  ISBN-13: 978-1-57542-371-5
  ISBN-10: 1-57542-371-5
  1. Literacy—Study and teaching (Elementary) 2. Language arts (Preschool) 3. Language arts (Elementary) 4. Language arts (Early childhood) 5. Children—Language. 6. Child development. I. Schlemmer, Dori. II. Title.
  LB1576.S3254 2001
  372.6'044—dc22   2011000125

eBook ISBN: 978-1-57542-705-8

The teachers and students described in examples are composites based on the authors' experience. The names used do not refer to real people.

Some of the information about differentiated instruction in Part 1, pages 10–20, is based on material in *Teaching Beyond the Test: Differentiated Project-Based Learning in a Standards-Based Age* by Phil Schlemmer, M.Ed., and Dori Schlemmer (Minneapolis: Free Spirit Publishing, 2008) and is adapted with permission of the publisher.

Edited by Eric Braun and Marjorie Lisovskis
Cover and interior design by Michelle Lee
Some cover/interior icons © istockphoto.com/NLshop; all other cover/interior icons by Michelle Lee
Cover photos: left and middle: © 2009 Jupiterimages Corporation; right: © Image99/Corbis
Illustrations on p. 88 by Paul Agner
BIP font © Maciej Ostanski

10 9 8 7 6 5 4 3 2 1
Printed in the United States of America

Free Spirit Publishing Inc.
217 Fifth Avenue North, Suite 200
Minneapolis, MN 55401-1299
(612) 338-2068
help4kids@freespirit.com
www.freespirit.com

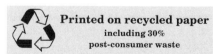

Printed on recycled paper
including 30%
post-consumer waste

Dedication

To the millions of kids across America who are trusting
the adults in their lives to prepare them for
a demanding, unpredictable world, and to the
teachers who work to fulfill that trust.

Acknowledgments

Thank you to the many students and educators
who have provided valuable input over the years as
these materials were developed. Their insights,
discoveries, and affirmations were helpful in designing
openings projects that work on many levels.

Contents

Part 1: Differentiation, Social-Emotional Learning, and Content Standards for Openings

Part 2: First Steps: Starter Openings

Part 3: The Openings

Forms for Extending Openings *(bonus material included on CD-ROM only)*

Poster Templates *(bonus material included on CD-ROM only)*

List of Reproducible Pages

Additional Handouts

Student Preparation Materials

Assessment Materials

Audience Feedback Materials

Teacher Tools

Bonus Material Included on CD-ROM Only

Forms for Extending Openings

Openings Student Contract (Middle Elementary)

Openings Student Contract (Upper Elementary)

Tips for a Successful Opening

Featured Opening Article (text & graphic)

Featured Opening Article (text only)

Featured Opening Article (graphic only)

My Favorite Opening Fact

On-the-Job Communication

Word Power

Skills for Life

Poster Templates

Poster Basics

Poster Design 1

Poster Design 2

List of Figures

Preface

What Is an Opening Presentation?

by Phil Schlemmer

The scene unfolded as if in slow motion. The teacher saw what was coming but it was beyond his control. The football hit the ground, bounced, and flipped end over end directly toward its inevitable target. Allen, a sixth-grade student, stood frozen in place, a deer-in-the-headlights look of panic in his eyes, his hands dangling uselessly at his side. He was on the playground reluctantly, having been cajoled by his teacher to get out there and "give it a try," and now the ball was headed directly for the bull's-eye. He was not the least bit athletic and he had little self-confidence when it came to physical activity, preferring to hang out by himself during recess rather than face painful teasing about his lack of athletic prowess. The ball did in fact hit Allen squarely in the nose, resulting in hurt, embarrassment, tears, and flight.

It was the fall of 1973, the teacher's first year on the job. Operating on instinct in the absence of experience, he followed Allen to his refuge on the empty bleachers. There, he accepted full blame for talking Allen into becoming an unwilling football magnet. Then the teacher listened as, through tears and sobs, Allen unloaded his insecurities and feelings of ineptness. As the teacher took in all of Allen's burden, an idea began to germinate. Knowing that Allen had a goal of being a veterinarian and was actively becoming a self-motivated expert on animals, his teacher suggested that the boy pour his energy into developing a presentation on a topic of his choice related to animals. He could make the presentation to his classmates as a way of educating them about something they knew little about. Allen would be the expert and he would teach his peers. The tears subsided. The sobs diminished to sporadic hiccups. Allen liked the idea.

One morning a couple weeks later, the teacher explained to the class that Allen was going to open the day by conducting a lesson about the gray wolves on Isle Royale in Lake Superior. Allen did a fine job, and at the conclusion of the presentation there was respectful applause. The applause (and the respect!) surprised Allen, and he was quite pleased. His self-confidence increased visibly and dramatically. Impressed by the potential of what Allen had done, and in a spontaneous flash of inspiration, the teacher announced a quickly improvised plan for everyone to do a presentation in the upcoming weeks. Because the presentations would be given first thing in the morning, to open *the day, they would be called* openings.

In this way a classroom tradition was born. The class continued doing openings for the rest of the year. As the fledgling openings program took root, the teacher began to see a real impact on his students. They were becoming engaged learners and confident presenters, and they were taking more responsibility for their own learning as they bought into the idea of being "resident experts." The young teacher experienced a lot of success with openings that year, and it didn't take long for the concept to become a permanent part of his instructional repertoire.

As you may have guessed, I was that novice teacher. Since that time in 1973, I have refined and developed the concept of openings and shared the idea with hundreds of teachers. Over the years, Dori and I saw openings successfully implemented with students of all ages, from kindergarten through college. That success led us to install openings at the heart of this book.

What do openings have to offer you and your students? We all know that the challenges you face in your classroom are far different and more intense than those of decades past. Every day you must navigate the demands of teaching a standards-based curriculum, preparing students for benchmark tests, and meeting the needs of a student body that is culturally, socio-economically, intellectually, and temperamentally diverse. In the midst of these many instructional pressures, your goal is to help your students succeed as confident, self-directed, lifelong learners. As they move through elementary school and on to middle and high school, their schoolwork will increasingly focus on rigorous differentiated learning that requires them to demonstrate understanding in a wide variety of ways. Openings provide a deceptively simple, yet effective and meaningful, approach to preparing students for these educational demands and rewards. They are a form of project-based learning in which even the youngest elementary students can engage. As students research topics and present what they have learned to their peers, they grow not only in knowledge but also in confidence, motivation, and responsibility.

If you are an early elementary teacher, you may have a classroom full of excited communicators who will talk anywhere at anytime with anyone about anything. As students get older, however, this situation tends to change, often dramatically, for many students. Enthusiasm and spontaneity evolve into discomfort, self-consciousness, and even panic for some.

This fear can keep students from full participation in active, project-based learning. It is unfortunate that many students are held back not by their lack of understanding, but by their perceived inability to effectively communicate what they know and can do. Why this aversion to making presentations? One big hurdle lies in the fact that kids generally do not understand that "presenting" is a skill that can be mastered right along with reading and writing. When students do not recognize oral communication as a skill, many end up thinking of it as an inherited trait, like being tall or having brown eyes: a person either is or isn't a good speaker, and that's just the natural order of things. As these students grow older, they typically become more self-conscious, more inhibited, more concerned with peer impressions, and consequently less confident. By the time they are in middle school and beyond, many have become convinced that they cannot make a presentation and actively seek any excuse to avoid doing so—often into adulthood.

We wrote this book to help students master the skills of oral presentation in an engaging, differentiated, project-based way. The premise of the book is that students who learn at an early age how to clearly and confidently research and present their knowledge, understanding, discoveries, and opinions orally are well prepared to meet the demands and challenges of a rigorous middle school and high school curriculum that requires students to demonstrate their understanding in a variety of ways.

Openings accomplish this goal effectively. This book provides ready-to-use openings projects designed for those who can benefit most from them: early, middle, and upper elementary students in grades K–6. Openings are an excellent way to help students become effective communicators and self-directed learners. They readily incorporate the core curriculum and differentiation strategies that will allow students to learn in ways that suit them best.

While originally the word *opening* referred specifically to a student presentation given first thing in the morning, the term has taken on additional meaning. It can be a metaphor for a new challenge or a chance to explore something never before experienced, opening a window of opportunity. It can suggest opening students' eyes to the world, allowing them to go in many different directions with their learning. It can refer to opening a door to understanding, a pathway to knowledge, or a mind to new ideas. It can indicate that students are doing something for the first time, as in opening a play or opening a business. You will certainly be able to attach further meaning to the word as you reflect on its use with students and its relationship to learning.

We created this book in the hope that you would find as much success and satisfaction from openings as we have over the years. Feel free to share your experiences and to ask questions as well. Please write in care of:

Free Spirit Publishing
217 Fifth Avenue North, Suite 200
Minneapolis, MN 55401-1299
help4kids@freespirit.com

Introduction

We wrote this book to help teachers of all students grades K–6 accomplish four goals that are keys to school success for even the youngest students:

1. **Forming a foundation of oral, visual, and written presentation skills to prepare kids for more in-depth project-based learning in later grades.** As they move through the grades toward middle school and high school, students will become increasingly involved in complex projects that require a range of capabilities. Your students will benefit significantly from having developed needed skills to research and present what they think, know, and are able to do.

2. **Providing opportunities for differentiated learning experiences.** As classrooms have grown increasingly diverse and we have come to understand more about the unique learning strengths and needs of individual children, differentiated instruction has become a necessary part of quality teaching practice. Knowing and using effective differentiation strategies allows you to support every student in acquiring knowledge and cultivating critical learning and communication skills.

3. **Promoting social-emotional learning in the classroom.** Students should see themselves as contributing members of a safe, welcoming, inclusive learning community that values (and expects!) participation and input from everyone. Most teachers recognize that students' social and emotional well-being contributes to their sense of capability and engagement with learning. Current trends in the field of education are adding new emphasis to the value of social-emotional learning (SEL), with some national organizations and states establishing competencies and standards teachers can use to measure students' growth in this area. Delivering oral presentations not only engages children intellectually and creatively but also cultivates a set of personal skills and experiences that contribute to their overall emotional well-being and social facility.

4. **Balancing the need to meet standards in the core content areas with the goal of providing a rich classroom environment where students thrive.** Academic achievement is, of course, the primary focus in schools, and children need to master grade-level content and demonstrate that mastery on standardized tests. In this book, the oral presentations students undertake are tied to standards in English language arts, social studies, math, and science. Reading, writing, computing, and gaining and applying knowledge in a range of subject areas can be accomplished within a balanced classroom environment where students stretch and grow personally and interpersonally and have their unique learning needs addressed.

Emphasizing these goals will undoubtedly have a lasting, positive impact on your students. All of their learning—both that which can be measured and tested and that which cannot—is certainly worth the time, energy, and effort it takes to address it. The projects in this book are crafted to help you achieve all four goals with your students.

Kids Teaching Kids

Teaching is a great way to learn! As a professional educator, you know the truth of this from your own classroom experiences: you can't teach something if you don't understand it. This concept applies to children as well as adults. Just watch any group of kids when left on their own. They teach each other constantly. They may not always teach about things you consider important, or even appropriate, but you can be sure that they are teaching and learning. A child who teaches draws on personal expertise, finds important connections, models how to do things, recognizes similarities and differences, uses clarifying language, explains in a variety of ways, and in the end strengthens his or her own understanding. If our focus is on helping students demonstrate what they know and can do, it makes sense to give them opportunities to teach. Do you encourage students in your classroom to explain, describe, demonstrate, report, present, exhibit, debate, and perform? When you allow students to formally share meaningful information with their classmates, you are putting a premium on kids teaching kids.

Kids teaching kids is a powerful concept. It places the student at the center of the learning process and emphasizes rigor, relevance, motivation, understanding, differentiated instruction, and project-based learning. When students are responsible for becoming "experts" and teaching what they know to others, the stage is set for self-directed, lifelong learning. These are very important goals for today's children. The ability to find information, organize it, and present it confidently and effectively to an audience is a fundamental key to success in your students' future. This book is all about kids teaching kids, beginning with the youngest children in the school (yes, the best place to start is kindergarten).

Why Do Openings?

Openings are projects in which students prepare and make presentations to other students. Openings combine standards from all six English language arts strands (reading, writing, speaking, listening, viewing, and visually representing) into one integrated project. You can use openings to help students learn and understand information about almost any subject taught in your classroom. It's a model that can be used over and over while focusing on different content. Even the most basic opening involves complex thinking and promotes the high learning retention that comes from the process of teaching others. By doing openings, students become contributing members of the class and gain confidence in their abilities to make presentations. Before moving on to the rest of the book, take a few minutes to reflect on what openings can offer you and your students.

Openings:

- support the existing curriculum and reinforce content standards already being covered

- provide a clear structure for students to follow while also offering the freedom to be unique

- emphasize key skills that will be extremely useful in later grades

- create a context within which learning takes place (students become "teachers" or "experts")

- provide clearly defined expectations for authentic student demonstrations of knowledge and skills

- establish a useful assessment system for self-directed learning as well as content knowledge and oral presentation skills

- allow teachers to concentrate on individual students for the purpose of in-depth observation, assessment, and feedback

- provide a natural opportunity for differentiation; the assignment is the same for everyone, but each student's opening can be customized or personalized (for example, by topic choice, content requirements, resources, visual aids, presentation style, or teacher support)

- give students confidence in their abilities to give oral presentations

Setting Up Your Openings Program

Students gain the most benefit from openings if they do multiple openings over the course of the school year, although if you can manage only one you will still be giving your students an extremely valuable learning experience. The optimal number of openings is three per year—one each in fall, winter, and spring. Following this basic schedule, you will see a tremendous difference in presentation quality, skill development, and confidence on the part of your students between the first and second opening, and again between the second and third opening. Thereafter, the dramatic increase in quality and confidence diminishes, simply because by then students have begun to master the basic skills, and they truly believe in themselves as presenters and teachers. Keep in mind that openings can focus on virtually any area of the curriculum, so having students present openings throughout the year allows them to work with critical content in an engaging, different way than they otherwise might.

Full-fledged openings call for students to settle in with a topic, research it, plan a presentation, create visuals, and then present their opening to the class following a clear and interesting format. The first question to consider as you plan to implement an openings program is, "Are my students ready for this?" Many students can do a fine job with openings immediately and do not need much training to get started. If, in your judgment, the majority of students in your class are prepared to handle openings without a preliminary support system, you should start with the full-fledged openings found in Part 3 of this book. You can differentiate openings in many ways if there are students in your class who need extra help.

However, if you have a significant number of students who are not accustomed to making formal presentations, who have not been taught the basics of speaking in front of a group, who are struggling socially or academically, or whose primary language is not English, you may wish to begin with starter openings, which are in Part 2.

As you plan an openings program for your classroom, consider the following factors:

- the age of your students
- the amount of openings prep work you assign as homework and the amount of work you plan to have students do in class
- the number of openings you intend to have students present each day
- the number of rounds of openings you want to have your students do over the course of the year

Early elementary openings require about one hour of student work time spread over several days—perhaps 15–20 minutes a day for three days prior to beginning the presentations. The actual opening presentations take approximately 2–3 minutes per student, with another minute or two for getting started and wrapping up. If you have a class of twenty-five students and have one student present an opening each day, it will take five weeks to finish one round of openings. Adding the preparation week, it will take six weeks to complete the round. If you have two students present openings each day, the week of preparation remains the same and the round of openings will take two to three weeks. Some teachers do three or more early elementary openings each day, reducing the number of days required to ten or fewer.

Middle elementary openings require about two hours of student work time spread over several days—perhaps 20–30 minutes a day for four days prior to beginning the presentations. The actual opening presentations take approximately 3–4 minutes per student, with another two or three minutes for getting started and wrapping up. If you have a class of 25 students and have one student present an opening each day, it will take five weeks to finish one round of openings. If you have more students present openings each day, the round of openings will be shorter.

Upper elementary openings require about four hours of student work time spread over several days—perhaps 40–60 minutes a day for four or five days prior to beginning the presentations. The actual opening presentations take approximately 5–6 minutes per student (and potentially longer for some students who really become engaged in the openings process), with another three or four minutes for getting started and wrapping up. If you have a class of 25 students and have one student present an opening each day, it will take five weeks to finish one round of openings. If you have more students present openings each day, the round of openings will be shorter.

These guidelines are general rules of thumb and may vary depending on your assignments and expectations.

> You can use openings to help students learn and understand information about almost any subject taught in your classroom.

A Word About State and National Standards

As noted earlier, openings reinforce content standards because they effectively support learning in almost any subject being taught in your classroom. As you examine this book, you will find many ways to use openings to emphasize science, social studies, mathematics, and English language arts. However, it is exciting to discover that most states clearly recognize the intrinsic value of teaching elementary students to make presentations, regardless of the content. A careful examination of curriculum standards posted at each of the fifty state departments of education websites in the winter of 2008 revealed that more than 75 percent of the states (39 of 50) have rigorous standards that focus specifically on oral presentation expectations for kindergarten through at least eighth grade. The table on pages 6–7 shows three typical examples for the elementary grades. There is a good chance that your state has similar standards. In addition, the Common Core State Standards, which many states have adopted, specify the need for elementary students to be able to present knowledge and ideas to their peers. As you glance over the expectations established by California, Indiana, and New York, think about how these standards might be accomplished. If you don't have a ready answer, here is a clue: you can do all of this with openings.

The standards listed in the table are selected portions of K–6 speaking standards taken directly from the states' departments of education websites. The purpose of the chart is to illustrate with specific examples how speaking standards from representative states align with openings. A complete set of your state standards is available via the Education World website (www.educationworld.com), as are the Common Core State Standards.

> By participating in openings, students will practice and develop skills, discover their strengths, recognize their potential, and become confident presenters.

About This Book

Teaching Kids to Be Confident, Effective Communicators: Differentiated Projects to Get All Students Writing, Speaking, and Presenting is divided into three parts. "Part 1: Differentiation, Social-Emotional Learning, and Content Standards for Openings" summarizes basic differentiation elements and provides specific differentiation strategies to help you individualize openings. This will allow you to accommodate students' unique learning styles and needs and optimize the benefits of openings in helping students develop self-awareness, self-management, and social awareness. Part 1 also provides background information about how openings support students' social-emotional learning (SEL). Finally, this first part includes overview charts correlating the openings with curriculum content standards.

"Part 2: First Steps: Starter Openings" introduces and provides starter openings, brief presentations (one minute or shorter) that help students learn the basics of openings. Starter openings are designed to help you and your students become familiar with the requirements, expectations, and potential of student presentations and set the stage for later success with more extensive openings projects. Having each student do one or two starter openings is the best way to prepare your students for their first experience with openings. We encourage you to spend some time examining Part 2, which will help you visualize how openings may be introduced to your students and utilized in your classroom.

"Part 3: The Openings" provides five fully developed, ready-to-use projects for each of the three levels of learners (a bonus opening for each level is provided on the CD-ROM): early (grades K–1), middle (grades 2–3), and upper (grades 4–6) elementary. The projects are content-based and require students to present their final work to the class as openings. Each project description includes all of the information and materials you will need to implement it with your students.

Following Part 3 are student preparation materials, assessment materials, audience feedback materials, and teacher tools. Forms for extending openings and poster templates are included as bonus materials on the CD-ROM. If you design your own assignments and develop your own openings projects, these forms and bonus materials will be extremely useful to you. The materials are not content specific and may be used for any topics you want to emphasize.

- **Student Preparation Materials.** These include visual aids that you can use when introducing your students to openings as well as to cue them when they are giving their presentations. These also include Is My Opening Ready? checklists, a Parent-Student Opening Agreement, and a Challenge Option Request Form.

- **Assessment Materials.** These include forms to provide feedback and assessment to your students.

- **Audience Feedback Materials.** These include an Audience Feedback Participation Form you can use to assess students' contributions as audience members as well as five forms students can use as tools to provide peer review of presenters.

- **Teacher Tools.** These include an Openings Planner and a Certificate of Achievement.

- **Forms for Extending Openings.** These include forms for publishing openings as well as several other forms students can use to take their openings further. It also includes a Tips for a Successful Opening form. These forms are not in the book and appear on the CD-ROM only.

- **Poster Templates.** This section has instructions and forms you can use to help upper elementary students create posters that are carefully constructed and uniform in appearance. These forms are not in the book and appear on the CD-ROM only.

The CD-ROM that accompanies this book includes all of the book's reproducible student forms and teacher forms as well as the bonus materials available only on the CD-ROM. All forms are view-only PDF documents.

Getting Started with This Book

Jump right in! Use this book in the way that best fits your interests and the needs of your students. You may want to read some or all of Part 1 to familiarize yourself with differentiation strategies and SEL concepts that will support you and your students as your class works with openings. Or you may wish to begin by browsing through the starter openings (Part 2) and more fully developed openings (Part 3) as a first step to familiarizing yourself with openings and with the types of projects included. Be sure to peruse openings for all three levels—early, middle, and upper elementary—because you may find an idea in one level that you can modify to use with students in a different grade range or ability level.

Once you give openings a try in your classroom, you will discover that the process truly engages students in their learning. Because students assume the role of experts with information to share, they are often highly motivated to study their topics and as a result they really know what they are talking about when they give their presentations. By participating in openings, students will practice and develop skills, discover their strengths, recognize their potential, and become confident presenters.

Teaching students to become effective communicators is similar to coaching an athlete to excel at a sport or helping a musician master an instrument. It's all about skills, motivation, and repetitions. As the coach, your job is to help students recognize how people become effective speakers, make the process of getting there fun and interesting, and give them lots of opportunities to practice and develop. You will reap your own rewards as well: You will have the satisfaction of having imparted to your students the knowledge that comes with being resident experts, skills for preparing and presenting that knowledge, and a lasting belief in themselves as effective, confident communicators.

Enjoy the wonderful world of openings with your students!

Examples of State Oral Presentation Standards

Grade	California	Indiana	New York
K	Deliver brief recitations and oral presentations about familiar experiences or interests, demonstrating command of organization and delivery.	Describe people, places, things (including their size, color, and shape), locations, and actions; tell an experience or creative story in a logical sequence (chronological order, first, second, last).	Report information briefly to peers and familiar adults, with assistance; retell more than one piece of information in sequence; share observations from classroom and home; share information, using appropriate visual aids, such as, puppets, toys, and pictures, to illustrate a word or concept, with assistance; share what they know and have learned about a topic.
1	Deliver brief recitations and oral presentations about familiar experiences or interests that are organized around a coherent thesis statement. Student speaking demonstrates a command of standard American English and organizational and delivery strategies.	Relate an important life event or personal experience in a simple sequence; provide descriptions with careful attention to sensory detail; use visual aids, such as pictures and objects, to present oral information.	Report information to peers and familiar adults; retell multiple pieces of information in sequence; share observations from the classroom, home, or community; share information using appropriate visual aids to illustrate a word or concept; share what they know, want to know, and have learned about a theme or topic.
2	Organize presentations to maintain a clear focus; speak clearly and at an appropriate pace for the type of communication (e.g., informal discussion, report to class); recount experiences in a logical sequence; report on a topic with supportive facts and details.	Organize presentations to maintain a clear focus; speak clearly and at an appropriate pace for the type of communication (such as an informal discussion or a report to class); tell experiences in a logical order (chronological order, order of importance, spatial order); report on a topic with supportive facts and details, drawing from several sources of information; use descriptive words when speaking about people, places, things, and events.	Present a short oral report, using at least one source of information, such as a person, book, magazine article, television program, or electronic text; state a main idea with supporting examples and details, with assistance; role-play to communicate an interpretation of real or imaginary people or events.
3	Organize ideas chronologically or around major points of information; provide a beginning, a middle, and an end, including concrete details that develop a central idea; use clear and specific vocabulary to communicate ideas and establish the tone; clarify and enhance oral presentations through the use of appropriate props (e.g., objects, pictures, charts).	Organize ideas chronologically (in the order that they happened) or around major points of information; provide a beginning, a middle, and an end to oral presentations, including details that develop a central idea; use clear and specific vocabulary to communicate ideas and establish the tone; clarify and enhance oral presentations through the use of appropriate props, including objects, pictures, and charts. Make brief narrative presentations that: • provide a context for an event that is the subject of the presentation. • provide insight into why the selected event should be of interest to the audience.	State a main idea with supporting details; present a short oral report, using at least two sources of information, such as a person, book, magazine article, or electronic text (speak loudly enough to be heard by the audience); use logical order in presentations; present original works, such as stories, poems, and plays, to classmates.
4	Present effective introductions and conclusions that guide and inform the listener's understanding of important ideas and evidence; use traditional structures for conveying information (e.g., cause and effect, similarity and difference, posing and answering a question); emphasize points in ways that help the listener or viewer to follow important ideas and concepts; use details, examples, anecdotes, or experiences to explain or clarify information; use volume,	Present effective introductions and conclusions that guide and inform the listener's understanding of important ideas and details; use logical structures for conveying information, including cause and effect, similarity and difference, and posing and answering a question; emphasize points in ways that help the listener or viewer follow important ideas and concepts; use details, examples, anecdotes (stories of a specific event), or experiences	State a main idea with supporting examples and details; present a short oral report, using a variety of sources (speak loudly enough to be heard by the audience; use gestures appropriate to convey meaning); use logical order in presentations; present original works, such as stories, poems, and plays, to classmates.

Examples of State Oral Presentation Standards

Grade	California	Indiana	New York
4 (cont.)	pitch, phrasing, pace, modulation, and gestures appropriately to enhance meaning. Make informational presentations: a. Frame a key question. b. Include facts and details that help listeners to focus. c. Incorporate more than one source of information (e.g., speakers, books, newspapers, television or radio reports).	to explain or clarify information; engage the audience with appropriate words, facial expressions, and gestures. Make informational presentations that: • focus on one main topic. • include facts and details that help listeners focus. • incorporate more than one source of information (including speakers, books, newspapers, television broadcasts, radio reports, or websites).	
5	Deliver focused, coherent presentations that convey ideas clearly and relate to the background and interests of the audience. Select a focus, organizational structure, and point of view for an oral presentation; clarify and support spoken ideas with evidence and examples; and engage the audience with appropriate verbal cues, facial expressions, and gestures. Deliver informative presentations about an important idea, issue, or event by the following means: a. Frame questions to direct the investigation. b. Establish a controlling idea or topic. c. Develop the topic with simple facts, details, examples, and explanations.	Select a focus, organizational structure, and point of view for an oral presentation; clarify and support spoken ideas with evidence and examples; use volume, phrasing, timing, and gestures appropriately to enhance meaning; emphasize points in ways that help the listener or viewer follow important ideas and concepts. Deliver informative presentations about an important idea, issue, or event by the following means: • frame questions to direct the investigation. • establish a controlling idea or topic. • develop the topic with simple facts, details, examples, and explanations.	Share information from personal experience; share information from a variety of texts; state a main idea and support it with facts, details, and examples; compare and contrast information; present reports of approximately five minutes for teachers and peers; summarize main points; use notes, outlines, and visual aids appropriate to the presentation.
6	Deliver informative presentations: a. Pose relevant questions sufficiently limited in scope to be completely and thoroughly answered. b. Develop the topic with facts, details, examples, and explanations from multiple authoritative sources (e.g., speakers, periodicals, online information). Deliver persuasive presentations: a. Provide a clear statement of the position. b. Include relevant evidence. c. Offer a logical sequence of information. d. Engage the listener and foster acceptance of the proposition or proposal. Deliver presentations on problems and solutions: a. Theorize on the causes and effects of each problem and establish connections between the defined problem and at least one solution. b. Offer persuasive evidence to validate the definition of the problem and the proposed solutions.	Select a focus, an organizational structure, and a point of view, matching the purpose, message, and vocal modulation (changes in tone) to the audience; emphasize important points to assist the listener in following the main ideas and concepts; support opinions with researched, documented evidence and with visual or media displays that use appropriate technology; use effective timing, volume, tone, and alignment of hand and body gestures to sustain audience interest and attention. Deliver informative presentations that: • pose relevant questions sufficiently limited in scope to be completely and thoroughly answered. • develop the topic with facts, details, examples, and explanations from multiple authoritative sources, including speakers, periodicals, and online information.	Synthesize and paraphrase information; make connections between sources of information; present reports of five to seven minutes for teachers and peers on topics related to any school subject; summarize main points as part of the conclusion; use notes, outlines, and visual aids appropriate to the presentation.

Standards are from *English-Language Arts Content Standards for California Public Schools, Kindergarten Through Grade Twelve,* California Department of Education; *Indiana's Academic Standards for Grades K–12 English/Language Arts,* Indiana Department of Education; and *English Language Arts Core Curriculum, Kindergarten–Grade 12,* University of the State of New York and the New York State Education Department. Accessed online July 21, 2008, at Education World (www.educationworld.com).

Part 1

Differentiation, Social-Emotional Learning, and Content Standards for Openings

Differentiation and Openings

What Is Differentiated Instruction?

Differentiated instruction means allowing students to learn and demonstrate understanding in ways that take advantage of their strengths and support their weaknesses. It's about bringing out each student's unique intelligence and spark. One approach to this is through the use of openings. By carefully developing oral-presentation projects that take into account the range of learning needs and motivational factors in your class, you make it possible for all students to become actively and successfully engaged in their learning. An important key to effectively infusing differentiated openings into your instruction is a clear understanding of what to differentiate and how to differentiate in your classroom in general.

Differentiate What?

There are three areas of classroom instruction that can be differentiated: content, process, and product.

- Content is what we want students to know and be able to do.

- Process means the activities students engage in as they make meaning of the content.

- Product is the way in which students provide evidence of understanding.

Teachers have some level of control over these areas. They have the ability to decide how each will be addressed within the curriculum and to make modifications when necessary. You will find that openings are wonderfully adaptable for differentiating any combination of content, process, and product. The differentiation strategies described in this section of the book have been organized around these three areas to help clarify which aspect of classroom instruction they are most likely to support (although they naturally interconnect and overlap in places). For a more in-depth discussion of differentiating content, process, and product, see *How to Differentiate Instruction in Mixed-Ability Classrooms* (ASCD, 2001), by Carol Ann Tomlinson.

Differentiating Content

We live in a standards-driven age where content is mandated by federal and state governments. Even with government mandates, though, it is possible to differentiate much of the content students are expected to master. Here are some suggestions:

- Give students a choice of specific topics about which to learn. Choice is a powerful strategy for differentiating content.

- Focus on concepts, principles, essential questions, and big ideas related to the required content. These things may be differentiated by adjusting the level of complexity, based on the needs of individual learners.

- Use varied resources. Resources may be differentiated by reading level, depth, and complexity.

- Provide varied support systems (scaffolding). Help all students master the same content by giving more or less support to students, depending on their needs.

Differentiating Process

Tomlinson suggests calling the processes students go through as they learn new ideas, information, or skills "sense-making activities." There are many such activities, which can be differentiated in various ways. For example:

- Use small groups to allow more flexibility in matching activities to the needs of students.

- Allow students to use graphic organizers as a way of visually representing information.

- Establish learning centers that focus on specific content and skills.

- Develop tiered assignments (assignments designed for struggling learners, on-target learners, and advanced learners; see pages 17–18).

- Provide as many ways as possible for students to compare and contrast information.

- Build oral presentation options into otherwise basic learning activities, giving students varied opportunities to demonstrate what they know and can do.

Differentiating Product

Products are a motivating factor in the learning process. Students take ownership in the products they create, and thus the product is a personal statement: tangible evidence of creativity, understanding, and effort. Products may take many forms, but they have some traits in common. Products should make students think, demonstrate real learning, be based on standards, incorporate skills that the content expectations demand, and place a high premium on quality. Products may be differentiated by allowing students to choose from a menu of product options, or by letting them design their own product option that reflects standard-level work. You may also establish completion criteria that allow students to add their own complexity or incorporate areas of personal interest beyond the product requirements. With openings, every presentation requires a visual aid that can take many different forms, thereby providing an effective way of differentiating the products students produce.

Differentiate How?

Three fundamental student characteristics can be used to determine how to differentiate instruction: readiness to learn, interest areas, and learning profile. Teachers have no control over these things. Students walk into the classroom as they are, and therefore it is necessary to know your learners if instruction is going to be differentiated appropriately.

- Readiness to learn refers to what students currently know and are able to do.

- Interest areas are the things students enjoy doing or learning about.

- Learning profile is related to intelligence preference, learning style, gender, and culture.

Using openings, you can differentiate content, process, and product to accommodate each of these three characteristics. The following guidelines explain how to do this effectively. Again, if you want additional information, Carol Ann Tomlinson's work is an excellent reference.

Differentiate by Readiness

Pre-assessment is necessary in order to differentiate by readiness. In some reliable way, you must determine what students know and can do and plan to accommodate the continuum of needs that you identify.

Since it is impractical to create an individual learning plan for every student, differentiating by readiness is often done by developing three tiered levels of instruction or student activity: for struggling learners, on-target learners, and advanced learners. Ways of differentiating by readiness include individualized support during presentations, varied texts by reading level, tiered assignments, scaffolding based on need, small group instruction, curriculum compacting, varied homework options, and learning contracts.

Differentiate by Interest

The primary reason for differentiating by interest is to tap into student motivation. Students who are learning about something of interest naturally bring increased enthusiasm to the task. That's how the brain works. There are two ways of approaching the idea of student interest. One is to determine what students are interested in and allow them to pursue those interests. The other is to create new interests in students by getting them excited about various aspects of the content being studied. Ways of differentiating by interest include interest groups, student choice, learning contracts, resident experts, WebQuests, literature circles, independent study, and optional applications of technology.

> Students take ownership in the products they create, and thus the product is a personal statement: tangible evidence of creativity, understanding, and effort.

Differentiate by Learning Profile

While students can be smart in many ways, they do have natural strengths. And if we want their best work, we try to align with those strengths. Students also have individual preferences about their learning environment and personal approach to learning. If these factors can be determined for individuals, for example, by using Howard Gardner's theory of multiple intelligences (see pages 18–19), their learning will be more effective and efficient. They will do better in class and they will understand themselves better as they become lifelong learners. Ways of differentiating by learning profile involve offering varied methods of gathering, organizing, analyzing, synthesizing, and presenting information. Giving students choices will lead to a natural self-selection of learning preferences.

Here is a simple chart to summarize the *how* and *what* of differentiated instruction:

Differentiate How? Differentiate What?			
Differentiate What?	**Differentiate How?**		
	By Learner Readiness	By Learner Interest	By Learner Profile
Differentiate Content			
Differentiate Process			
Differentiate Product			

You can differentiate openings by focusing on any combination of the nine empty cells. For example, you could choose to differentiate content based on learner interest, or differentiate product based on learner readiness. The items in the "Differentiate What?" column on the left are the things you control (content, process, product). The items in the "Differentiate How?" row at the top are the unique attributes that students bring with them into the classroom that are not under your control and must be determined through assessment, survey, or other means.

Why Differentiate Through Openings?

You undoubtedly want every child to be a confident, productive, contributing member of the learning culture that you nurture every day in your classroom. A differentiated openings program will help you achieve this goal. When students work on structured, curriculum-aligned openings, they:

- participate at an appropriate readiness level
- take ownership in and accept responsibility for their own learning and for supporting the learning of their peers
- take part actively rather than observe passively
- build confidence in themselves as self-directed learners and presenters
- demonstrate in personalized ways what they know and can do
- make personal choices and decisions that result in individualized learning experiences
- work independently, with a partner, or in small groups
- focus on topics of interest and relevance
- develop unique final products

A well-designed opening involves students in applying and developing an array of important skills:

1. Reading
2. Writing
3. Research
4. Planning
5. Problem solving
6. Self-discipline
7. Self-evaluation
8. Presentation

These are the same key skills that constitute the basis for successfully participating in project-based learning that students encounter more and more as they move into middle school and high school. We encourage you to talk with students about these skills and the importance of each one. The more you use openings with your students, the more they will begin to grow in the different skill areas and understand how the skills tie together, and the more deeply you will be laying the groundwork for meaningful and rich educational experiences for students throughout their school days.

Strategies Used in Classroom Differentiation Examples

Differentiation Strategies	Early Elementary Openings	Middle Elementary Openings	Upper Elementary Openings
Anchor Activities	The Storyteller	The Shape Hunter	Buying the Car of My Dreams
Choice-as-Motivator	I Made a Pattern I Understand Food Chains The Storyteller	Alien Broadcast System This Place Is a Zoo Community Cam	It's Written in the Stars Family Ties to History Featured Expert Series Heroes
Flexible Grouping	I Understand Food Chains	These Objects Are Classified The Shape Hunter	Featured Expert Series
Kids Teaching Kids	I Understand Food Chains		
Multiple Intelligences	My Home and Family Did You Know? I Made a Pattern	Local Hero of the Year	The Naturalist Buying the Car of My Dreams Family Ties to History Featured Expert Series
Reflection Card		Local Hero of the Year	Heroes
Resident Experts	Did You Know?	This Place Is a Zoo	
Scaffolding	My Home and Family Did You Know? Words All Around Us I Understand Food Chains The Storyteller	These Objects Are Classified Alien Broadcast System Local Hero of the Year This Place Is a Zoo The Shape Hunter Community Cam	The Naturalist Buying the Car of My Dreams Family Ties to History Heroes
Tiered Assignments	My Home and Family Did You Know? Words All Around Us The Storyteller	These Objects Are Classified Alien Broadcast System This Place Is a Zoo	Buying the Car of My Dreams It's Written in the Stars Family Ties to History

Differentiation Strategies for Openings

As you examine the strategies described in this section, you will see that many will apply to the starter openings you will use to introduce students to the fuller presentations (Part 2) and every one of them could be built into any of the opening projects described in Part 3. At the end of each project description, you will find a "Classroom Differentiation Example." These vignettes demonstrate how one or more differentiation strategies might be incorporated into the opening to accommodate students with diverse readiness needs, a variety of interests, and different learning profiles. The Classroom Differentiation Example is a suggestion, not a prescription. You may decide

to differentiate a selected opening in entirely different ways—those described in this book or others that you prefer to use—but it's always good to have a place to begin. The chart above shows which differentiation strategies are used in the Classroom Differentiation Example vignette for each opening.

Differentiating Content
Scaffolding
Scaffolding means to provide the support that is necessary for each student to reach learning goals. The most common use of scaffolding is to help struggling learners complete assigned tasks and demonstrate understanding. Scaffolding and tiering are sometimes used interchangeably, but there is a fundamental difference. Tiering provides

multiple assignments, typically for three types of learners: struggling, on-target, and advanced. The teacher determines which level best fits each student's readiness and gives that student the appropriate assignment (see "Tiered Assignments" on pages 17–18 for more detail). By contrast, scaffolding often begins with the same assignment for everyone. The teacher differentiates by determining how much support each student needs in order to complete the assignment.

Scaffolding is a great way to support students who struggle with the assignment or need to overcome difficulties that might inhibit their ability to complete the requirements of an opening. One of the most direct and obvious ways to scaffold with openings is by differentiating the resources students will use. Be sure that the topics assigned to struggling learners have plenty of resource materials available, at a reading level that makes them accessible and useful. Simultaneously, challenge more advanced learners with resources that require higher reading levels and topics that demand more synthesis of information. You can accomplish this by knowing beforehand how the available resources match the needs of your students and then carefully managing the topic selection process.

> Scaffolding is a great way to support students who struggle with the assignment or need to overcome difficulties that might inhibit their ability to complete the requirements of an opening.

The starter openings in *Teaching Kids to Be Confident, Effective Communicators* were designed as a form of scaffolding for the entire class. It is possible that your students are ready for full-fledged openings and do not need preliminary training and support. However, in many cases, starter openings provide a convenient and effective way to scaffold in classes where positive reinforcement and an introduction to basic presentation skills are needed.

With starter and full-fledged openings, build in scaffolded support systems that can be gradually modified or removed as each student masters skills and gains confidence. For example:

- Give struggling students more detailed guidance, additional examples, extra clarification of assignment expectations, and plenty of modeling.

- Basics first: Provide time in class for students to work on the fundamental parts of their openings (research, written report, and visual aid), and set a due date when they are expected to show you what they have finished. When you check the products they have developed, you are verifying that they have successfully completed the necessary basics. This gives you an opportunity to intervene with (provide a scaffold for) students who are struggling or procrastinating. From this point, each student may enhance his or her project with additional information, extended writing, or improved visual materials, but no student will be left in the uncomfortable position (for whatever reason) of not being ready when it is time to make the presentation.

- Scaffold the visual aid requirement by providing detailed templates for students to follow (such as the poster templates on the CD-ROM), options for additional flexibility (such as letting students use visual materials found on the Internet), extra guidelines to clarify what must be done, or even ready-to-use posters or other visual devices for students who need such help.

- Support the written report with templates or guided assistance. Allow students who struggle with writing to work with a "writing buddy" from your class or from a higher grade, or ask parents to help their children with the written component of the opening. Some students may be allowed to dictate to you or a designated scribe what they want to say.

- Support the oral presentation by setting firm expectations at the outset of the project. Many students who fear speaking in front of the class will participate if they see no other choice. Some students, though, will try to opt out if possible. Here are some scaffolds to use with a student who fears or avoids speaking to the class:

  - Let the student work with a partner who can help with the presentation.

  - Offer to be a student's partner yourself. Or, simply tell everyone, "If you don't want to do the opening by yourself, you will get to have me as a partner."

- Schedule the student to be one of the last presenters so that he or she can benefit from seeing others model how to do the opening.

- Allow the student to present to a small group instead of to the entire class.

- If there is a language barrier, let the student present in his or her first language and provide an interpreter for the class.

- Make a video recording of a student's presentation and play the movie for the class. Following the video, have the student ask if there are any questions.

- Look for strengths in the student, and build them into the opening. For example, if the student has art skills, place an increased focus on the visual aid.

- Work closely with the student's parent to have the student practice at home.

- Provide opportunities for the student to practice at school with you or classmates. Each practice is really an opening presentation and a confidence builder.

- Have a meeting with the student and parent to discuss the reasons for not wanting to present, and work together to come up with solutions.

- Celebrate the completion of an opening. Help the student see it as a real accomplishment that proves he or she can do it.

- Create a set of "prompt cards" to use while students are presenting, with words or pictures that tell what to do next, and hold up the appropriate card as a prompt if the student stumbles, freezes, or forgets how to proceed. (See pages 193–199 for reproducible forms you can use for this purpose.) Or, develop specific verbal cues to use with students who struggle.

- Help struggling students prepare for the question-and-answer portion of an opening

by giving them sample questions ahead of time. Be sure that at least one of the samples is actually asked (by you or someone else) so that students can experience success by being prepared to give a good answer.

Flexible Grouping

The wide range of learning needs found in every classroom is a dilemma faced by all teachers. Each child is different, and this fact alone can be overwhelming to teachers who recognize that student differences require a variety of strategies. One solution to this dilemma is flexible grouping. When you group flexibly, you create instructional groups and prescribe specific activities that respond to students' individual learning needs. Flexible grouping is often used to differentiate content, by varying the type or level of instruction and resources for each group, but can also be used to differentiate process, by varying the nature or complexity of each group's task.

Openings are generally thought of as individualized projects, but they also can have a grouping component. Allowing students to work with partners or in small groups particularly helps those students who benefit from having other people to collaborate with while planning and presenting their openings. Students may work in groups to prepare for their openings, or they may actually present their openings together. For example, a group of three students could work together to learn about a common topic or three closely related topics. Three options for their presentations could be to do one of the following:

- Plan a joint opening in which each student has a specified role.

- Plan individual openings that are directly connected and presented consecutively on the same day.

- Support each other in the development of separate openings that are presented individually on different days.

You may choose to group students in any of these ways:

- **Randomly:** Group students by drawing names, numbering off, or using some other method of creating groups without regard to any selection criteria.

- **By Student Choice:** Allow students to choose their own partners or form their own groups.

- **By Compatibility:** Group students whose skills or temperaments make them good matches, and separate students who can't get along or get along too well.

- **Heterogeneously:** Form each group so that it has a range of student readiness, from struggling to advanced learners.

- **Homogeneously:** Form each group so that it has students at the same readiness level.

It is important to understand that flexible grouping does not create permanent groups or label students in any way. "Flexible" means that students are grouped and regrouped as appropriate for particular activities. For example, students may sometimes be grouped heterogeneously and at other times homogeneously; for one activity students may be grouped by interest and for another by intelligence type. One day students may be grouped randomly and the next by student choice. In other words, student groups are routinely rearranged as the situation demands.

Differentiating Process
Kids Teaching Kids

Kids teaching kids is fundamental to openings. It is also one of the most powerful strategies for process differentiation that you can build into your instructional repertoire. In his book *How the Brain Learns*, educational consultant David Sousa presents a learning pyramid developed from studies of how well students retain information learned via different teaching methods.

The pyramid shows the average percentage of new learning that students recall twenty-four hours after being taught. (Retention after twenty-four hours indicates the memory is in long-term storage.)

Given these research findings, what can you do to ensure your students retain essential information? You should have them teach it! Children naturally and routinely teach one another all the time, and when they do, you can observe the bottom two levels of the pyramid in action: "Practice by Doing" and "Teach Others/Immediate Use of Learning." Your goal is to harness the power of that process and incorporate it into the classroom through the use of openings.

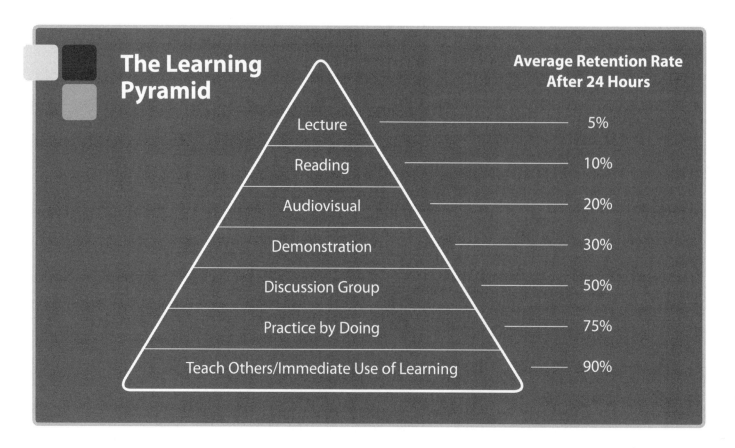

The Learning Pyramid

Average Retention Rate After 24 Hours

Lecture	5%
Reading	10%
Audiovisual	20%
Demonstration	30%
Discussion Group	50%
Practice by Doing	75%
Teach Others/Immediate Use of Learning	90%

* *How the Brain Learns* by David A. Sousa. Copyright 2006 by Sage Publications Inc Books. Reproduced with permission of Sage Publications Inc.

Resident Experts

Resident experts is an idea developed by Susan Winebrenner.* A resident expert is a student who has developed a unique area of expertise by focusing on a topic of interest that other students have not studied. A class that contains resident experts typically makes use of them whenever information is needed that is related to topics they know about. Openings provide an excellent opportunity to build a cadre of resident experts in your classroom by focusing on topics that are related to the content being covered. The implementation of resident experts can be differentiated in at least three ways:

- Students can focus on topics that are interesting and have personal relevance.

- Students can learn at their own level of readiness. In other words, *every* student can become an expert, not just advanced or gifted and talented students.

- Students who become exceptionally engaged in their areas of expertise may be allowed to pursue them independently, beyond the scope of the class.

Tiered Assignments

Tiered assignments are intentional efforts to accommodate the range of learning needs found in any classroom by providing more than one way for students to reach the same basic learning goals. Each assignment is a tier (think of stairway steps); the higher the tier, the more complex or challenging the assignment. All students are expected to focus on essential content and skills, but the assignments are differentiated so that each student is faced with tasks that meet his or her individual needs. The most common reason for creating tiered assignments is to differentiate by readiness, as a way to provide for struggling, on-target, and advanced learners.

In a typical classroom, there might be three tiered assignments developed for a given opening. Using pre-assessment information to determine readiness, the teacher gives each student whichever assignment is most appropriate. There is no rule for how many students should be at each tier. There may be only a few assigned to the top tier while the majority work at the middle tier.

It is critical that each tier provides respectful work that reflects the learning goals of the opening. Assignments should be similar, and everybody in the class should be equally engaged in their work.

Diane Heacox identifies six ways assignments can be tiered:**

1. **Challenge:** Each tier focuses on a different thinking level (as in Bloom's taxonomy: knowledge, comprehension, application, analysis, synthesis, evaluation).

2. **Complexity:** Each tier focuses on a different level of abstraction, analysis, in-depth investigation, or advanced concepts.

3. **Resources:** Each tier utilizes different resources at appropriate reading levels or depth of coverage.

4. **Outcome:** Each tier utilizes the same resources, but requires a different application of learning (outcome).

5. **Process:** Each tier has the same outcome, but utilizes a different process to get there.

6. **Product:** Each tier has a different product expectation, often based on intelligence type.

To increase the rigor and relevance of a project, especially for top tier assignments, consider these options:

- Include a "So What?" component in the opening. This is an opportunity for students to explain why anyone should care about the topic just presented: Why is this topic important to us? Who cares?

- Add a technology option that allows students to build tables, charts, graphs, spreadsheets, databases, multimedia, interactive whiteboards, podcasts, Web pages, blogs, or other technology into their openings.

- Offer students a "point/counterpoint" option, where they could say: "Some people believe this . . . but others believe this . . ." or "This is one point of view, and here is another. . . ." In other words, let students tell the audience that there is more than one way to look at a topic.

---

* *Teaching Gifted Kids in the Regular Classroom* by Susan Winebrenner (Free Spirit Publishing, 2001), pp. 157–158.
** *Differentiating Instruction in the Regular Classroom* by Diane Heacox, Ed.D. (Free Spirit Publishing, 2002), pp. 91–94.

- Give students the option of providing an "If you want to know more" conclusion to the opening. This would allow students to tell their audience about good resources they discovered and where interesting information about the topics may be found.

- Allow students to simply do more of what the opening assignment calls for. If the topic or presentation requirements appeal to a student and he or she really engages with the assignment, provide an opportunity to go beyond the basic requirements by creating additional visual aids or producing enhanced written materials or making an extended presentation.

- Students may choose to include a "connections" section in their openings. This is where students tell how their openings are connected to the work of other students. For example, a student who is adding a connections component to his or her opening might say, "My topic is connected to Jeremy's. Here's how." Of course, making connections becomes progressively easier the further you go through the openings process. However, early presenters can make connections to course content, a teacher-presented opening, openings from previous assignments, and topics that will be covered in future openings.

Reflection Card (or Exit Card)

More commonly known as an exit card, a reflection card is an index card or half sheet of paper on which each student records personal reflections about his or her just-completed opening. Ask that the card be turned in to you within a certain time following the opening presentation, and provide a prompt to help students focus their thoughts about their performance. Examples of reflection prompts include:

- **Glow and Grow:** Please record on your reflection card two things that you think you did well during your opening (two "glows") and one thing that you think could be improved (one "grow").

- **Add-On:** Please record on your reflection card something you wish you could have added to this opening.

- **Help, Please!** Please record on your reflection card an area you feel you need help with when you are preparing for your next opening.

- **I Feel Good:** Please record on your reflection card something that made you feel good about this opening.

- **Important Point:** Please record on your reflection card the most important thing you learned from doing this opening.

You will gain important insights into the students' perceptions of themselves as learners and presenters when you read the cards, and you can use their responses as a basis for personalized feedback and future support.

Differentiating Product
Multiple Intelligences

Emphasize multiple intelligences in student presentations by working with your students to identify and take advantage of their strongest intelligence areas. Here are brief descriptions of what can be done with students who are strong in each of the eight intelligences identified by Harvard professor Howard Gardner:

- **Verbal/Linguistic ("Word Smart"):** Students prefer to learn by listening, talking, and following written directions. These students thrive on the basic opening format because their strengths are heavily emphasized in both the oral and written portions of the assignment.

- **Visual/Spatial ("Picture Smart"):** Students prefer to learn by working with pictures, models, and graphic organizers. Because they like to create and manipulate images to represent ideas, they are generally excited to make drawings, models, concept maps, multimedia, posters, or other graphic representations of information for the visual portion of an opening.

- **Logical/Mathematical ("Number Smart"):** Students prefer to learn by applying number, computing, and logic skills. They like to look for patterns and relationships through classifying and sequencing activities. Students with a logical/mathematical bent will enjoy creating graphic organizers, using numbers and geometric shapes, or producing tables, graphs, and charts in support of their openings.

- **Bodily/Kinesthetic ("Body Smart"):** Students prefer to learn through physical activities such as building models or using manipulatives; they like to be active and move while they learn. These students might be allowed to construct models for their openings and to perform, demonstrate, or dramatize ideas, opinions, procedures, and information.

- **Musical/Rhythmic ("Music Smart"):** Students prefer to learn by listening to, and engaging in, musical and rhythmic activities. They like to dance and compose, play, or conduct music. With openings, these students could have the option of singing or rapping to the audience.

- **Naturalist ("Nature Smart"):** Students prefer to learn by observing and categorizing; they like to explore nature and understand the world of plants and animals. Nature smart students can choose topics related to nature and focus on classifying things and organizing objects by their natural attributes.

- **Interpersonal ("People Smart"):** Students prefer to learn and benefit from interacting with other students, so they might be group leaders or collaborate with others on ways to produce and present openings.

- **Intrapersonal ("Self Smart"):** Students prefer to learn independently and should have opportunities to be reflective thinkers and provide their personal insights and feelings about topics being studied.

It is not necessary (or realistic) to give students options from all eight intelligences all of the time. Being aware of these kinds of differences among children, however, will help you make good decisions about differentiating openings for your students.

Choice-as-Motivator

Give students opportunities to make choices about important elements of their openings. When students are allowed to make choices, they generally

take more ownership in their work and tend to apply themselves more seriously to the task. They gain a sense of independence and feel that they are trusted to make decisions. Most important, they will naturally choose things that fit them best as learners. Choice may be built into openings in any of the following ways:

- Allow students to choose their own topics (even if they are from a predetermined list) so that they are focusing on areas of interest and making a personal commitment to the project.

- Give students options about the type of visual aid they may use with their openings, such as choosing to create a poster, construct a chart, produce a movie, or develop a PowerPoint presentation.

- Let students make choices about how to present their openings, based upon preferred multiple intelligences.

- Provide options for the type of writing students may produce to accompany their openings. For example, students may choose to compose a journal entry, a newspaper article, a report, a poem, a story, an imaginary historical document, a fictional eyewitness account, a script, or a letter.

- Let students choose one aspect of the opening (oral presentation, written report, or visual aid) and increase the assessment value for that part of the presentation. For example, you might tell students that you will double the points awarded for one part, and each student may decide which one it will be. By letting a student place added weight on one part of the opening, you are essentially allowing him or her to identify a personal strength that will be taken into account during assessment.

> Emphasize multiple intelligences in student presentations by working with your students to identify and take advantage of their strongest intelligence areas.

Anchor Activities

In any classroom setting it is inevitable that some students will complete basic learning requirements before others. The answer to the age-old question "What do I do now?" lies in providing meaningful, engaging tasks to which students can turn their attention once they have completed an assignment or activity. These tasks are not merely time-fillers, but are intended to ensure that all kids are focused on the curriculum at all times, so as to extend learning. Such tasks are called anchor (or "sponge") activities, and they are important to successfully differentiating instruction. Openings provide a wonderful opportunity to offer students anchor activities. When a student has time available, he or she may be allowed to independently develop an opening presentation on a mutually agreed-upon topic.

Putting It All Together

The chart on page 29 presents the complete sequence for conducting starter openings and openings. Any part of the openings process can be differentiated, depending on your learning goals and the needs of your students. For a given stage, consider *what* (content, process, product) and *how* (by learner readiness, interest, profile) you can differentiate to support your students and help ensure their success.

Social-Emotional Learning (SEL) and Openings

Openings can be instrumental in helping students gain the essential social and emotional skills that build confidence, enhance learning, and promote self-esteem. These skills—or competencies—according to The Collaborative for Academic, Social, and Emotional Learning (CASEL), include:

- Self-awareness—the ability to identify one's emotions and strengths

- Social awareness—the ability to identify and understand the thoughts and feelings of others and to appreciate diversity

- Self-management—the ability to monitor and regulate one's feelings as well as establish and work toward pro-social goals

- Responsible decision-making—the ability to analyze situations, assume personal responsibility, respect others and treat them with compassion, and solve problems

- Relationship skills—the ability to communicate effectively using verbal and nonverbal skills, establish and maintain relationships, achieve mutually satisfactory resolutions to conflict by addressing the needs of all concerned, and refuse to engage in unwanted, unsafe, unethical, or unlawful conduct*

In short, social and emotional learning is the development of the skills, attitudes, and values all people need to manage life tasks and grow up healthy and happy. Research done by CASEL and others strongly suggests that social and emotional health is also an important key to academic success.

How Openings Support SEL

One of the most important outcomes of an openings program may be the introspection that is required and the resulting insights that students gain into their own often unrecognized and untapped capabilities. A much different process is necessary to prepare for an opening and present it publicly than to simply complete an assignment and hand it in. Openings encourage students to analyze their personal strengths and weaknesses.

Openings also provide opportunities for students to interact with others. There is no doubt that students learn a great deal about diversity by watching their classmates present openings. Even more compelling are the insights each student gains about communicating and interacting with others by presenting to an audience of peers. Openings are individualized projects that require students to think about their feelings and emotions as they face the prospect of making public presentations. This is not an easy task for many students. Openings require students to make decisions, solve problems, and take responsibility for their work because each presentation is uniquely the result of choices a student makes. By being involved in such a program, students are naturally engaged in a process of learning about themselves and developing relationships with others.

How Discussing SEL Helps Develop It

Illinois is a leading state in developing SEL education goals, standards, and descriptors. The chart** on page 22 shows a selection of the Illinois SEL goals, standards, and descriptors for grades 1–5 that relate to the discussion questions in the next section. Complete standards are available at www.isbe.net.

Beyond the social and emotional value kids get from doing openings, they can learn SEL skills directly by talking about those skills as they relate to openings. Use the following discussion questions to conduct class or individual discussions about feelings and openings. (Each question is linked directly to Illinois goals, standards, and

---

* SEL competencies taken from www.casel.org/basics/skills.php. Accessed November 3, 2008.
** Illinois SEL goals, standards, and descriptors used with permission of the Illinois State Board of Education (ISBE). The ISBE does not endorse this book.

Illinois SEL Goals, Standards, and Descriptors

Goal	Standard	Descriptor
Goal 1: Develop self-awareness and self-management skills to achieve school and life success.	A: Identify and manage one's emotions and behavior.	Stage B #1: Describe how various situations make you feel.
		Stage C #5: Distinguish among intensity levels of an emotion.
		Stage C #6: Demonstrate ways to deal with upsetting emotions.
	B: Recognize personal qualities and external supports.	Stage A #7: Describe situations in which you feel you need help.
		Stage B #2: Describe an achievement that makes you feel proud.
		Stage C #7: Demonstrate ways to ask for help when needed.
Goal 2: Use social-awareness and interpersonal skills to establish and maintain positive relationships.	A: Recognize the feelings and perspectives of others.	Stage A #4: Explain how interrupting others may make them feel.
		Stage B #6: Demonstrate an ability to listen to others.
		Stage C #5: Demonstrate a capacity to care about the feelings of others.

descriptors.) Use the follow-up information, as appropriate, in your discussions.

Discussion Questions

What emotions (feelings) might students have who are getting ready to talk to the class?
Students may answer that they feel nervous, scared, excited, self-conscious, prepared, or even like they have to go to the bathroom. Let students know it's normal to feel these things before giving an opening. Everyone gets a little nervous, even if they don't look it. The important thing for students to remember is that when it's their turn, you and the whole class will support them. They can feel proud that they did something that wasn't easy.
Illinois SEL Standard 1A: Identify and manage one's emotions and behavior. Descriptor Stage B #1: Describe how various situations make you feel.

If you are *excited* about giving your opening, would you say you feel a little bit excited, quite excited, or very excited?
Some people get very excited about certain things, while others are calm most of the time. Help

students understand that people have different personalities, and everyone reacts differently in situations. If they feel very nervous about doing an opening, you can help them with that beforehand. You will also be right there to help during the opening if students can't remember what to talk about next.
Illinois SEL Standard 1A: Identify and manage one's emotions and behavior. Descriptor Stage C #5: Distinguish among intensity levels of an emotion.

If talking to the class makes you feel *nervous,* can you think of something you could do to feel calmer?
Students may mention one of the following examples, all of which can be helpful. If these answers don't come up, you may want to suggest them:

- deep breathing

- be prepared so you know what you're going to say

- talk with a friend who may know a joke to tell you or be supportive in other ways

Students may not be able to make the nervous feelings go away completely before their openings, but they will feel good when it's done. The important thing is for them to do their openings and think about how the class will enjoy hearing about their topics.

Illinois SEL Standard 1A: Identify and manage one's emotions and behavior. Descriptor Stage C #6: Demonstrate ways to deal with upsetting emotions.

What kinds of things have you done well in the past that you are proud of?

Let students know that as they learn to do openings in your classroom, they will likely feel a great sense of pride in what they have done. No one is expecting them to do everything perfectly. Just getting up to talk to the class makes their first opening a success! Students' confidence will improve as they learn how to make a good presentation.

Illinois SEL Standard 1B: Recognize personal qualities and external supports. Descriptor Stage B #2: Describe an achievement that makes you feel proud.

Can you think of things you might want help with as you get ready to do your opening? Who might you ask for help? How might you ask?

Emphasize for students that you are there to help them with any questions, and so is everyone in your class. Students are learning to do openings together so they need to help each other with a smile. That will make doing openings more fun. Each student has different strengths; each is a unique and important individual; and each will have his or her own presentation style.

Tell students: Don't wait for someone to ask if you need help. Be sure to let someone know you need help, even if no one asks you that day.

Illinois SEL Standard 1B: Recognize personal qualities and external supports. Descriptor Stage A #7: Describe situations in which you feel you need help.

If someone is standing in front of the class making his or her presentation and suddenly someone in the audience starts talking to a neighbor or tapping a pencil on the desk, how do you think the presenter would feel?

Possible answers students may suggest include feeling insulted, frustrated, upset, distracted, or mad. Explain to students that it is very rude to talk or not pay attention to the presenter. Each of them

will be the presenter at some point and they will want their audience to listen to what they have to say. Even if students are not interested in the topic being presented, it is important to show their respect for the speaker by not interrupting or being a distraction in any way. If they think of a question they want to ask about the presentation, they should save it until their classmate is done talking.

Illinois SEL Standard 2A: Recognize the feelings and perspectives of others. Descriptor Stage A #4: Explain how interrupting others may make them feel

Picture yourself standing in front of the class giving your opening. As you look out at the audience, what types of things would you like to see your audience doing?

Most students would like to see the audience looking at them with interest, sitting still, and listening quietly. Remind students that openings are not just about the person giving the presentation. They are about everyone in the class doing their part to make the presentation a good one. The audience does their part by paying attention, thinking quietly about what the presenter is saying, having a pleasant and supportive attitude, and sitting still and facing the presenter. This is how people show respect.

Illinois SEL Standard 2A: Recognize the feelings and perspectives of others. Descriptor Stage B #6: Demonstrate an ability to listen to others.

When the presenter has finished talking, what can the audience do to show their appreciation?

Encourage your students to give a round of applause, to smile and look at the presenter, and to have thoughtful questions to ask. Another nice thing to do is to find a moment later in the day to tell the classmate what a good job he or she did. Openings give students a chance to teach the rest of the class about something they've learned, and it's important for the audience to show their appreciation for the hard work their peers have done. Giving an opening is not easy, but when other people show their appreciation, it makes a huge difference.

Illinois SEL Standard 2A: Recognize the feelings and perspectives of others. Descriptor Stage C #5: Demonstrate a capacity to care about the feelings of others.

Content Standards and Openings

Use the following chart to see at a glance which national standards are supported by which openings.

Level	Content Area	Strand	Standard/Benchmark	Project Name	Page
K–1	Any Content	Any Strand	Any Standard	Did You Know?	71
K–1	English	Evaluation Strategies	Students apply a wide range of strategies to comprehend, interpret, evaluate, and appreciate texts. They draw on their prior experience, their interactions with other readers and writers, their knowledge of word meaning and of other texts, their word identification strategies, and their understanding of textual features (e.g., sound-letter correspondence, sentence structure, context, graphics).	The Storyteller	CD-ROM
K–1	English	Applying Knowledge	Students apply knowledge of language structure, language conventions (e.g., spelling and punctuation), media techniques, figurative language, and genre to create, critique, and discuss print and nonprint texts.	The Storyteller	CD-ROM
K–1	English	Participating in Society	Students participate as knowledgeable, reflective, creative, and critical members of a variety of literacy communities.	The Storyteller	CD-ROM
K–1	English	Applying Knowledge	Students apply knowledge of language structure, language conventions (e.g., spelling and punctuation), media techniques, figurative language, and genre to create, critique, and discuss print and nonprint texts.	Words All Around Us	77
K–1	English	Participating in Society	Students participate as knowledgeable, reflective, creative, and critical members of a variety of literacy communities.	Words All Around Us	77
K–1	Math	Representation	Create and use representations to organize, record, and communicate mathematical ideas.	I Made a Pattern	81
K–1	Math	Communication	Organize and consolidate their mathematical thinking through communication.	I Made a Pattern	81
K–1	Math	Connections	Recognize and apply mathematics in contexts outside of mathematics.	I Made a Pattern	81
K–1	Math	Algebra	Understand patterns, relations, and functions: • *recognize, describe, and extend patterns such as sequences of sounds and shapes or simple numeric patterns and translate from one representation to another; analyze how both repeating and growing patterns are generated.*	I Made a Pattern	81
K–1	Science	Science as Inquiry	All students should develop abilities necessary to do scientific inquiry: • *ask a question about objects, organisms, and events in the environment; communicate investigations and explanations.*	I Understand Food Chains	85
K–1	Science	Life Science	All students should develop understanding of organisms and their environment: • *all animals depend on plants. Some animals eat plants for food. Other animals eat animals that eat the plants.*	I Understand Food Chains	85
K–1	Social Studies	Individual Development and Identity	Describe personal connections to place—especially place as associated with immediate surroundings.	My Home and Family	66
K–1	Social Studies	People, Places, and Environments	Describe how people create places that reflect ideas, personality, culture, and wants and needs.	My Home and Family	66

Level	Content Area	Strand	Standard/Benchmark	Project Name	Page
K–1	Social Studies	Individual Development and Identity	Describe the unique features of one's nuclear and extended families.	My Home and Family	66
K–1	Social Studies	Individual Development and Identity	Identify and describe ways family, groups, and community influence the individual's daily life and personal choices.	My Home and Family	66
2–3	Any Content	Any Strand	Any Standard	Alien Broadcast System	102
2–3	Math	Geometry	Analyze characteristics and properties of two- and three-dimensional geometric shapes and develop mathematical arguments about geometric relationships: • *recognize, name, build, draw, compare, and sort two- and three-dimensional shapes; describe attributes and parts of two- and three-dimensional shapes.*	The Shape Hunter	126
2–3	Math	Geometry	Use visualization, spatial reasoning, and geometric modeling to solve problems: • *recognize geometric shapes and structures in the environment and specify their location.*	The Shape Hunter	126
2–3	Science	Scientific Inquiry	All students should develop abilities necessary to do scientific inquiry and understandings about scientific inquiry: • *ask a question about objects, organisms, and events in the environment; plan and conduct a simple investigation, communicate investigations and explanations.*	These Objects Are Classified	90
2–3	Science	Physical Science	All students should develop an understanding of properties of objects and materials.	These Objects Are Classified	90
2–3	Science	Life Science	All students should develop an understanding of the characteristics of organisms, life cycles of organisms, and organisms and their environments.	This Place Is a Zoo	118
2–3	Social Studies	Time, Continuity, Change	Demonstrate an ability to use correctly vocabulary associated with time such as past, present, future, and long ago; read and construct simple timelines; identify examples of change; and recognize examples of cause and effect.	Community Cam	CD-ROM
2–3	Social Studies	People, Places, & Environments	Describe how people create places that reflect ideas, personality, culture, and wants and needs.	Community Cam	CD-ROM
2–3	Social Studies	Individual Development & Identity	Describe personal connections to place, as associated with community, nation, and world.	Community Cam	CD-ROM
2–3	Social Studies	People, Places, & Environments	Describe ways that historical events have been influenced by, and have influenced, physical and human geographic factors in local, regional, national, and global settings.	Community Cam	CD-ROM
2–3	Social Studies	Individual Development & Identity	Work independently and cooperatively to accomplish goals.	Community Cam	CD-ROM
2–3	Social Studies	Civic Ideals & Practices	Recognize and interpret how the "common good" can be strengthened through various forms of citizen action.	Local Hero of the Year	110
2–3	Social Studies	Individual Development & Identity	Identify and describe the influence of perception, attitudes, values, and beliefs on personal identity.	Local Hero of the Year	110

Level	Content Area	Strand	Standard/Benchmark	Project Name	Page
4–6	Any Content	Any Strand	Any Standard	Featured Expert Series	178
4–6	Math	Algebra	Analyze change in various contexts: • *investigate how a change in one variable relates to a change in a second variable; identify and describe situations with constant or varying rates of change and compare them.*	Buying the Car of My Dreams	146
4–6	Math	Communication	Communicate their mathematical thinking coherently and clearly to peers, teachers, and others.	Buying the Car of My Dreams	146
4–6	Math	Representation	Create and use representations to organize, record, and communicate mathematical ideas.	Buying the Car of My Dreams	146
4–6	Math	Algebra	Use mathematical models to represent and understand quantitative relationships: • *model problem situations with objects and use representations such as graphs, tables, and equations to draw conclusions.*	Buying the Car of My Dreams	146
4–6	Math	Connections	Recognize and apply mathematics in contexts outside of mathematics.	Buying the Car of My Dreams	146
4–6	Science	Earth & Space Science	All students should develop an understanding of Earth in the solar system.	It's Written in the Stars	159
4–6	Science	Life Science	All students should develop an understanding of the characteristics of organisms, life cycles of organisms, and organisms and environments.	The Naturalist	135
4–6	Social Studies	Individual Development & Identity	Identify and describe the influence of perception, attitudes, values, and beliefs on personal identity.	Heroes	CD-ROM
4–6	Social Studies	Civic Ideals & Practices	Recognize and interpret how the "common good" can be strengthened through various forms of citizen action.	Heroes	CD-ROM
4–6	Social Studies	Individual Development & Identity	Relate such factors as physical endowment and capabilities, learning, motivation, personality, perception, and behavior to individual development.	Heroes	CD-ROM
4–6	Social Studies	Individual Development & Identity	Relate personal changes to social, cultural, and historical contexts.	Family Ties to History	168
4–6	Social Studies	Individual Development & Identity	Describe personal connections to place, as associated with community, nation, and world.	Family Ties to History	168
4–6	Social Studies	Global Connections	Analyze examples of conflict, cooperation, and interdependence among groups, societies, and nations.	Family Ties to History	168
4–6	Social Studies	Time, Continuity, Change	Demonstrate an ability to use correctly vocabulary associated with time such as past, present, future, and long ago; read and construct simple timelines; identify examples of change; and recognize examples of cause and effect.	Family Ties to History	168

Standards for the English Language Arts, by the International Reading Association and the National Council of Teachers of English, Copyright 1996 by the International Reading Association and the National Council of Teachers of English. Reprinted with permission. See www.ncte.org/standards.

Principles and Standards for School Mathematics are listed with the permission of the National Council of Teachers of Mathematics (NCTM). NCTM does not endorse the content or validity of these alignments.

Expectations of Excellence: Curriculum Standards for Social Studies are from the National Council for the Social Studies (NCSS).

"National Science Education Standards," © 1995 by the National Academy of Sciences, courtesy of the National Academies Press, Washington, D.C. Reprinted with permission.

Part 2

First Steps: Starter Openings

Introduction to Starter Openings

Starter openings are a way of scaffolding. They provide a helpful first step for students because they do not require all the preparation of full openings. Rather, students get in front of their classmates to present things they already know about. This way, the emphasis is placed on students' learning and mastering a format and skill set. This will give them confidence when they later begin working on more substantial, individualized presentations.

Your primary task when implementing starter openings is to give your students a format to follow and to work with them as they become comfortable using the format to present information.

There is a standard sequence of tasks and activities to follow in conducting openings; some, but not all, of that sequence applies to starter openings. The chart on page 29 shows the complete openings process. The right-hand column of the chart represents the areas emphasized by starter openings. By looking at this chart, you can see what the key components of starter openings are and how they fit into the bigger picture of openings in general. Please note that each component of the process is a potential place for differentiating the project for students. More about this will be said in Part 3.

Conducting Starter Openings

Twelve starter openings are provided in this section: four each for early elementary (grades K–1), middle elementary (grades 2–3), and upper elementary (grades 4–6). Each is described in enough detail for you to use it immediately with your class. You may use the starter opening ideas exactly as they are described or modify them to fit your needs and those of your students. (See pages 33–34 for suggested adaptations.)

Regardless of the grade level you teach, be sure to examine all twelve starter openings for ideas. With slight modifications, each idea may be useful with any age group. For example, one of the middle elementary starter openings is called "What Is the Same? What Is Different?"

This is an important concept that you might want to work on with older students as well, perhaps titled "Looking for Similarities and Differences" or "How Can Objects Be Compared and Contrasted?"

For each of the three levels, the first starter opening includes a detailed explanation of how to introduce it along with procedures, guidelines, and expectations of students. The remaining three starter openings for each level are clearly described but with fewer examples and less detail.

Choose a Starter Opening

In your planning, choose or adapt a starter opening that appeals to you. Although these beginning presentations are not content focused and rely on basic personal prior knowledge, students will be working on skills that fulfill oral presentation standards in English language arts (see pages 6–7).

Plan the Specifics

Before you begin any presentations, decide in what order students will do their starter openings. You may want to ask for volunteers first; the volunteers will provide modeling for the more reluctant students. Also decide how many starter openings you will do each day.

Review the "Options to Consider with Starter Openings" and "Differentiating Starter Openings" on pages 33–34 for ideas about adapting the topic, preparing students to present, adding visual interest, and other differentiation strategies and variations. Also review additional variations suggested for the specific starter opening you are conducting.

Introduce Students to Starter Openings

When using starter openings for the first time, students will likely have two basic questions: What is an opening and why should we do them? First, introduce the idea of openings and talk about what the term *openings* means. You might begin with words like the following:

Standard Sequence for Openings and Starter Openings

Process Component	Openings	Starter Openings
Identifying a Content Area	The teacher identifies a content area on which to focus, based on the curriculum.	The teacher may or may not focus on content. The emphasis is on prior knowledge and student readiness.
Identifying Content Standards	The teacher identifies appropriate grade level content standards to provide alignment between the opening project and the curriculum.	In general, content standards are not emphasized beyond speaking. Speaking standards are a major emphasis of starter openings.
Determining the Order of Presentations	The teacher determines the order of presentations, based on readiness, willingness, logical sequence of topics, random selection, student choice, or other criteria.	The teacher determines the order of presentations, based primarily on readiness and emotional needs.
Choosing Topics	Students generally choose their own topics within parameters established by the teacher.	The teacher identifies topics and generally assigns them to students or gives them a narrow range of choices.
Conducting Research	Students conduct research to find information that is relevant to their selected topics.	NA
Using Resources	Students use resources provided by the teacher, that are available in the classroom or school, or that they find on their own.	Where necessary, students use resources that are directly provided by the teacher.
Writing the Report	Students use the information they gather to write a report, which is the basis for their oral presentations.	NA
Creating the Visual	Students produce a visual aid to support their oral presentation.	NA
Preparing for the Oral Presentation	Students make notes or outlines and practice at home or, in some cases, at school with peers.	Students give impromptu presentations that require little or no preparation.
Presenting to an Audience	Students present their openings to the class on a scheduled day and time.	Students present their starter openings to the class when called upon.
Answering Questions	At the conclusion of a standard opening, the student presenter asks if there are any questions.	NA
Assessing the Opening	The teacher assesses the presentation using an assessment form.	The teacher provides feedback using a Starter Opening Feedback Form.

"Let's talk about a new project that we're going to begin soon. The project is called 'Openings.' An opening is an opportunity for you to share things you know with your classmates. When you do an opening, you will stand in front of the class and present information or ideas to the rest of us. We'll begin slowly so that each of you can learn how to do openings and so that you will get better and better at being presenters. At first we'll do 'starter openings' that last less than a minute. Later we will do more challenging openings."

To help students understand the value of learning to make classroom presentations, you might begin by asking, "Why do you think learning how to be a presenter is important?" or "How can learning to present to the class help you in school? What about later in life?" Guide the discussion so students recognize that becoming capable presenters can help them feel comfortable and confident, communicate more effectively, make what they have to share more interesting to others, and have their opinions and ideas heard and understood.

Take some time to discuss why the presentations are called openings. Ask students what the word *opening* means to them. They might suggest these or other ideas:

- going from one place to a new place

- opening a door or a gate and walking through

- being ready for business, as when a store opens

- being open-minded

- unwrapping a gift

- doing or seeing something new, like a new movie or play or the first ball game of the season

If you wish, have students work in small groups to come up with ideas, and then create one or more "We call our presentations openings because . . ." posters.

Explain the Assignment

For each starter opening, begin with a brief explanation of the topic that students will talk about. State the assignment. Then present or review the required steps for the starter opening. Experience has shown that, regardless of which starter opening idea you use, your greatest success will come from expecting students to follow a clearly defined format when they present. The presentation format for any type of opening consists of the following five key elements:

> ### The Presentation Steps for a Starter Opening or an Opening
>
> **1.** Introduce yourself.
> **2.** Explain your topic.
> **3.** Present your information.
> **4.** Conclude the opening.
> **5.** Answer questions (optional for starter openings).

You may find it helpful to have a set of prompts to help students remember these five steps. Copy the reproducible forms on pages 193–199, setting the copier at 200% and using 11" x 17" paper. Or, if you wish, create your own poster, perhaps showing pictures in panels like a comic strip depicting the elements you expect students to include. Display the poster or the forms where the presenters can see them and where you can point to them if necessary. It usually doesn't take much of a prompt to remind a student of what to do or say next. If you are more comfortable giving oral prompts, that is fine as well.

Use the first starter opening as an opportunity to teach these steps to students. Before inviting individual students to present a starter opening, present your own so that they will see an example of what you expect. As students go through their openings, reiterate the steps and take time to gently guide students who struggle with the format. Keep in mind that starter openings are a way of differentiating instruction for the whole class through scaffolding—their purpose is to help children learn a presentation format and gain confidence in speaking to the group. Give unrestrained positive reinforcement to students as they work their way toward mastery. (See below through page 33 for more about the use of feedback when using starter openings.) Once students internalize the format, it becomes the standard framework for presenting any opening.

The charts on pages 31 and 32 present the twelve starter openings and give examples of how this presentation format might be followed. The first example for each grade level shows all five steps. The remaining examples illustrate some or all of step 3, "Present your information."

Establish Audience Expectations

Be sure to set clear expectations for the students in their role as listening audience. Specific, age-appropriate audience expectations for each level are provided in the guidelines for conducting the starter openings later in Part 2; see pages 35, 39, and 44.

Give Feedback

Starter openings are designed to introduce novice presenters to the concept of kids teaching kids. They are like rehearsals for musicians: a chance to master skills prior to performing for an audience. With this in mind, starter openings should not be formally graded or assessed because they are meant to be low-stress, low-stakes practice sessions during which students learn how to present an opening. However, it is important to give students feedback about their presentations, so they can grow and improve.

Skills and behaviors to emphasize with early, middle, and upper elementary students are detailed in the introduction to each level's starter openings. A Starter Opening Feedback Form is included on page 205. There are several ways to make use of the form, depending on your goals and the age of

Starter Openings Presentation Examples

Early Elementary

Title	Basic Assignment	Example	Page
Who Am I?	Tell your full name, how old you are, where you go to school, and your teacher's name. Then tell one thing you like to do.	"Good morning. My name is Emma Sue O'Gara and I have an opening for you. My opening is called 'Who Am I?' It is about me. I am six years old. I go to Santa Juana Elementary School. My teacher's name is Ms. Mollet. One thing I like to do is tap dance. Thank you for listening."	35
I Like Recess	Tell one thing you like to do at recess and tell why, using the word *because*.	"I like to run around the playground with my friends *because* we have lots of energy."	38
The Weather Outside	Tell two things that can be observed about the weather today. Use two descriptive words and connect them with the word *and*.	"Today it is foggy *and* really wet. It looks like it is going to rain all day."	38
I Have a Friend	Tell about your friend. Give the friend's name, describe the friend with a word or phrase, and tell something you do together.	"My friend's name is TaShawn Berry. He can do cartwheels without getting dizzy. TaShawn and I like to tell jokes."	39

Middle Elementary

Title	Basic Assignment	Example	Page
What I Do in School	Tell a few things that you do at school and one thing that you like.	"Good morning. My name is Danh Nguyen and I have an opening for you. My opening is called 'What I Do in School.' I will tell you some things I do at school. I do sit-ups in gym class and I like to paint pictures in art. Thank you for listening."	40
What Is the Same? What Is Different?	Tell one thing that is the same and one thing that is different about the two objects you were given. Use the words *objects*, *same*, and *different*.	"These *objects* are the *same* because they are both cereal boxes made of cardboard and they each hold 18 ounces of cereal. But they are *different* from each other, too. Look at the way the top flaps close. The box I'm holding has a tab that you have to insert into the other flap. This other box has a flap that is designed to be pushed in one easy motion under the other flap. It's not a huge difference but it is different."	42
Choose One of Three	Choose one of three topics listed (something you like to do) for your opening. Describe one activity and tell why you like it, using the word *because*. Give two reasons.	"I help my dad deliver newspapers on weekends. I like to help him *because* I earn my allowance that way and sometimes we get a doughnut afterward."	43
Welcome to My Morning	Describe how you start your day. Present at least four activities, events, tasks, or routines in chronological order.	"I don't like getting up in the morning so my mom sends Skittles, our cat, in to wake me up. He licks my face. Then I check my hamster to see what it's doing. My mom usually hollers at me to get in the kitchen to eat my breakfast so I do. Then I brush my teeth and comb my hair."	43

Upper Elementary

Title	Basic Assignment	Example	Page
It's a Rule of the School	Tell about a rule at school and why you think we have that rule.	"Hello. My name is Emira Durakovic and I have an opening for you about school rules. I will tell you about a rule in this school and explain why I think we have that rule. In our school we are supposed to treat everyone with respect. That is a good rule to have because otherwise people can treat others like they aren't as important and that makes them feel bad. My teacher last year said that you shouldn't ever start thinking you aren't good enough because someone disrespects you; and you shouldn't act mad either. Just smile and quietly walk away. Thank you for listening to my opening about school rules."	44
What I Want to Be	Tell about a career that you are interested in. Tell the name of the career, at least two things that someone does in that career, why these are personally interesting to you, and at least two things you need to know or do to prepare for that career.	"I'm interested in developing video games that help students learn about school subjects. My uncle says that in the future, schools will offer online modules that students 'play' to learn chemistry and biology or any other subject they need to take. Developing a video game involves people who are computer engineers, graphic designers, storywriters, animators, and marketing specialists. I'd like to be the person who is the subject expert so I can help develop the story and provide accurate information about the school subject. I need to find a good college to learn about the gaming industry and become an expert in the sciences. My uncle says that people our age will have careers that don't even exist yet. That's cool! That completes my opening. Thank you."	47
Analyze This	Describe what kind of data is provided on a graph or chart and give your explanation of what can be concluded from the data.	"The 'My Pyramid' food chart shows what foods you should eat to have a healthy diet. It shows that we should be eating whole grains and lots of dark green vegetables each day. How many of us do that? When I think about what I choose to eat in the lunchroom every day, I have to admit that it doesn't help very much with the grains and vegetable recommendations. The chart also shows that we need physical activity and . . .'"	47
Luck of the Draw	Draw a topic from a bowl and think about it for 30 seconds; then use what you already know to provide details and examples about this topic.	"My topic is 'Explain the difference between an adjective and an adverb, giving at least two examples.' We just worked with this when we did our 'Vivid Descriptions' writing last month. An adjective is a word that adds a new idea to a noun or pronoun. You could say that the goat ate the pie, but it would be more interesting or accurate to say that the renegade goat ate the entire pie! Adverbs, on the other hand . . .'"	48

your students. Here are a few suggestions to help you decide how to use the form. You will likely find that some combination of the following ideas will suit your purposes best:

- Post the form in the room for everyone to see and spend some time discussing it. It is important for students to know specific project expectations ahead of time.

- Record your observations while the student is presenting, and then refer to the form as you provide instant oral feedback to the student and the audience following the presentation. This is especially useful for the youngest students since you can translate your observations into age-appropriate language.

- Record your observations while the student is presenting, and then schedule a brief meeting for later in the day when the two of you can discuss the presentation.

- Ask members of the audience to provide suggestions for "glows" and "grows" that can be provided to the presenter. A "glow" is something that was done well. A "grow" is something that needs to be improved. Generally the audience is asked to offer two "glows" for every "grow." Be sure to record the things mentioned by audience members on the feedback form.

- Give the student presenter a copy of the form to fill out as a self-assessment. Then arrange to meet with the student to compare his or her impressions with yours.

- Complete the form by the end of the day and give it to the student presenter before he or she goes home. The reason for waiting until the end of the day is to allow you to find a few minutes in your busy schedule to record more fully your observations and comments before giving it to the student.

- Store the form in a student record folder for future reference so that you can track improvement over time as the student does more openings.

- Include the form in parent conference meetings to serve as a basis for discussing each child's strengths as a presenter, and to document areas that might need to be improved (both as a presenter and as an audience member).

Options to Consider with Starter Openings

You can fine-tune and adapt starter openings in a variety of ways to meet the needs of your class and of individual students. Consider the options and differentiation strategies suggested in the next few pages, and also check the additional options recommended for each individual presentation.

- Prepare students by discussing key words and concepts that they are expected to use in their starter openings.

- Use the key words in sentences to model the use of each term.

- Brainstorm topic ideas or descriptive words that relate to the assignment.

- Record a specific topic for each student (if the assignment allows) to avoid redundancy.

- Find photos or other resources that students could use as visuals (visuals are not required in starter openings).

- Help students feel more comfortable by giving them the option of sitting at a table to present rather than standing.

- Simplify the assignment with fewer requirements for students who struggle.

- Allow kinesthetic learners to enhance their presentations with acting or motions.

- Have cue cards ready for students who may need help remembering what to talk about next: ("Hello, my name is . . . ," "My opening is about . . . ," "Thank you for listening.")

- If students need more challenge, allow them to include more information in their openings.

- Give students the option of using the whiteboard or chalkboard or other visuals with their openings.

- Allow students to find a unique way to begin or end their presentations.

- Challenge students to use descriptive or interesting words in their openings.

- Allow students to add a component to the opening based on their strongest multiple intelligence.

- Increase the assignment requirements or add a new component.

- Have a student in the back of the classroom hold up a "Louder Please" sign if the presenter is talking too quietly. Similarly, have two or three students hold up signs that say "Look at me" to remind the presenter to make eye contact with people in the audience.

- Vary the assignment by changing the content/topic area of the starter opening or letting students choose from two or three content areas to keep the audience interested.

- Change the way the order of presentations is determined: alphabetically, by birth date, randomly, by drawing a number, and so forth.

- Build a technology component into the presentation, such as an overhead graphic, video camera, microphone, or Internet site.

- Structure the opening topic around some aspect of the curriculum.

- Invite a guest audience member.

- At the end of a student's presentation, ask the audience to mention something positive about the opening. (Select one or two students to comment.)

The starter openings offer you ready-to-use ideas to accomplish the important task of introducing students to openings without overwhelming or intimidating them. Feel free to use the starter openings as they are, modify them, or simply view them as templates and take off on your own to create entirely new ideas. Just keep in mind that the goal is to help students take that all-important first step toward becoming confident communicators.

Differentiating Starter Openings

Despite the simplicity of starter openings, they can be differentiated by content, process, and product to fit students' needs. Differentiating students' early presentations can help you meet your goal of supporting students to become comfortable, confident, effective presenters. You can differentiate any or all of the elements in the "Standard Sequence for Openings and Starter Openings" (page 29). Use any of the following suggestions, or come up with ideas of your own. You will also find additional ideas for differentiating specific starter openings in the "Options to Consider" for each presentation.

Differentiating content. While the topics described in this section comprise a complete set of starter openings, you may wish to differentiate the content by providing different topics for students to present. Topics might relate to prior knowledge from students' own lives or to information recently covered in class.

Differentiating process. Because openings are grounded in the concept of kids teaching kids, you are automatically differentiating the teaching and learning process simply by having students present their openings. Other ways to differentiate process with starter openings include using flexible grouping to allow kids to team up to plan or present starter openings and allowing time for students to think about a particular topic prior to presenting, making the starter opening a bit less impromptu. Scaffolding the assignment by using prompts for students who need them, such as posters or verbal reminders, is another helpful way to differentiate process.

Differentiating product. Finally, differentiate the product itself by allowing students to read prepared material aloud rather than speak extemporaneously, or by incorporating the use of other mediums (songs, pictures, photos, role plays, and so forth).

The Starter Openings

Early Elementary Starter Openings

This section presents four starter openings to use with early elementary students (grades K–1):

- Who Am I?
- I Like Recess
- The Weather Outside
- I Have a Friend

The following information will be helpful to you in working with early elementary students doing starter openings.

Student Introductions: The first step in presenting any opening is the introduction. Kindergarten and first-grade teachers report that requiring students to write their names on a whiteboard or chalkboard at the time they introduce themselves is a good way to personalize the opening and to allow for observation of writing skills such as legibility, use of an uppercase initial letter, and proper letter formation. If you wish, use a digital camera to make a record of progress over the year. At the completion of each opening, take a picture of the student standing next to his or her handwritten name on the whiteboard or chalkboard. At the end of the year, you will have a set of photographs for each child that show a year's growth in writing skills.

Presenter Expectations: There are six skills and behaviors to emphasize with early elementary students. You will want each child to:

- Write his or her name on the board.
- Show willingness to present in front of the class.
- Use good posture.
- Make appropriate eye contact.
- Use strong voice projection.
- Follow the assignment.

Use the Starter Opening Feedback Form on page 205 to evaluate children's presentations and to help you guide them to work on specific skills during future openings.

Audience Expectations: Be sure to set clear expectations for the students in their role as listening audience. Here are five rules that you can give to students in the audience:

- Sit in a listening position (you can establish this in a class discussion).
- Look at the speaker.
- Don't talk.
- Think about what the speaker is saying.
- Clap when the speaker is finished.

These are ways to show respect and appreciation toward the speaker and to ensure that everyone is able to see and hear the complete presentation.

Be sure you have explained the concept of openings to students. (For information on introducing openings, see pages 28–30.) Also have a plan for determining which child will present first and how the sequence for subsequent presenters will be determined.

This first starter opening, "Who Am I?", presents detailed procedures and guidelines for introducing it. Since the remaining three starter openings are described more succinctly, we recommend that you fully review the first starter opening even if you plan to have your students begin with a different one.

Who Am I?

Materials and Preparation

Handouts or posters: Copy and display the handouts from pages 193–199 in a large format to prompt students when they get stuck during their presentation. You can also prepare your own posters using the language from the handouts. (You will want these displays for all starter openings.)

Topic and Assignment

State the topic and explain what students are to do. The assignment for "Who Am I?" is: *Tell your full name, how old you are, where you go to school, and your teacher's name. Then tell one thing you like to do.*

Setting the Stage by Modeling

Present your own opening on the topic so students can see and hear an example. You might set up your example by saying, "I will do an opening first. For the opening, I'll tell about myself and the school I went to when I was six. We'll pretend I'm six years old." Next, you would write your first name on the whiteboard or chalkboard. Then you could continue: "Hello. My name is Howard. My opening is called 'Who Am I?' It's all about me. My full name is Howard Protzki. I'm six years old and I go to Belview School. My teacher's name is Mrs. Curtis. One thing I like to do is play with toy cars. Thank you for listening to my opening." If you will be asking students to do so, add, "Does anyone have a question?"

Procedure

Call on the first presenter. The following is an example of a well-formatted starter opening on the topic "Who Am I?" presented by a kindergartner or first grader.

Joshua is presenting the starter opening. He has already seen you model a "Who Am I?" starter opening, so he knows what it should look like and understands what he is supposed to do. He is also comfortable in the knowledge that you will help him by guiding and coaching him if he struggles or forgets any of the requirements. He knows you want him to be successful. Joshua begins to follow the steps you have explained.

1. Introduce yourself. Joshua introduces himself by carefully writing his name on a whiteboard or chalkboard and then turning to the audience and saying, "Good morning. My name is Joshua and I have an opening for you." Initially, it is important that each student be required to use the same introduction, whether it is this one or something different. While using a standard introduction is helpful as students begin presenting openings, once they are comfortable with the process you may want to let them be more creative with how they begin their presentations.

2. Explain your topic. Joshua follows his introduction by saying, "My opening is called 'Who Am I?' It is about me." The key requirement here is that, in one or two sentences, the student tells the audience exactly what is going to be presented, thereby setting the stage for audience members to focus on the topic.

3. Present your information. Joshua now presents his information in a systematic way, one that you have already modeled for him and the class. He says: "My full name is Joshua M. Rosales. I am six years old. I go to Lincoln School. My teacher is Mrs. Jones. One thing I like to do is go fishing with my dad." Notice that this is all prior knowledge for Joshua. It is not something that has been learned at school, but rather is information that Joshua already knows and is now sharing with others. Before giving the starter opening, Joshua thought of one thing to tell the class that he likes to do, which gives him choice and personalizes the starter opening. It's still prior knowledge, but it's personal prior knowledge that is unique to Joshua.

If Joshua needed help at any point when he spoke, you could draw his attention to the posted steps or prompt him with a few words ("My topic is . . . ","One thing you like to do . . . ").

4. Conclude your opening. Joshua now ends his starter opening by saying, "Thank you for listening." Using this standard conclusion statement allows students to bring the opening to a definite end. You may wish to add other components to the conclusion. For example, Joshua could be expected to say: "That is the end of my opening. Thank you for listening." Without providing this way of wrapping up, many young students find themselves standing awkwardly in front of the audience with nothing left to say. Later, when students have become comfortable with the openings process, you may allow presenters to vary the way they conclude.

At the conclusion of Joshua's opening, you will want to begin a round of applause. You could then affirm Joshua by saying, "Thank you so much, Joshua. You did a great job." At this point you may want to use the feedback form on page 205 to reinforce the presentation skills and behaviors that your students are practicing with openings.

5. Answer questions. A regular opening requires students to ask if there are any questions at the conclusion of their presentation. However, you may want to dispense with this requirement during starter openings, particularly with younger children. In Joshua's case, the main opportunity for questions is the information he provides when he says: "One thing I like to do is go fishing with my dad." Questions *can* be developed based on this information (*Where do you and your dad go fishing? What kind of fish do you catch? Do you eat the fish you catch? Do you ever go fishing with friends?*), but it is often difficult for young students to think of questions based on such limited input. The Starter Opening Feedback Form includes an optional item about answering questions from the audience. If you choose to have the audience ask questions, be prepared to provide guidance. For example, you might prompt the class by asking, "Does anyone have a question about Joshua's fishing trips with his dad?"

Following the first student's starter opening, remind the class of what you expect them to do when they make their own presentations. You might say: "Now, I want you all to remember what I look for when you are doing an opening. First, I expect each of you to do one. When you are in front of the class I want you to stand nice and tall, look at people in the audience, wait for everyone to be quiet, speak loudly, and follow directions. When you are done with your opening, say 'Thank you for listening.' These are things that help make you good presenters. I am very excited about helping you get better and better at it. Now, let's have another person do an opening."

Options to Consider for "Who Am I?"

You may differentiate any element of a starter opening to fit the needs of your class and of individual students. Pages 10–20 present a variety of options. Here are a few specific ideas you might try for this starter opening:

- Simplify the assignment for students who need a more gradual introduction to giving a presentation: *Tell us your name and one thing you like to do.*

- Add challenge by letting students include more information to their openings. For example, a child might include the fifth step, answering questions, or tell something he or she likes to do at school and at home.

The next few pages provide descriptions of three additional starter openings that you may want to try with your students.

I Like Recess

Topic and Assignment

For this starter opening students talk about what they like to do during recess (or any other activity time that you want to emphasize) and tell why, using the word *because*. Example: "I like to go on the spinner, because it makes me dizzy."

Procedure

Proceed with "I Like Recess" starter openings as you have planned them. As necessary, prompt children to fulfill the key elements of the starter opening as they speak. Remind them to tell something they like about recess and why they like it, using the word *because*. Model the required language

that is unique to this opening ("I like to watch children play because I know it's good for them to be active").

Options to Consider for "I Like Recess"

- Conduct a brainstorming session with the class to make a list of things students like to do during recess. Each student may choose a topic from this list.

- Practice using the word *because* with the class: "I like to _____ because _____."

- Replace recess with a different activity for students to talk about, such as art, physical education, or reading.

The Weather Outside

Topic and Assignment

For this starter opening students give a report about the weather outside. Students think of at least two words that describe what they observe about the weather today and connect them with the word *and*. Example: "Today it is warm and rainy outside."

Procedure

Proceed with "The Weather Outside" starter openings as you have planned them. As necessary, prompt children to fulfill the key elements of the starter opening as they speak. Remind them to describe two things about the weather, connecting them with the word *and*. Model the required language that is unique to this opening ("My opening is about what I observe—what I notice—about the weather today. When I look outside I observe that it is cloudy and windy.").

Options to Consider for "The Weather Outside"

- Challenge students to use descriptive words that have not been used by previous presenters. For example, students might use words such as *blustery, chilly, calm, stormy, muggy,* or any number of other descriptive weather words.

- Invite students to enact weather conditions physically. For example, they might use their fingers to show rain falling gently, blow or wave like wind, or open their arms to show full sun.

I Have a Friend
Topic and Assignment
For this starter opening students tell about a friend. They give the friend's first name, describe the friend with a word or phrase, and tell something the two of them do together, using the words *and I.* Example: "My friend's name is Maggie. Maggie is good at singing. Maggie and I make up songs together."

Procedure
Proceed with "I Have a Friend" starter openings as you have planned them. As necessary, prompt children to fulfill the key elements of the starter opening as they speak. Remind them to say *and I* (rather than *and me*). Model the required language that is unique to this opening ("My friend Stephanie likes to read. She and I talk about books together").

Options to Consider for "I Have a Friend"
- Brainstorm with the class about things friends often do together.
- Challenge students to use descriptive words that have not been used by previous presenters. For example, students might use words such as friendly, strong, intelligent, talented, or any number of other words to describe their friends. Or they might use language like *has black hair, is a strong swimmer, likes to tell jokes,* or *is good at addition.*

Middle Elementary Starter Openings

This section presents four starter openings to use with middle elementary students (grades 2–3):

- What I Do in School
- What Is the Same? What Is Different?
- Choose One of Three
- Welcome to My Morning

The following information will be helpful to you in working with middle elementary students doing starter openings.

Presenter Expectations: There are seven skills and behaviors to emphasize with middle elementary students. You will want each child to:

- Demonstrate a positive attitude (show willingness to present in front of the class).
- Introduce herself/himself by name.
- Use good posture.
- Make appropriate eye contact.
- Use strong voice projection.
- Use appropriate vocabulary.
- Follow the assignment.

Use the Starter Opening Feedback Form on page 205 to evaluate children's presentations and to help you guide them to work on specific skills during future openings.

Audience Expectations: Set clear expectations for the students in their role as listening audience. Here are five rules you can give to the audience:

- Use respectful listening manners (you can establish these in a class discussion as needed).
- Use appropriate body language.
- Ignore distractions from others.
- Think about what the speaker is saying.
- Provide positive feedback at the end of the opening.

The Starter Opening Feedback Form includes a section for monitoring the audience as well.

Be sure you have explained the concept of openings to students. (For information on introducing openings, see pages 28–30.) Also have a plan for determining which child will present first and how the sequence for subsequent presenters will be determined.

This first starter opening, "What I Do in School," presents detailed procedures and guidelines for introducing it. Since the remaining three starter openings are described more succinctly, we recommend that you fully review the first starter opening even if you plan to have your students begin with a different one.

What I Do in School

Materials and Preparation

Copy and display the handouts from pages 193–199 in a large format, or prepare your own posters using the language from the handouts. (You will want these displays for all starter openings.)

Topic and Assignment

State the topic and explain what students are to do. The assignment for "What I Do in School" is: *Tell a few things that you do at school and one thing that you like.*

Setting the Stage by Modeling

Present your own opening on the topic so students can see and hear an example. You might set up your example by saying, "I will do an opening first. My name is Mrs. Santorini. My opening is called 'What I Do in School.' I'm going to tell you some things I do here at school and one thing I especially like. I teach second and third graders at Plum Valley Elementary School. I help students learn reading, writing, and speaking skills. I also teach them arithmetic and science. I especially enjoy teaching and talking with students about the solar system. Thank you for listening to my opening."

Procedure

Call on the first presenter. The following is an example of a well-formatted starter opening on the topic "What I Do in School" presented by a second or third grader.

Alison is presenting a starter opening. She has already seen you model a "What I Do in School" starter opening, so she knows what it should look like and understands what she is supposed to do. She is also comfortable in the knowledge that you will help her by guiding and coaching her if she struggles or forgets any of the requirements. She knows you want her to be successful. Alison begins to follow the steps you have explained.   .

1. Introduce yourself. Alison introduces herself by facing the audience from the front of the room and saying, "Good morning. My name is Alison Drew and I have an opening for you." Initially, it is important that each student be required to use the same introduction, whether it is this one or something different. Once students are comfortable with the process you may want to let them be more creative with how they begin their presentations.

2. Explain your topic. Alison follows her introduction by saying, "My opening is called 'What I Do in School.' I'll tell you about some things I do and one thing I really like." The key requirement here is that, in one or two sentences, the student tells the audience exactly what is going to be presented, thereby setting the stage for audience members to focus on the topic.

3. Present your information. Alison now presents her information in a systematic way, one that you have already modeled for her and the class.

She says: "At school I read books and learn about lots of interesting things, and I play at recess with my friends. I'm also learning to multiply. One thing I really like is singing songs with Mrs. Miller." This is all prior knowledge for Alison. It is not something that has been learned at school, but rather is information that she already knows and is now sharing with others. (She reports that she is learning to multiply; she does not demonstrate *how* to multiply.) Before giving the starter opening, Alison thought of one thing to tell the class that she likes to do at school, which gives her choice and personalizes the starter opening. It's still prior knowledge, but it's personal prior knowledge that is unique to Alison.

If Alison needed help at any point when she spoke, you could draw her attention to the posted steps or prompt her with a few words ("One thing you like to do at school . . . ").

4. Conclude your opening. Alison now ends her starter opening by saying, "Thank you for listening." Using this standard conclusion statement allows students to bring the opening to a definite end. Later, when students have become comfortable with the openings process, you may allow presenters to vary the way they conclude.

At the conclusion of a student's opening, you will want to begin a round of applause. You could affirm Alison by saying, "Thank you, Alison. We all enjoyed your opening." At this point you may want to use the feedback form on page 205 to reinforce the presentation skills and behaviors that your students are practicing with openings.

5. Answer questions. A regular opening requires students to ask if there are any questions at the conclusion of their presentation. However, you may want to dispense with this requirement during starter openings. For Alison, students might ask questions that relate to her enjoyment of music class *(Why do you like music? Are you involved in music outside of school?).* It is often difficult for students to think of questions based on such limited input, though. The Starter Opening Feedback Form on page 205 includes an optional item about answering questions from the audience. If you choose to have the audience ask questions, be prepared to provide guidance. For example, you might prompt the class by asking, "Would anyone like to ask Alison a question about how much she enjoys music?"

Following the first student's starter opener, remind the class of what you expect them to do when they make their own presentations. You might say: "Now, I want you all to remember what I look for when you are doing an opening. First, I expect each of you to do one. When you are in front of the class I want you to stand nice and tall, look at people in the audience, wait for everyone to be quiet, speak loudly, and follow directions. When you are done with your opening, thank your audience for listening to you. These are things that help make you good presenters. I am very excited about helping you get better and better at it. Now, let's hear another opening."

Options to Consider for "What I Do in School"

You may differentiate any element of a starter opening to fit the needs of your class and of individual students. Pages 10–20 present a variety of options. Here are a few specific ideas you might try for this starter opening:

- Vary the content by focusing on a subject area ("What I Do During Science Time") or on an activity outside the classroom ("What I Do on the Playground").

- Simplify the assignment: *Tell us your full name and one thing you do each day at school.*

- Add challenge by letting students name something they *like* and *do not like* to do at school.

- Let children show or perform something they like to do at school.

The next few pages provide descriptions of three additional starter openings that you may want to try with your students.

What Is the Same? What Is Different?

Materials and Preparation

- *Multiple pairs of objects for students to compare and contrast:* Gather enough objects so that each student can present a unique set of objects. Geometric shapes of different sizes, colors, and materials are useful for this purpose.

Choose objects that have definite similarities and differences, such as two blue triangles, one large and one small, one made of wood and one of cardboard. It is important to have several different pairs of objects so that students are not repeatedly comparing and contrasting the same things.

Topic and Assignment

For this starter opening each student is given two objects to compare and contrast. They tell one way the items are alike and one way they are not alike, using the words *objects, same,* and *different.* Example: "These objects are the same because they are rectangles. They are different because one is large and one is small."

Procedure

Proceed with "What Is the Same? What Is Different?" starter openings as you have planned them. As necessary, prompt children to fulfill the key elements of the starter opening as they speak. Remind them to tell a way the items are alike and a way they are not alike, using the words *objects, same,* and *different.* Model the required language that is unique to this opening ("These two objects are the same because they are both recorders. They are different because one is made of plastic and the other is made of metal").

Options to Consider for "What Is the Same? What Is Different?"

- Focus on a variety of different objects and conduct a brainstorming session with the class to practice identifying similarities and differences. Either use different objects from those that will be used during the starter openings or use the same objects in different combinations.

- Let students choose their own objects to compare and contrast.

- Require students to identify two (or more) similarities and differences, rather than just one.

- Put a number of objects on a table and let each student choose any two objects to compare and contrast for the starter opening.

Choose One of Three

Materials and Preparation

On a bulletin board, whiteboard, or chalkboard, write the following topics:

- Something I Do with My Family
- Something I Do as a Hobby
- Something I Do with My Friends

Topic and Assignment

For this starter opening, students choose from three given topics; they describe something they do related to their chosen topic and two reasons why they enjoy the activity, using the word *because* before giving their reasons. Example: "I go to the pool with my teenage brother. I like going to the pool because we play on the giant slide and jump off the diving board."

Procedure

Proceed with "Choose One of Three" starter openings as you have planned them. As necessary, prompt children to fulfill the key elements of the starter opening as they speak. Remind them to state a specific thing that they do (with family, at school, or with friends) and to use the word *because* when giving at least two reasons for liking it. Model the required language that is unique to this opening ("I enjoy building birdhouses for wetland birds, because I am helping ensure that water birds can safely raise a family each year and I like the way they look").

Options to Consider for "Choose One of Three"

- Choose a different set of three activities from which students may pick. For example, they could all be related to school, such as "Something I Do at Recess," "Something I Do in Music Class," and "Something I Do in Math."

- Make the requirements more extensive. For example, have students cite two things they do, rather than one. Or, ask them to give three reasons for liking the activity, rather than two.

- Tell students they will be doing one of the three options, but which one will be determined by a random drawing. Put each option on a separate slip of paper and have students draw one out of a hat or bowl. This becomes their assignment.

Welcome to My Morning

Topic and Assignment

For this starter opening students describe what their morning is like, from waking up until they walk into the classroom. They tell about at least four activities, events, tasks, or routines that take place each morning, in chronological order. Expect each student to present a sequence of events, using words that indicate the order in which they typically happen. Listen for terms such as *first, second, after that, then, before, later, next,* and *when.* Example: "First thing every morning I get dressed. Then I walk my dog Pepi. After that I eat breakfast before I brush my teeth and head out the door."

Procedure

Proceed with "Welcome to My Morning" starter openings as you have planned them. As necessary, prompt children to fulfill the key elements of the starter opening as they speak. Remind them to tell the events of their morning in order. Model examples of sequencing language that is unique to this opening ("The first thing that happens every morning is . . . Then I . . . When I have finished . . . Finally . . .").

Options to Consider for "Welcome to My Morning"

- Brainstorm with the class a list of typical morning activities, events, and routines that students may include in their starter openings.

- Focus on a different part of the day, such as after school, before bedtime, during recess, or during lunchtime. Or title the starter opening "Welcome to My Day" and let each student choose which time of day she or he prefers to talk about.

- Challenge each speaker to mention at least one thing that nobody has previously talked about. With this option, the students who go later have a more difficult task, since many more things will have been mentioned. Keep this in mind in determining the order of the presentations; you may want to encourage more confident presenters to go toward the end.

Upper Elementary Starter Openings

This section presents four starter openings to use with upper elementary students (grades 4–6):

- It's a Rule of the School
- What I Want to Be
- Analyze This
- Luck of the Draw

The following information will be helpful to you in working with upper elementary students doing starter openings.

Presenter Expectations: There are seven skills and behaviors to emphasize with upper elementary students. You will want each child to:

- Demonstrate a positive attitude.
- Provide an introductory statement.
- Maintain proper body posture.
- Establish eye contact with members of the audience.
- Speak clearly with strong voice projection.
- Use appropriate vocabulary.
- Fulfill all assignment requirements.

Use the Starter Opening Feedback Form on page 205 to evaluate children's presentations and to help you guide them to work on specific skills during future openings.

Audience Expectations: Be sure to set clear expectations for the students in their role as listening audience. Here are six rules that you can give to students in the audience:

- Use respectful listening manners (establish these as necessary before beginning).
- Use appropriate body language.
- Show interest in the presentation.
- Think about what the speaker is saying.
- Ignore distractions from others.
- Provide positive feedback at the end of the opening.

The Starter Opening Feedback Form includes a section for monitoring the audience as well.

Be sure you have explained the concept of openings to students. (For information on introducing openings, see pages 28–30.) Also have a plan for determining which child will present first and how the sequence for subsequent presenters will be determined.

This first starter opening, "It's a Rule of the School," presents detailed procedures and guidelines for introducing it. Since the remaining three starter openings are described more succinctly, we recommend that you fully review the first starter opening even if you plan to have your students begin with a different one.

It's a Rule of the School

Materials and Preparation

Copy and display the handouts from pages 193–199 in a large format, or prepare your own posters using the language from the handouts. (You will want these displays for all starter openings.)

Topic and Assignment

State the topic and explain what students are to do. The assignment for "It's a Rule of the School" is: *Tell about a rule of the school and why you think we have that rule.*

Setting the Stage by Modeling

Present your own opening on the topic so students can see and hear an example. You might set up your example by saying, "I will do an opening first. Good morning. My name is Mr. Chen. My opening is called 'It's a Rule of the School.' I'm going to tell you a rule here at school and why I think we have the rule. One rule we have is that no one can have a cell phone in the classroom. I think we have the rule so people will be able to concentrate on schoolwork without being interrupted while they work. Thank you for listening to my opening."

Procedure

Call on the first presenter. The following is an example of a well-formatted starter opening on the topic "It's a Rule of the School" presented by a fourth, fifth, or sixth grader.

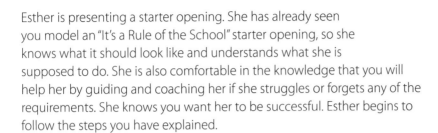

Esther is presenting a starter opening. She has already seen you model an "It's a Rule of the School" starter opening, so she knows what it should look like and understands what she is supposed to do. She is also comfortable in the knowledge that you will help her by guiding and coaching her if she struggles or forgets any of the requirements. She knows you want her to be successful. Esther begins to follow the steps you have explained.

1. Introduce yourself. Esther introduces herself by facing the audience from the front of the room and saying "Good morning. My name is Esther Wolfson and I have an opening for you." Initially, it is important that each student be required to use the same introduction, whether it is this one or something different. Once students are comfortable with the process you may want to let them be more creative with how they begin their presentations.

2. Explain your topic. Esther follows her introduction by saying, "My opening is called 'It's a Rule of the School.' I will describe a rule in this school and explain why I think we have the rule." The key requirement here is that, in one or two sentences, the student introduces the central idea of the opening, thereby setting the stage for audience members to focus on the topic.

3. Present your information. Esther now presents her information in a systematic way, one that you have already modeled for her and the class. She says: "In our school we have a rule that nobody can be in the hallways during class time without a pass from a teacher. I think we have that rule because it's important for the teachers to know where everyone is and because some students might do things they're not supposed to if they're alone in the halls." Notice that this is all prior knowledge for Esther. It is not based on academic learning, but rather is information that Esther already knows and is now sharing with others. Before giving the starter opening, Esther thought of one school rule and her beliefs about why the rule is important, which gives her choice and personalizes the starter opening. It's still prior knowledge, but it's personal prior knowledge that reflects Esther's own thinking.

If Esther needed help at any point when she spoke, you could draw her attention to the posted steps or prompt her with a few words ("To begin an opening, you introduce yourself to the audience").

4. Conclude your opening. Esther now ends her starter opening by saying, "Thank you for listening." Using this standard conclusion statement allows students to bring the opening to a definite end. Later, when students have become comfortable with the openings process, you may allow presenters to vary the way they conclude.

At the conclusion of a student's opening, you may need to begin a round of applause if students do not do this spontaneously. You could affirm Esther by saying, "Thank you for presenting that interesting opening, Esther." At this point you may want to use the feedback form on page 205 to reinforce the presentation skills and behaviors that your students are practicing with openings.

5. Answer questions. A regular opening requires students to ask if there are any questions at the conclusion of their presentation. However, you may want to dispense with this requirement during starter openings. In Esther's case, one opportunity for questions concerns the information she provides when she says: "I think we have that rule because it's important for the teachers to know where everyone is and because some students might do things they are not supposed to if they are alone in the halls." Questions can be developed based on this information *(Do you think this rule is fair? What happens to students who break this rule?)*. It is sometimes difficult for students to think of questions based on the limited input involved in a starter opening. The Starter Opening Feedback Form on page 205 includes an optional item about answering questions from the audience. If you choose to have the audience ask questions, be prepared to provide guidance. For example, you might prompt the class by asking, "Does anyone have a question for Esther about the school's hallway rules?"

Following the first student's starter opening, remind the class of what you expect them to do when they make their own presentations. You might say: "Now, I want you all to remember what I look for when you are doing an opening. First, I expect each of you to do one. When you are in front of the class I want you to use excellent posture, look at people in the audience, wait for everyone to be quiet, speak loudly, and follow directions. When you are done with your opening, thank your audience for listening to you. These are the things I will be assessing you on—they are things I'll watch for so I can see that you know how to give a talk to the rest of the class. I know that each of you will learn to be an excellent presenter and I'm very excited about helping you accomplish this important skill. Now, let's hear another opening."

Options to Consider for "It's a Rule of the School"

You may differentiate any element of a starter opening to fit the needs of your class and of individual students. Pages 10–20 present a variety of options. Here are a few specific ideas you might try for this starter opening:

- Differentiate the content by refocusing the assignment. After stating the rule, students might defend it by telling one or two reasons they believe it is a worthwhile rule or argue against it by explaining why they believe it is unfair or suggesting a way to change the rule to make it more fair.

- Place students in small groups and have the groups brainstorm rules and reasons for the rules.

The next few pages provide descriptions of three additional starter openings that you may want to try with your students.

What I Want to Be

Topic and Assignment

For this starter opening, students tell about their career goals. They name a career they are interested in, describe at least two things that a person in the chosen occupation does, briefly explain why those two things are personally interesting to them, and tell at least two important things that a student must do to prepare for that career.

Procedure

Proceed with "What I Want to Be" starter openings as you have planned them. As necessary, prompt children to fulfill the key elements of the starter opening as they speak. Remind them to specify reasons for wanting to pursue a certain career. This will help students recognize for themselves what might be appealing in careers they have thought about.

In your modeling, you may want to place yourself in the role of an elementary school student, as in this example: "To do this opening, I'm going to pretend to be in fifth grade. When I grow up, I want to be an astronaut. One thing an astronaut does is fix satellites that are orbiting Earth. I think doing space walks would be very challenging and exciting. Another thing an astronaut does is conduct experiments in outer space. I love science and so it would be interesting to do experiments in weightlessness. Two things I should do to prepare to be an astronaut are study as much math and science as possible and do lots of exercising to stay in really good shape."

Options to Consider for "What I Want to Be"

- Conduct a brainstorming session with the class to talk about a variety of careers, what people do in them, and how people prepare for them.

- Provide a list of careers and ask students to choose from the list for their presentations. The list can be generated through class discussion. This is mostly to avoid the possibility that students will say they want to be professional athletes, movie stars, or musicians.

- Require students to identify more than two ways to prepare for their chosen careers, to make them think more deeply about what it might take to get there.

- Ask students to identify people they know or have heard of who currently work in the career areas they have chosen.

- Include a requirement for students to identify skills that someone in their chosen career area would benefit from having.

- Allow students to physically demonstrate aspects of their chosen career.

- Add a short research component so students have a chance to learn more about a career before giving their opening.

Analyze This

Materials and Preparation

Graphs, tables, charts, and lists for students to analyze and show during their starter openings: Gather a number of these from textbooks, newspapers, magazines, or any other source, including making some of your own. You will want a range of forms of data representation on different topics, so the openings will be varied.

Topic and Assignment

For this starter opening, each student examines a set of data in the form of a graph, chart, table, or list; tells what type of data has been provided; and explains at least one key observation about what the data shows or represents based on examining or analyzing the data.

Procedure

Proceed with "Analyze This" starter openings as you have planned them. As necessary, prompt children to fulfill the key elements of the starter opening as they speak. Remind them to tell what kind of data is being presented and give an explanation of what they can tell from examining or analyzing the data, providing at least one observation of what the data show. In your modeling, you may wish to express more than one observation ("What I noticed when I looked at the graph is that smaller cars began to sell better about five years ago, and each year since then more were sold than the year before. The graph also shows that at the same time small car sales were going up, big car sales were going down").

Options to Consider for "Analyze This"

- Conduct a brainstorming session with the class, to identify a list of typical sources of data to be used with these starter openings. Students may be asked to find tables, graphs, and other data representations in publications or online and to bring these from home.

- Differentiate the opening by giving struggling students less complex sets of data to analyze and advanced students more complex sets of data.

- Focus on one content area and gather charts and graphs that relate to that area. For example, if the social studies curriculum is addressing human movement and population in the state, nation, or world, then a wide variety of population data sets could be used to have students think about and analyze these things.

- Make overhead transparencies of the charts and graphs so that they can be displayed for the class to observe while each starter opening is being presented. Or scan them into a computer and project them for all to see. This is an important consideration for this particular starter opening because seeing the data will help the audience fully understand the analysis.

"Think Time" Strategies

It can be helpful with some starter openings to allow the presenter half a minute or so to reflect on a prompt before talking to the class. This raises a question about what the other students in the class do during the 30-second "think time." Some ways for everyone to make good use of the time include the following:

- Have the students keep a "Starter Opening Journal" in which they write their ideas for each of the prompts given to individual presenters. While one student reflects on a prompt before presenting, the rest of the students think about the same prompt before writing. Following the 30-second think time, the student giving the starter opening presents to the class while everyone listens respectfully (pencils down!). Following the starter opening, everyone writes a brief journal entry telling his or her own response to the prompt. You might randomly collect a few of the journals after each starter opening to check that they are being completed according to your expectations.

- While the presenter is thinking of what to say to the class, have students work in pairs to share ideas about the same prompt. Following the starter opening presentation, randomly ask one or two pairs to share with the class one idea they came up with in their conversation that is different from what the presenter talked about. This means that the partners must think of at least two things to be sure they have something that is different.

Luck of the Draw

Materials and Preparation

Write a variety of topics on slips of paper and place them in a bowl. Provide as many topics as you have students. Here are some suggested topics to get you started:

- Recite for the class a poem that you know.

- Sing a song for the class.

- Tell what your morning is like each day before you get to school.

- Explain in step-by-step detail how to make a peanut butter and jelly sandwich.

- Tell what you typically do after school.

- Explain what a hero is.

- Tell about a time when you helped someone.

- Tell about a time when someone helped you.

- Describe something you like to do with your family or with a family member.

- Introduce yourself to the class and tell two things that nobody knows about you.

- Describe a hidden object (provided by the teacher) and see if anyone can guess it.

- Explain the concept of _____ that you are currently studying in science.

- Explain the concept of _____ that you are currently studying in social studies.

- Explain how to solve this math problem: _____.

- Define the word _____ and use it in a sentence.

Topic and Assignment

For this starter opening, each student begins by drawing a slip of paper and reading it. The student has the option of rejecting that topic and drawing another, but can do this only once; if the first topic is rejected, the second topic must be accepted. The student then has 30 seconds to think about the topic before presenting the starter opening. (See "'Think Time' Strategies" on page 48 for ideas of what the rest of the class can be doing during this 30 seconds.) In their openings, students need to provide enough details and examples to make their meaning clear and informative.

Procedure

Introduce students to the topic bowl. Spend some time discussing the kinds of topics that might be found in the bowl. It is up to you whether to reveal all of the topics or keep them a secret to add to the challenge and intrigue of the assignment.

Discuss the guidelines for drawing a topic and presenting a "Luck of the Draw" starter opening, remembering that the presentations will be different because each student randomly draws a topic. Since students are given 30 seconds to reflect on the topic before presenting, explain that they should use this time to decide what they will say and how they will say it. Encourage them to write down a few notes if that will help them organize their thoughts.

To model "Luck of the Draw," draw a topic from the bowl; keep it or draw again. Then reflect on your topic for 30 seconds, jotting down a few notes. Make sure students observe you as you do this. Then present your starter opening, using words like these: "Hello. My name is Mr. Withers, and I have an opening for you. I drew a topic from the bowl, but I didn't want to do that one, so I have drawn a second topic that I will now present. My topic is: 'Explain how animals are classified.' It is a concept we are currently studying in science. Animals are classified by their structure. Two big divisions are animals with backbones and animals without backbones. I will tell you about animals with backbones. Animals with backbones are called vertebrates. There are five classes of vertebrate animals. They are fish, amphibians, reptiles, birds, and mammals. Each class is identified by these characteristics: body covering, heating system, breathing system, and type of reproduction. I can use reptiles as an example. A reptile is a vertebrate that is covered with dry scales and is cold blooded (scientists call this exothermic because the reptile's heat comes from outside its body). Reptiles breathe with lungs only and lay leathery-shelled eggs on land. Thank you for listening."

Proceed with "Luck of the Draw" starter openings. As necessary, prompt children to fulfill the key elements of the starter opening as they speak and assist them with ideas of how to present the various topics in the bowl. Remind students to provide details and examples to help explain what is being presented.

Options to Consider for "Luck of the Draw"

- Develop your class's own distinctive set of topics to put in the bowl. For example, they could all be related to local issues that are of special interest to you and your students.

- Focus on one aspect of the curriculum. For example, have all of the topics be related to science concepts that have been covered over the past several weeks.

Part 3

The Openings

Introduction to the Openings

Openings place students at the center of the learning process and emphasize rigor, relevance, motivation, understanding, differentiated instruction, project-based learning, social-emotional development, and workplace readiness. Openings are all about developing the strengths and talents of students so they become capable, confident, curious, and creative learners. These are very important qualities for today's elementary-age children, preparing them for the demands of a modern middle school and high school curriculum that will likely require them to demonstrate in a variety of ways what they know and are able to do.

The chart on this page shows the complete openings process in a logical sequence. Please note that each component of the process is a potential place for differentiating the project for students.

If you have conducted any of the starter openings in Part 2, students will be familiar and comfortable with the openings process. If you did not conduct starter openings with your group, you will want to introduce the concept of openings at this time. See pages 28–30.

Explain the process of developing and presenting an opening. You can do this in the context of the first opening everyone will work on. Go over the topic choices, and carefully describe the research that will be required and the resources that are available. Tell your students they will write a report, create a visual aid, present their information orally to the class, and then answer questions from the audience. Be sure to discuss the purpose of a visual aid and what type of visual aid you would like students to produce. Assure students that they will have time to prepare and that you'll want them to practice their talks at home or with the support of another student prior to presenting their openings.

From the moment you present the openings concept, convey to students that you are enthusiastic about their becoming effective communicators and that you will be there to support them each step of the way. The transformation that occurs in the minds of children who realize they can learn from each other and be responsible for teaching others is worth every effort it takes to get to that point. Students who believe they have ownership of their learning will become tomorrow's leaders; they will know that school is about much more than learning to read, write, compute, and take tests.

An opening has four key tangible products that you can assess: written report, visual aid, oral presentation, and questions from the audience. Middle and upper elementary students also generally conduct research (following your preferred method), though research is not assessed. Younger students typically do not conduct research but rather work with information that is provided to them.

Standard Sequence for Openings

Process Component	Description
Identifying a Content Area	The teacher identifies a content area on which to focus, based on the curriculum.
Identifying Content Standards	The teacher identifies appropriate grade level content standards to provide alignment between the opening project and the curriculum.
Determining the Order of Presentations	The teacher determines the order of presentations, based on readiness, willingness, logical sequence of topics, random selection, student choice, or other criteria.
Choosing Topics	Students generally choose their own topics within parameters established by the teacher.
Conducting Research	Students conduct research to find information that is relevant to their selected topics.
Using Resources	Students use resources provided by the teacher, that are available in the classroom or school, or that they find on their own.
Writing the Report	Students use the information they gather to write a report, which is the basis for their oral presentations.
Creating the Visual	Students produce a visual aid to support their oral presentation.
Preparing for the Oral Presentation	Students make notes or outlines and practice at home or, in some cases, at school with peers.
Presenting to an Audience	Students present their openings to the class on a scheduled day and time.
Answering Questions	At the conclusion of a standard opening, the student presenter asks if there are any questions.
Assessing the Opening	The teacher assesses the presentation using an assessment form.

Discuss with your students the four basic parts and the corresponding skills they involve—writing, speaking, showing, and answering questions—before beginning an openings project. On pages 189–192, you will find reproducible forms titled Focus Wheels to use in guiding students to understand each of the four parts of an opening and the skills each part requires. Each focus wheel highlights what students need to focus on for that part of their opening and asks why. Use the forms as guides for discussion, as posters in the classroom, or to show to parents.

After explaining the basic skills students will use, explain the five steps required for the oral presentation:

1. **Introduce yourself.**
   All students introduce themselves, using their first name or first and last name, depending upon your guidelines. Early elementary students also sign in by writing their name on the whiteboard, which is a very useful writing assessment strategy that allows you to observe letter formation and spacing.

2. **Explain your topic.**

3. **Present your information.**
   As part of the presentation, students will explain their visual aid.

4. **Conclude your opening.**

5. **Answer questions.**

You can use the reproducible forms on pages 193–199 as visual cues to help students remember the parts and sequence of their oral presentation. You will notice two extra forms not included in this sequence. The Sign In form is used with early elementary students only as part of their writing requirement. The Talk About Your Visual Aid form is included because students will benefit from a reminder about their visual aid. Talking about the visual is part of step 3, "Present your information."

You may find it helpful to copy the forms on 11" x 17" paper, setting the copier at 200 percent. Or, create your own poster, perhaps showing pictures in panels like a comic strip depicting the elements you expect students to include. Display the poster or the forms where the presenters can see them and where you can point to them if necessary. It usually doesn't take much of a prompt to remind a student of what to do or say next. If you are more comfortable giving oral prompts, that is fine as well.

Getting Started

Following this introduction section are fifteen fully developed openings projects—five each for early, middle, and upper elementary classrooms. (One more for each level is on the CD-ROM.) Choose or adapt openings that fit the content area you wish to work in. Consider the standards for your grade level. With any opening, students will be working on skills that fulfill oral presentation standards in English language arts (see pages 6–7). The openings are also designed to focus on other specific standards in English language arts, mathematics, social studies, and science.

You may use the openings as they are described or modify them to meet the specific needs in your classroom. For example, the upper elementary opening "Heroes" (on the CD-ROM) may be modified in a variety of ways. In its current form it focuses on social studies standards, but without changing the assignment in any significant way, it can be modified to emphasize science standards (scientists and their discoveries) or English/language arts standards (authors and their stories). In addition, the project can be redesigned to simplify it for younger students and used successfully with middle and even early elementary classes.

The project description for each opening includes all of the information and materials you will need to implement it with your students. Use these descriptions to help you decide which openings to implement. Every project includes these elements:

- *Content Focus*—Identifies the content area the project is built around.

- *Topic and Assignment*—Briefly describes the opening project and the tasks and expectations for students.

- *Materials*—Lists the resources and materials you will need to gather so that students can complete their assignments and make their presentations.

- *Student Handouts*—Lists each student handout that is included with the project; for middle and upper elementary students, this includes a student assignment sheet. (All of the required student forms are included at the end of the project and on the CD-ROM.)

- *Content Standards*—Lists nationally aligned content standards as the targeted learning expectations for the opening.

- *Ideas for Introducing the Opening*—Recommends ways to familiarize students with the topic area and lay the groundwork for the project.

- *Project Steps*—Presents a step-by-step procedure for implementing the opening project.

- *Ideas for Extending or Modifying the Opening*—Offers additional suggestions for narrowing or enhancing the project focus, expanding the topic, creating visual aids, and extending learning.

- *Classroom Differentiation Example*—Presents a short classroom example with ideas for differentiating components of the opening.

Review the opening you have selected. Familiarize yourself with the resources and materials needed and the steps you will follow as you guide students through the project. Consider differentiation and support strategies you wish to use as well. For any opening, you will want to adhere to the "Standard Sequence for Openings and Starter Openings" on page 29. Use the Openings Planner on pages 218–219 to assist you in planning and preparing for any opening project.

Choosing or Assigning Topics

One of the defining characteristics of openings is that each student has a unique topic to present to the class. Here are several ways to choose, assign, or identify topics for your students:

- Assign each student a topic that is directly related to the content area or theme of the opening. This allows you some discretion in determining the difficulty or challenge of the topic each student tackles. It also lets you give struggling students topics for which you are certain there is plenty of information available at an appropriate reading level.

- Develop a list of acceptable topics and let students choose from the list. A list of possible topics may be developed with student input through a class discussion. Conduct a random drawing to determine the order in which students are allowed to choose their topics, to avoid duplication.

- Let students choose their own topics, with some guidelines for appropriateness. You may establish criteria for accepting a request,

such as requiring students to verify that their topics are located somewhere within a specified section of a textbook.

- Randomly assign topics. Put all of the identified topics in a bowl and have each student draw one. Alternatively, include some choice by having each student draw two topics and pick which of the two he or she prefers. Or, add a sense of adventure by allowing students to draw a second time if they don't want the first topic drawn, with the stipulation that the rejected topic may not be reclaimed and whatever topic is drawn the second time must be accepted.

- Reward students who volunteer to be early presenters by letting them choose their topics ahead of other students who do not volunteer to go first. Put all of the volunteers' names in a bowl and draw them one at a time to determine the presentation order. Students choose their topics in the same order, so the first student drawn gets first choice of topic, and so forth.

You will also need to decide how many openings to do each day (see "Setting Up Your Openings Program" on pages 2–3).

Assigning Written Reports

Students are expected to research their topic and write a report to prepare for their opening. After presenting, the student hands in the report to be graded. You may decide to let students reference their written reports instead of note cards or an outline while giving their openings. If you want to be sure students have prepared enough information for their presentations, you can check their reports before their oral presentations are given.

Creating Visual Aids

A visual aid is a basic requirement of an opening. Many of the openings projects in this book include a template for students to use when planning or developing their visual aids. For early elementary openings, students can use their filled-out templates as their actual visual aids. For middle and upper elementary students, we recommend you have them use the template to create a design and then make larger, more polished visual aids on poster board, through the use of technology, or with another medium. Here are some suggestions:

- Assign students to produce their visual aids on poster board or art paper. We make the assumption that posters will be the preferred method of producing visual aids for most projects in this book, and we have included poster supplies in the "Materials" list provided with each opening project. The size of posters may be anywhere from 12" x 18" up to much larger formats, depending on the project and availability of resources.

- Encourage students to use multimedia, models, dioramas, exhibits, maps, timelines, artifacts, authentic objects, and the like as visual aids.

- Allow students to develop demonstrations, reenactments, dramatic performances, and so forth as ways of presenting information about their topics.

- Use a document camera and data projector to display images, or make transparencies of 8½" x 11" visual aids for use with an overhead projector.

- Scan 8½" x 11" visual aids into a computer and enlarge or project them.

- Take digital photographs of 8½" x 11" visual aids and enlarge or project them.

- Have students create visual aids directly on computers so that they can be projected.

Modeling

It is very important for students of all ages to have openings modeled for them. You can play a crucial role in their overall success by modeling yourself what it is that you are looking for in any given opening. Every opening assignment has a unique focus and its own special "flavor." By modeling, you establish certain expectations up front, and you can refer to your own performance when reminding students of what you are looking for. For example, you might say something like, "Do you remember when I did my opening and I held up the two required science vocabulary words as I told what they mean? That's what I expect each of you to do. You need to hold them up, tell what they mean, and explain how they are related to your topic, just like I did."

As the year progresses and the class has presented one or two full cycles of openings, you may choose to simplify your modeling. Depending on the topic and on the needs of your group, you might want to do any or all of the following:

- Explain and demonstrate how to use particular resources for their research and how to create the visual aid.

- Show students examples of what a visual aid might look like when complete.

- Read or provide a brief written report in the format you want students to follow.

- Demonstrate ways to begin and end the opening, or prepare a complete presentation as an example.

Another form of modeling comes from the students themselves. Because openings are done one at a time, students who go first are automatically modeling for those who come later. You can take advantage of this by having the class provide feedback to the presenters. Ask audience members to name for the presenter two things that were done well and one thing that could be improved. Some teachers provide extra credit to students who volunteer to go first, with the understanding that they are modeling and therefore will receive some critical feedback for the benefit of others. (See "Using Student Checklists and Audience Feedback Forms" on pages 56–57 for additional discussion of student feedback.)

Beginning and Ending the Presentation

It is very useful to have a standard introduction and closing for openings. You can assess students on their use of these presentation guidelines, but their true value is that they provide a way to get an opening started and a way to wrap it up. It can be quite challenging for a nervous student to begin a presentation smoothly and confidently if there is no prescribed method of doing so. And it can be even more awkward finishing if the audience doesn't have a clear indication that the presentation is over.

A standard introduction can be as simple as having every student say, "Good morning. My name is _____, and I have an opening for you. My opening is about . . ." (Part of the introduction for the very youngest students is to have them write their names on the whiteboard.) The standard closing can be even simpler: "Thank you for listening. Are there any questions?" For students who have a lot of experience making opening presentations, a more general expectation can be that they provide an inviting introduction and a clearly defined conclusion, and then allow them to devise their own. But for inexperienced and younger students, it is advisable to establish a specific expectation for beginning and ending an opening.

Using Student Checklists and Audience Feedback Forms

To be effective presenters, students need to learn to plan their projects and assess how prepared they are to fulfill the different parts of the assignment. Giving students a checklist that identifies the key elements of an opening is a good way to set the stage for success. The checklist clearly tells students what the expectations for the opening are and helps them prepare for the presentation. It may be shared with parents so that they know what their children are preparing for and how support may be provided at home.

Audience feedback on presentations can also be helpful to students as they prepare and make openings and other oral presentations in the future. Enlisting the help of students in providing constructive feedback to the presenter is also a way of engaging the audience during an opening. Audience feedback is generally more successful with older students, but it may be useful with even the youngest children if simple guidelines and procedures are carefully spelled out.

Is My Opening Ready? Checklists

An Is My Opening Ready? checklist is a series of simple, straightforward yes-or-no questions that cover the basic requirements of the opening assignment. If a student can mark yes for each of the questions, he or she is ready to go. If the answer to any of the questions is no, then further work probably is needed. There are separate Is My Opening Ready? checklists for early, middle, and upper elementary students. See pages 200–202.

Here are several options for using the Is My Opening Ready? checklist:

- Give the checklist to students and let them self-analyze their readiness. This option is the quickest and easiest, but it offers the least opportunity for you to provide feedback and support because students are expected to independently respond to each item. If they are "stuck" or not prepared, you may not know it until it's too late to help.

- Have students meet with partners and ask each other the questions on the checklist. Each student fills out the checklist for his or her partner. This method helps overcome the tendency of some students to claim they are prepared when in fact they are not.

- Require students to take the checklist home to complete and then turn it in with a parent signature. A signed checklist can be extremely valuable for you to use when providing feedback following an opening and at conference time when discussing student performance with parents.

- Arrange to meet with each student separately. At that time, either complete the checklist together or have the student present you with a completed checklist that you can then discuss. A signature from both you and the student signifies your agreement that each item has been completed and that the student is ready to present.

Audience Feedback Forms

The purpose of audience feedback is to help the presenters improve as public speakers. Presenters should understand this. It is absolutely critical that feedback be offered in a positive manner. Students should report on "what was good" and "what could be improved."

Five forms for constructive audience feedback are provided on pages 213–217, focusing on eye contact, voice projection, visual materials, questions for the presenter, and the central idea of the opening presentation. These forms are designed for use with middle and upper elementary students, and not younger children. Use the forms in any combination at your discretion. Here are some recommendations:

Eye Contact

Identify three or four students to monitor eye contact from the presenter. Do not let the presenter know who these students are, but try to have them be scattered around the room. These students watch carefully to see if the presenter looks at them, and also if they notice him or her look at other students in the audience. Not knowing who will be providing eye contact feedback, the presenter has incentive to look at a variety of audience members.

Voice Projection

Identify two or three students to gauge voice projection from the presenter. It is not necessary to keep the identity of these students a secret, and in fact you might want to have special seats for them in the farthest reaches of the room. Their job is to report on how well the presenter could be heard and understood during the opening.

Visual Materials

Identify two or three students to report on how visible and understandable the presenter's visual materials are. The key here is that a presenter should provide a poster or other visual with text that is readable and graphics that are easy to see and understand.

Questions for the Presenter

A standard requirement of opening presenters is to ask if there are any questions and to be able to answer reasonable questions from the audience at the end of the presentation. It can be somewhat awkward if there are no questions. To overcome this problem, identify three or four students prior to the opening whose job it is to think of questions to pose at the conclusion of the opening. Students in the audience are much more likely to think of good, meaningful questions if they specifically know ahead of time that they are expected to do so.

Central Idea

Identify two or three students whose job it is to record what they believe to be the central idea of the opening, and to report their opinion to the class at the opening's conclusion. This lets you gauge both whether the presenter has made the central idea clear and how readily the audience can discern the central idea.

Assessment with Openings

Openings represent a "structured freedom" approach to instruction. Based on the premise that students need to accept increased responsibility for their own learning, structured freedom establishes a framework within which they can comfortably and confidently become self-directed learners. One of the keys to providing structure is a well-designed assessment that clearly articulates criteria for an effective presentation while simultaneously establishing a basis for useful feedback. Given sufficient structure, even the youngest students can manage a great deal of freedom.

Presenter Assessments

On pages 206–208, you will find assessment forms that focus on the four parts of a typical opening: oral presentation, visual aid, written report, and answering questions from the audience. The expectations for fulfilling these aspects, of course, may be modified depending on the age and skill level of the students. For example, the writing requirement for kindergartners may consist of students writing their names on a whiteboard, chalkboard, or easel before addressing the audience. Given the assessment ahead of time, students may use it as a set of preparation guidelines. Following the opening presentation, the teacher will use the assessment to offer constructive feedback.

Take some time to examine the assessment form for your grade level (early, middle, or upper elementary, pages 206–208). It is also very important that students know what they are being assessed on, so be sure to show them the assessment form and carefully go over it with them. As you listen to a student presenter, you should have the assessment form in front of you so that you can record your observations on the fly.

Finally, always try to give students some immediate feedback while they are still standing in front of the room. For example, you might say, "Okay, Miguel, thank you for that opening. As I watched you present, I noted two things that you did well and one thing that you could improve the next time you give an opening. Let me tell you what they are." Remember to provide positive feedback as well as to (gently!) help students improve by pointing out something that could be improved.

Call this "two glows and one grow" and explain to students that they should expect such feedback.

Here are a few things to consider about assessment as you prepare to implement an openings program:

- You may decide to give certain items on the assessment added weight because they are special areas of emphasis. You can do this by giving the point value of each item a "multiplied" factor. In other words, if you really want to emphasize voice projection, you can tell students that you are multiplying that item on the assessment form by two, giving it twice the weight it would otherwise have.

- You can involve your students more deeply in the assessment process by having them contribute to a rubric that is based on the assessment form. Ask them to develop language that describes various levels of mastery for each item.

- Have your students do more than one opening during the year. Assessment feedback is more meaningful if students have opportunities to demonstrate improvement in areas of weakness, rather than just being told "these are things you need to do better the next time you make a presentation."

- Ask each student to complete a self-assessment and compare his or her perceptions of the presentation with yours.

- Build into the assessment any content expectations that you feel need to be emphasized. For example, if the openings focus on topics from the science curriculum, then you should identify specific science content that needs to be covered in each opening. The assessments provided here focus mostly on presentation skills, not on content.

- Share the assessments with parents before students give their presentations, so they know what the expectations are.

Assessment forms for early, middle, and upper elementary students are provided. If you prefer to develop your own custom-designed assessment, these forms may be useful as a starting point.

Listening Assessments

Openings focus primarily on students standing at the front of the room making oral presentations, but it is also possible to emphasize another key communication skill during openings: listening. It is very important to have conversations with your students about being good listeners. One way to motivate students to put listening skills into practice is to assess them as listeners.

Students need to understand that being a good listener involves more than sitting still and being quiet. This requires teaching, because most students really don't know what it means to be "active" listeners. Here are some of the attributes of a good listener.

A good listener:

- employs listening manners (listens quietly without interrupting)

- displays appropriate body language

- shows interest in what is being said

- ignores distractions

- shows patience (listens to the whole message)

- asks clarifying questions when appropriate

- demonstrates understanding of what was said (can paraphrase the speaker's ideas or answer questions about what was said)

- participates in discussions about what was said

- acts on what was said (follows directions, forms opinions, makes plans, etc.)

Three listening assessments are on pages 209–211, one each for early, middle, and upper elementary. Keep in mind that it is impossible to do a listening assessment for every student in the audience during every opening. Your attention will be focused primarily on the presenter, which is where it should be. In order to also conduct listening assessments, try this:

Prior to each opening, identify two students to assess. Do not tell the students who they are. Write the names of these two students on two listening assessment forms. During the opening, pay attention to only these two students with regard to listening assessment. You may choose to give students their finished assessments immediately following each opening, or you can keep them until all openings have been completed. If you keep them, students can't deduce who has and has not been assessed. By doing two during each opening, you will end up with two formal listening assessments for each student in the class. Of course, if there are "special cases" in your classroom, you may choose to complete additional assessment forms to document specific behavior.

Communicating with Parents About Openings

It is important to keep parents informed about the requirements, expectations, and benefits of the openings their children have been assigned to present. Parents generally want to know what their children are being asked to do, and they want to help. A letter home will ensure that parents know what an opening is and what their children have been assigned to do.

Another way to inform parents is to send assignment and assessment sheets home for them to examine and talk about with their children. Beyond this, you might want to attach a simple agreement for students and parents to sign. Such an agreement would ask students to do their best and be ready when the opening is due, and it would ask parents to agree to support their children at home. An example of a parent-student agreement is provided on page 203.

Besides informing parents, it's a great idea to involve them. Practicing at home is the single most effective way for students to improve their performance on presentations at school. Ask parents to talk with their children about openings and to listen to them make their presentations. You may even want to require that most of the preparation for an opening be done as homework. Parent involvement will make a huge difference in your students' attitude, confidence, motivation, and preparedness. That's quite a contribution for parents to make.

A parent letter may be used to do any of the following:

- emphasize the importance of self-directed learning
- explain the value of mastering presentation skills
- provide basic information about the assignment
- inform parents about presentation topics
- give dates and times for opening presentations
- share assessment criteria and expectations
- suggest ways in which parents can help their children become accomplished presenters

On the following pages, you will find examples of letters that may be sent home to parents. It is not possible to anticipate precisely how you plan to organize openings or what you will want to say to your parents, so the examples provide suggestions to help you craft your own letter. The point is that parents need to be informed and you will want to plan on communicating with them early and often about their children's participation in your openings program.

Sample Parent Letter Introducing Openings (Any Grade Level)

Date: September 14

Announcing a New Class Project: Openings!

Dear Parent/Guardian/Caregiver:

We all know it is important for students to learn to read, write, and use math in their lives. There is another skill all children need as they grow up in the 21st century: the skill of effective communication. It is important for children to learn to discuss and present ideas with confidence.

Most people do not magically acquire the skill of effective communication without working at it. This is why we are doing a project called "Openings" in our classroom this year. With openings, children research a topic, prepare a report and a visual aid, and formally present what they have learned to the class. The openings process teaches important learning skills for middle school and beyond:

- choosing and researching a topic

- organizing information

- preparing written and visual material

- practicing for an oral presentation

- presenting information to an audience

- responding to questions about the topic

- reflecting on what was effective about the presentation and what could be improved

- listening with attention

Students will prepare and present their openings in a way that fits their individual levels of development, learning styles, interests, and strengths. In the process, each student will become an expert about a part of the content area we are studying. When your child presents an opening, he or she will be teaching something new to the rest of the class. The openings are aimed at helping students learn important subject-area content and share what they have learned capably and confidently.

Next week your child will bring home a letter telling you about his or her first opening assignment. The letter will include ideas for how you can help your child practice the opening presentation. Look for the letter, and be sure to ask your child about the openings we are doing.

Sincerely,

  Mrs. Arianzi

Sample Parent Letter Introducing an Early Elementary Opening

Date: <u>September 14</u>   Student's Name: <u>Chad B.</u>

Dear Parent/Guardian/Caregiver:

Our class is preparing to begin a new project. The project is called "Openings." An opening is an oral presentation made to the class. We call these presentations openings because they "open" a new door to learning for the children. They are my way of helping your child become a confident and effective communicator. I believe this ability will be a key to your child's future success as a student and as a productive citizen.

Opening Topic: <u>environmental print</u>

Visual Aid Assigned: <u>create a drawing or cutout of printed text that can be found in our environment (such as a sign, billboard, logo, etc.)</u>

Your child's opening presentation will be on: <u>September 27</u>

How can you help?

You can help your child by talking with him or her about the assignment. The most important thing is practice. Ask your child to present the opening to you at home several times:

- Have your child practice signing in. The first thing a student does at the beginning of an opening in my class is write his or her name on the board. I will be looking for legibility, an upper case initial letter, and proper letter formation.

- Talk to your child about speaking loudly enough for all to hear and standing straight and tall.

- Help your child make eye contact at least once with the audience during the opening.

- Emphasize a good beginning: "Good morning. My name is <u>Chad</u> and I have an opening for you. My opening is about . . ."

- Emphasize a good ending: "Thank you for listening."

Finally, please let your child do all of the work. The visual component needs to be entirely the student's work. I expect your child to do his or her own printing or writing. Your job is to encourage your child as he or she learns how to talk to an audience.

Thank you for your support—I know your child will enjoy sharing the opening with you.

Sincerely,

<u>Mr. Bauer</u>

Sample Parent Letter Introducing a Middle Elementary Opening

Date: <u>September 12</u>

Dear Parent/Guardian/Caregiver:

The students in my classroom are preparing to begin a new project called "Openings." An opening is an opportunity for your child to talk to the class about something we are learning. Openings are my way of helping your child become comfortable talking to a group. I believe this ability will help your child be successful as he or she moves toward upper elementary and middle school.

Here are some details:

Topic: <u>geometric shapes</u>

Writing Assignment: <u>write a report about the shapes found in your assigned picture</u>

Visual Aid: <u>use the assigned picture; trace the shapes in it</u>

Due Date: <u>November 17</u>

How can you help?

Please talk to your child about this project and ask him or her to practice at home (several times!). Here are the important parts of a good opening:

- Include accurate information.

- Speak loudly enough for everyone to hear.

- Look at people in the audience.

- Make good use of the visual aid.

- Have a clear beginning ("Good morning. My name is _____ and I have an opening for you. My opening is about . . .").

- Have a clear ending ("Thank you for listening. Are there any questions?").

Thank you for helping your child prepare for this project. By working together, we can guarantee your child a positive learning experience.

Sincerely,

<u>Mrs. Donahue</u>

Sample Parent Letter Introducing an
Upper Elementary Opening

Date: September 12

Dear Parent/Guardian/Caregiver:

The students in my classroom are preparing to begin a new project called "Openings." An opening is an opportunity for each student to become an expert and teach his or her classmates by making an oral presentation to the class. Openings are my way of helping your child become a confident and effective communicator. I believe this ability will be a key to your child's future success in middle school and high school.

Here are some details:

Topic: pond ecosystem and one thing that lives in ponds

Research/Writing Assignment: write a report about your assigned life form

Visual Aid: educational sign that explains your life form

Due Date: September 17

How can you help?

Please talk to your child about this assignment. The most important thing is practice. Ask your child to present his or her opening to you at home and be ready to discuss these parts of the assignment:

- the importance of finding accurate information from reliable sources

- voice projection and inflection (how to sound excited about the topic and interesting while speaking)

- body posture and use of hands

- making good eye contact with the audience

- beginning with an engaging introduction

- ending with a clear conclusion or wrap-up

- being able to answer reasonable questions by knowing the information well

Thank you for your support in this effort to help your child learn how to become an effective communicator. By working together, we can make a major contribution to his or her education.

Sincerely,

  Mr. Porcello

Ideas for Extending Openings

You may want to make openings a bigger part of your classroom, extending their value. The following extension options provide ways for students to learn more about their own topics as well as those of other students, gain greater exposure for their openings, and challenge themselves further. Reproducible forms described in the extensions are included on the CD-ROM included with this book.

1. Plan an open house. Have students stand at "Topic Stations" with their opening materials so that parents and guests can circulate to listen to presentations, look at visuals, ask questions, and talk to students about their projects. The Topic Stations are tables arranged in the classroom, in the gym, or along a hallway so that visitors can easily gather around and make a given student the center of attention. This culminating activity for openings will give students an opportunity to make a significant contribution to a common goal—the open house—and the satisfaction of being a featured expert for parents.

2. "Publish" featured opening articles in clear 8½" x 11" display stands. Place these somewhere in the classroom, on lunchroom tables, or elsewhere in the school. Three Featured Opening Article templates are provided: Text & Graphic, Text Only, and Graphic Only. One plastic stand can display the articles of two students, one on each side. Or one student's Text Only and a Graphic Only template could be set up as a front and back display. Another option for the Text & Graphic template is to have the graphic be a photo of the student giving the opening. This is possible if you photograph students at the beginning of their oral presentations.

3. Create a "Favorite Facts from Openings" wall in the classroom. Post favorite facts or pull-quotes from the written reports using the template My Favorite Opening Fact. You can have students design an interesting border around the favorite fact box. The template also asks the student to list good resources for someone who would like to learn more about the topic.

4. Have students use the On-the-Job Communication handout provided to talk with a parent or family friend about the types of communication formats he or she uses at work. Then hold a class discussion for students to share what they've learned about communication on the job.

5. Use openings as a vocabulary builder. Students use the Word Power worksheet to revise a sentence from their rough draft to make it more interesting, dynamic, descriptive, or understandable.

6. Help students realize the value of what they are learning with openings. After completing an opening, have students use the Skills for Life handout to identify skills they used during their project.

7. An Openings Student Contract can be used with middle and upper elementary students who would like to propose their own idea for an opening. A version for each level is provided, as well as a handout titled Tips for a Successful Opening.

8. Use the Challenge Option Request Form (page 204) with students who would like to add a challenge option to their assigned opening. A challenge option is an extra component agreed to by the student and teacher.

9. Award Certificates of Achievement to students after everyone has completed an opening. If you like, incorporate a photograph of the student teaching the class or a small school picture.

Making Your Own Openings

You can extend the use of openings in your classroom by creating your own. Use the Openings Planner on pages 218–219 to develop your own opening ideas.

If you decide to develop your own opening based on something you teach, consider the following questions before writing up your ideas on the Openings Planner. There are a lot of questions, but the final write-up will be well designed because you've thought it through.

1. What content area will the opening be focused on?

2. In addition to the six language arts strands, which content standard(s) will students learn?

3. Can you build in an engaging scenario or assignment to this opening idea?

4. What will the written portion of the opening be focused on and will it have a special format?

5. What will the visual aid be focused on, and will it have a special format?

6. What will students be expected to talk about for the oral presentation?

7. How will students choose topics?

8. How much class time will students have to prepare for their opening?

9. How will you determine the order of presentations?

10. Is any pre-teaching needed before you give out the openings assignment?

11. Will students be able to use technology to research or present their openings?

12. Which students may need special materials or special support to do an opening?

13. Will you be sending a letter home to parents about their child doing an opening?

14. Are there any special room requirements needed for these oral presentations (LCD projector, easel for posters, unique set, overhead projector, etc.)?

15. How will you ensure that the class pays attention during student presentations (listening skills)?

16. At what point will you do your model opening for the class and what will your topic be?

17. Is this opening project the only one you will have students do this year? (Whether the answer is yes or no, students can be asked to do one or more starter openings to prepare for their first opening.)

18. Do you have a starter opening idea that you would like the class to do to prepare for this opening?

19. How will you be sure students have resources to research their opening topic?

20. What materials, including handouts, will students need to complete their openings assignment?

21. Which assessment forms will you use for this opening?

22. On which date will you start student presentations?

23. On which date will you finish?

24. Will you photograph or videotape each student giving an opening?

25. What specific things can you do to help students be enthusiastic about the challenge of doing an opening?

And Finally . . .

Teaching students to become effective communicators is similar to coaching an athlete to excel at a sport or helping a musician to master an instrument. It's all about skills, motivation, and repetitions. Your job is to help students recognize how people become good communicators, make the process of getting there fun and interesting, and give them lots of opportunities to practice. With this book in your hands, you are well on your way.

Early Elementary Openings

- My Home and Family

- Did You Know?

- Words All Around Us

- I Made a Pattern

- I Understand Food Chains

 # My Home and Family

Content Focus: Social Studies
Topic and Assignment

To most young children, home and family are the center of the world. In their homes, children learn they are loved and belong, develop their values and self-concept, and experience their earliest person-to-person relationships. This opening project helps students recognize the diversity of families. They will get an opportunity to think about their own families and describe to their classmates things that make home and family special to them. Students likely will be able to see that many different kinds of families exist—large and small, two-parent and single-parent, extended and blended—and that families have a variety of places they call home. Some children may not have a permanent home or may have formed a special connection to a place or person outside the family, perhaps a caregiver, neighbor, or teacher. Through the openings process, students will have an opportunity to reflect on whatever people and places are of primary importance in their lives.

Materials

 Whiteboard or easel and marker; or chalkboard and chalk

 Crayons, markers, or colored pencils

 Drawing paper (optional)

Note: Use your knowledge of children's situations and your own discretion to adapt the topic so all children can comfortably engage in the assignment. For example, you might modify the opening topic to "My Favorite Place," "A Favorite Person," or "A Place I Like to Be." Any of these topics will allow you to focus on the concepts of family and community in a respectful way that helps children learn about and appreciate family diversity.

During this project students will:

- Sign in on a whiteboard, chalkboard, or easel to demonstrate writing skills.

- Create a drawing of something in their home that is special to them (such as a family member, a pet, or a particular room or space).

- Think of at least two things to say about the picture they have drawn to explain why this aspect of their home or family is important to them.

- Express their two ideas in writing (by dictating if necessary).

- Present an opening in which they describe something or someone that is special or important to them in their home and/or family.

Student Handouts

- My Home and Family (writing handout)
- My Home and Family (drawing handout)

Content Standards*

1. Describe personal connections to place—especially place as associated with immediate surroundings.

2. Describe how people create places that reflect ideas, personality, culture, and wants and needs.

3. Describe the unique features of one's nuclear and extended families.

4. Identify and describe ways family, groups, and community influence the individual's daily life and personal choices.

Ideas for Introducing the Opening

- Share photos of some of your family members and tell why each one is special to you.

- Look at a book together such as *Houses and Homes* by Ann Morris and Ken Hayman, *All Families Are Special* by Norma Simon, or *Families* by Ann Morris.

Project Steps

1. Introduce the project to the students. Tell them that they will be doing an opening titled "My Home and Family." During this project they will think about important places and people in their lives, and they will tell their classmates about someone or something at home that is special to them.

2. Have a brainstorming session with students to think of all the things that might make home special to someone. This might include family members or neighbors, pets, special places in the home, activities, family traditions, foods, and so forth.

3. Explain to students that they will create a drawing that shows two things about their home or family. When they present their opening, they will use the drawing to show the class something that's special to them at home.

4. Decide what your expectations will be for the written and visual parts of the assignment. Give students the My Home and Family writing handout. This handout asks students to write down two things that make their home special to them. Refer back to the brainstorming session as students think about what to write. If you have students who cannot write their ideas, ask them to dictate to you so that you can record their thinking.

5. Give students the My Home and Family drawing handout or, if you wish, provide drawing paper instead. The assignment is for students to make a drawing of the two things they wrote about that make their home special to them.

6. Communicate with parents about the upcoming opening, to inform them about the theme being covered and the requirements of students when making an opening. Ask them to practice with their children at home. (See pages 60–63 for parent letters to adapt.)

7. As needed, model part or all of a "My Home and Family" opening for the class. Demonstrate how to present the information ("This room is special to me because . . . and because . . .").

8. Schedule class time for students to prepare and present their openings. Preparation time will vary depending on your expectations and the readiness of your students. In general, this project should require no more than about one hour of class time prior to students making their presentations. This time is typically spread over several days.

9. *Optional:* Students who are done preparing early can create a "Home and Family" sign for students to stand next to while they do an opening.

10. Make copies of the assessment form on page 206. Complete a form for each student after he or she has presented an opening.

11. Proceed with "My Home and Family" openings as you have planned them. Have students write their names on the board before they introduce themselves to the class. As necessary, prompt children to fulfill the key elements of the opening as they make their presentations.

---

* Expectations of Excellence: Curriculum Standards for Social Studies are from the National Council for the Social Studies (NCSS).

Ideas for Extending or Modifying the Opening

1. Create an "Our Homes and Families" wall in the room. After each opening, put the presenting student's artwork on the wall to produce a public display.

2. Organize student drawings and writings into an "Our Homes and Families" book. Students become published authors and illustrators, and the book may be put on display for parents and others to view.

3. Make additional assignments related to home, such as telling about family traditions, drawing family portraits (including pets), taking digital pictures of homes, or describing specific activities that take place at home. Or extend the assignment to focus on the neighborhood, school, or community.

4. Do a "What Is the Same? What Is Different?" activity with the class related to favorite or special people in their lives. Ask students to answer these questions: *What are some things that are the same about your favorite people? What are some things that are different about them?*

Classroom Differentiation Example: Mrs. Goldstein

Strategies: scaffolding, tiering

Anna, Hu, and D'Andre are preparing to do a "My Home and Family" opening. Their kindergarten teacher, Mrs. Goldstein, has chosen to differentiate the assignment for each of these students.

Anna has not yet developed sufficient writing skills for her to independently complete the writing portion of the project. Instead, Mrs. Goldstein has decided to provide a scaffold by letting Anna dictate what she wants to say about her home to a parent volunteer.

Hu is shy and somewhat reluctant to do the opening. He benefits greatly from seeing others do things before he is asked to do them. Mrs. Goldstein knows that Hu will be more comfortable if the opening is modeled several times for him, so she provides a scaffold by scheduling his presentation near the end.

D'Andre has been a showman since the first day of school, and he thrives on performing for an audience. He has expressed a real interest in the concept of home and family, and wants to do more with it. Mrs. Goldstein has agreed to let him take digital photographs in his home and, as a challenge tier, give an extended presentation of things that make his home special to him.

My Home and Family

1. Think about your home and the people who live there. Write down one thing that makes your home and family special to you.

_____

_____

What makes this special?

_____

_____

2. Write down another thing that makes your home and family special.

_____

_____

What makes this special?

_____

_____

My Home and Family

Name: _____ **Date:** _____

Draw the two things you wrote about that make your home and family special to you. Show your drawing to the class when you give your opening.

Did You Know?

Content Focus:
Any Content Area
Topic and Assignment

This project will help you introduce students to the concept of finding and sharing information. Students assume the role of experts as they prepare to make opening presentations to their classmates. The openings are designed to let students identify specific topics and share interesting information that they find. After making their presentations, students contribute their visual and written material to a classroom "Did You Know?" collage.

"Did You Know?" can be easily adapted to fit into your existing curriculum. You may want to have students focus their research and findings on a particular topic that you are currently covering, such as animals, food, or weather. Or, you may simply ask students to discover and share facts that interest them. However you decide to set up the project, be sure to have a wide variety of informational texts and other resources available in your classroom or media center.

During this project students will:

- Sign in on a whiteboard, chalkboard, or easel to demonstrate writing skills.

- Choose topics that interest them.

- Use books and other resources to learn new facts.

- Create a "Did You Know?" visual that can be added to a classroom collage.

- Write at least two facts about their topic.

- Present an opening in which they share factual information they have found through their own research.

Materials

 Whiteboard or easel and marker; or chalkboard and chalk

 Books, magazines, and other resources for students related to their topics

 Crayons, markers, or colored pencils

Student Handouts

- Did You Know? (word cards)

- Did You Know? (word-and-picture cards)

- Did You Know? (picture cards)

Content Standards

This project can address standards in any core content area, depending upon your chosen topics.

Idea for Introducing the Opening

Look with students at a magazine such as *Ranger Rick, Click, Ask, National Geographic Kids,* or *Spider.* Demonstrate that the articles in the magazine include facts, and discuss how writers must know and find facts to write their articles. Use examples from the magazine to help children understand what *facts* are.

Project Steps

1. Determine the content area or theme that will be the focus. Compile a list of topics related to the theme and either assign one to each student or let them choose their own from the list. If you decide to let students choose their own topics, avoid any conflict over who gets which topic by drawing names from a bowl and letting the students choose in order as their names are drawn.

2. Designate space on a wall in the classroom or elsewhere in the school where the class can construct a collage. Make a large "Did You Know?" sign to display above the collage area.

3. Decide what your expectations will be for the written and visual parts of the assignment. Based on your expectations, determine which type of Did You Know? cards (pages 74–76) you will have students use. You might choose one style for everyone to use, assign a style to each student based on his or her

readiness, let students ask for the style they prefer, or require that students use a combination of styles.

4. Introduce students to the project. Explain that students will become experts on the topics they choose (or are assigned). Their job is to learn about their special topics so they can tell the rest of the class about them. Ask them to tell you what a fact is, and talk to them about finding and using facts. Help them understand how facts relate to topics.

5. Demonstrate for students how they might look through a book, magazine, or other resource to find interesting facts to share with the class.

6. Tell students that for their opening they will each find at least two interesting facts about a topic to present to the class.

7. Hand out the Did You Know? card templates. Photocopy or print out the pages that are provided to make as many card templates as you need. Two cards are on the page, so either you or the students should cut it into half-page cards. These cards will serve as the students' visual aids during their openings and following the openings they will be added to the collage. Model how the templates should be completed.

8. When the cards are finished, collect them and check for quality, using the guidelines and expectations you have given to students as criteria. After checking for quality, return the cards to the students with any comments or feedback that you wish to provide before the openings are presented. These cards are the students' visual aids, so do not write or mark directly on them unless you expect them to redo the work.

9. Schedule class time for students to prepare and present their openings. Preparation time will vary depending on your expectations and the readiness of your students. In general, this project should require no more than about one hour of class time prior to students making their presentations. This time is typically spread over several days.

10. Communicate with parents about the upcoming openings to inform them about the theme being covered and the requirements of students when making an opening. Ask them to practice with their children at home. (See pages 60–63 for parent letters to adapt.)

11. As needed, model part or all of a "Did You Know?" opening for the class. Each student is expected to present two facts about his or her topic.

12. *Optional:* Have students who finish their projects early create a "Did You Know?" sign or banner for students to stand next to when they present their openings. Or they can create a scene, such as a network newsroom or conference podium, to serve as the setting for students giving openings.

13. Make copies of the assessment form on page 206. Complete a form for each student after he or she has presented an opening.

14. Proceed with "Did You Know?" openings as you have planned them. Have students write their names on the board before they introduce themselves to the class. As necessary, prompt children to fulfill the key elements of the opening as they make their presentations. At the completion of each opening, add the student's Did You Know? cards to the collage.

Ideas for Extending or Modifying the Opening

1. With students, find and create additional types of visuals for the classroom's collage. Examples include drawings, cutouts, photographs, coloring-book pages, clip art, images from the Internet, news clippings, and so forth.

2. Place students in small groups and have each group focus on a similar theme. Each student still does an independent opening, but students in each group can help one another find facts. For example, if the class is studying animals, one group could focus on animals that swim, a second group on animals that fly, a third on animals that walk on four legs, a fourth on those with hair or fur, a fifth on those with horns or antlers, a sixth on those that eat meat, and so forth.

3. Use this opening idea more than once, in conjunction with different units through the year.

4. Have students focus on themselves. In this case the opening would include facts such as "Did you know that I have four brothers?" or "Did you know that I was born in Texas?"

5. Create your own "Did You Know?" templates on larger paper (by drawing your own or by photocopying the form at 200 percent on 11" x 17" paper) to give students more room to draw or write.

Classroom Differentiation Example: Mr. Younkis

Strategies: resident expert, scaffolding, multiple intelligences, tiering

Mr. Younkis's first-grade class is preparing to do a "Did You Know?" opening project. The focus will be on animals. He knows that for each student to gain as much as possible from the project, he must provide some differentiation. Here are three examples:

Assif is a struggling reader whose success depends on working from resources that are mostly pictures with simple text. Mr. Younkis has compiled a list of topics for which he knows there are plenty of such resources available in his classroom. He will work directly with Assif to be sure that he chooses one of these topics. He will also check in with Assif to review the facts he has found.

Neidra reads well, but she struggles with writing. She draws beautifully, so her best output of information is graphic rather than written. Mr. Younkis intends to encourage Neidra to use the pictures-only option for her visual aid.

Maggie is an exceptional reader who enjoys challenging text and is constantly expanding her reading choices to books that are beyond those on the classroom shelves. Mr. Younkis has made arrangements with the school media specialist to help Maggie find resources about her chosen topic that match her reading level and desire for challenge.

Topic: _____

Did You Know?

_____

_____

_____

_____

_____

By: _____ Teacher OK: _____

Topic: _____

Did You Know?

_____

_____

_____

_____

_____

By: _____ Teacher OK: _____

Topic: _____

Did You Know?

_____

_____

_____

_____

By: _____ Teacher OK: _____

Topic: _____

Did You Know?

_____

_____

_____

_____

By: _____ Teacher OK: _____

Topic: _____

Did You Know?

By: _____ Teacher OK: _____

Topic: _____

Did You Know?

By: _____ Teacher OK: _____

Words All Around Us

Content Focus: Language Arts
Topic and Assignment

Materials

 Photographs, magazine pictures, product labels, and other examples of environmental print

 Scissors

 Whiteboard or easel and marker; or chalkboard and chalk

 Glue

 Crayons, markers, or colored pencils

This project focuses on environmental print—the words that students see all around them every day. Students identify examples of environmental print such as street signs, product labels, signs on and in buildings, billboards, road maps, words printed on commercial vehicles, and so forth. Students choose an example of environmental print to present to the class as an opening.

During this project students will:

- Sign in on a whiteboard, chalkboard, or easel to demonstrate writing skills.

- Learn about environmental print to help them understand that printed words carry a message.

- Observe and identify environmental print.

- Choose an example of environmental print for a project.

- Create a visual (such as a drawing, cutout, or photograph) of printed text that can be found in our living environment.

- In writing, describe the environmental print, what it means, and where it might be found.

- Present an opening describing their environmental print.

Student Handout

- Words All Around Us

Content Standards*

1. Students apply knowledge of language structure, language conventions (e.g., spelling and punctuation), media techniques, figurative language, and genre to create, critique, and discuss print and nonprint texts.

2. Students participate as knowledgeable, reflective, creative, and critical members of a variety of literacy communities.

Idea for Introducing the Opening

Show students photos you've taken of environmental print from the school neighborhood to use as examples that students may recognize.

Project Steps

1. Determine at what level your students are prepared to examine and interact with environmental print. This project may be used with preemergent, emergent, or developing readers by adjusting the difficulty or complexity of the print students are asked to work with.

2. Give students opportunities to observe and identify environmental print:

   - Bring in photographs, magazine pictures, product labels, and other examples of environmental print and have students tell where someone might see each example and what it means.

   - Give students an assignment to bring in their own examples of environmental print in the form of magazine and newspaper pictures, photographs, or actual product labels, and talk about them in class: Where might they see each example? What does it mean?

   - Go for "print walks" outside and have students point out environmental print and tell what it means.

3. Tell students that for their opening they will each choose an example of "words all around us" to present to the class. Have them look through the materials you have gathered and select an example of environmental print to cut out or draw. You may also give students

---

* *Standards for the English Language Arts* by the International Reading Association and the National Council of Teachers of English. Copyright © 1996 by the International Reading Association and the National Council of Teachers of English. Reprinted with permission.

the option of finding examples on their own if you think it's appropriate.

4. Decide what your expectations will be for the written and visual parts of the assignment. Hand out the Words All Around Us form and model how the form should be completed. The template includes four places to record information:

   ▪ *"This is a picture of":* Students complete this statement by telling what kind of environmental print they will show on the handout. For example, they might write: "a stop sign," "a cereal box," "a soup can," "an advertising sign," or "a sign on the school."

   ▪ *Blank space for a picture:* Students cut out a picture from a magazine or newspaper to paste in this space; or they may make a drawing, use a photograph, or print an image from clip art or the Internet.

   ▪ *"The words in this picture mean":* Students finish this statement by explaining what the environmental text means. For example, they might write: "cars should stop," "the can has chicken noodle soup in it," "there is a furniture sale this week," or "the school is named Thomas Jefferson School."

   ▪ *"You could find these words":* Students finish this statement by telling where in their environment people might see the words in the picture. For example, they might write "at a street corner," "in the grocery store," "in front of a school," "on a billboard," or "on the side of a bus."

5. Schedule class time for students to complete their Words All Around Us templates and prepare their openings. Preparation time will vary depending on your expectations and the readiness of your students. In general, this project should require no more than about one hour of class time prior to students making their presentations. This time is typically spread over several days. You may also assign some of the work as homework.

6. When the templates are finished, collect them and check for quality, using the guidelines and expectations you have given to students

as criteria. After checking for quality, return the templates to the students with any comments or feedback that you wish to provide before the openings are presented. These templates are the students' final visual aids, so do not write or mark directly on them unless you expect them to redo the work.

7. Communicate with parents about the upcoming opening, to inform them about the theme being covered and the requirements of students when making an opening. Ask them to practice with their children at home. (See pages 60–63 for parent letters to adapt.)

8. As needed, model part or all of a "Words All Around Us" opening for the class. Demonstrate how to present the information in sequence ("This is a picture of a sign. The words mean . . . You could find this sign . . .").

9. *Optional:* Have students who finish their projects early create a "Words All Around Us" sign or a poster-sized example of environmental print to serve as a backdrop to the opening presentations.

10. Make copies of the assessment form on page 206. Complete a form for each student after he or she has presented an opening.

11. Proceed with "Words All Around Us" openings as you have planned them. Have students write their names on the board before they introduce themselves to the class. As necessary, prompt children to fulfill the key elements of the opening as they make their presentations.

Ideas for Extending or Modifying the Opening

1. Engage students in a treasure hunt for the unusual or uncommon: Give them a challenge assignment to identify an example of environmental print that nobody else will think of or bring in.

2. Ask students to think about what is the same and what is different among examples of environmental print. For example, what is the same and what is different about "Stop," "Yield," and "Speed Limit 35" signs? (They are the same in that they are street signs and they tell drivers what to do; they're different

in that they tell drivers to do different things and have different shapes and colors.)

3. Have students classify environmental print. Give them categories such as these: found inside, found outside, advertising, product names, street signs. Ask students to tell in which category each example of environmental print belongs. Watch for "ah-ha!" moments when students realize that some examples may be classified in more than one way.

4. Create a display called "Words Around Our School." Walk the school building and grounds with students and take pictures of every example of environmental print they can identify.

5. Create your own Words All Around Us templates on larger paper to give students more room to draw, paste pictures, or write. A simple way to do this is by photocopying the form at 200 percent on 11" x 17" paper.

Classroom Differentiation Example: Ms. Archer

Strategies: scaffolding, tiering

Ms. Archer has decided to use a basics-first approach with her students as they prepare for their opening projects. She has designated class time when they will work on their written and visual materials. At the end of this time, the students will show her what they have done. Students know that if their basic assignments need more work, Ms. Archer will provide whatever support (scaffolding) is needed to complete them. However, if a student is ready to go, he or she will be allowed to extend the project beyond the basics. Here are three examples:

Sammi has struggled with the assignment. She understands the concept of environmental print, but the task of finding an example and explaining in writing what it means has proven to be quite difficult for her. After examining what she has done, Ms. Archer asks Sammi to meet with her for guided support to complete the project before presenting it. Understanding that Sammi needs help with the writing expectation, Ms. Archer allows her to dictate what she wants to say in order to complete the assignment.

Dmitri has finished the project requirements, but it is not evident that he completely understands the concept of environmental print. Ms. Archer's judgment is that he could benefit from continuing to focus on the basic elements of the project. As a result, she gives Dmitri two very specific project extension options that he may choose from and asks him to work with a parent volunteer to build at least one of them into his project.

LaTasha has finished the assignment with a high level of quality and an obvious mastery of the concept. Ms. Archer tells LaTasha to choose any of the options provided on a list of extension ideas and include them in her presentation.

Words All Around Us

Name: _____ **Date:** _____

This is a picture of _____.

[ ]

The words in this picture mean _____

_____.

You could find these words _____

_____.

I Made a Pattern

Content Focus: Math
Topic and Assignment

Materials

Whiteboard or easel and marker; or chalkboard and chalk

Objects and materials for students to create patterns (see project step 2)

Glue

This project helps students master the concept of simple repeating patterns. Patterns are at the heart of mathematics, and helping students recognize and describe patterns is an important part of their mathematics training. As they participate in this project, students experience patterns in a variety of ways and create their own patterns to present to the class as openings.

During this project students will:

- Sign in on a whiteboard, chalkboard, or easel to demonstrate writing skills.

- Learn to recognize patterns.

- Discover patterns in everyday objects.

- Create patterns on paper or using a variety of objects.

- Describe patterns orally and in writing.

- Present an opening in which they show and describe a pattern they have made.

Student Handout

- I Made a Pattern

Content Standards*

1. Create and use representations to organize, record, and communicate mathematical ideas.

2. Organize and consolidate their mathematical thinking through communication.

3. Recognize and apply mathematics in contexts outside of mathematics.

4. Understand patterns, relations, and functions: Recognize, describe, and extend

patterns such as sequences of sounds and shapes or simple numeric patterns and translate from one representation to another; analyze how both repeating and growing patterns are generated.

Idea for Introducing the Opening

Bring objects that contain patterns to class, such as clothing items, fabric patterns, wallpaper, or wrapping paper. Ask students if they can find the pattern. Have students look at each other's clothing to see if they can find patterns.

Project Steps

1. Introduce students to simple visual and audio patterns using colors, objects, hand claps, finger snaps, and so forth. Do pattern repetitions with the class, and end each pattern sequence by asking, "What comes next?" For example, put this pattern of colored squares on the whiteboard: *blue, blue, red, blue, blue, red, blue, blue, red, blue.* Have the class say it with you and when you get to the end ask, "What comes next?"

2. Create patterns in class using objects of different colors, sizes, and shapes. Work with students to extend the patterns to be sure they understand "what comes next." If students begin to master simple repeating patterns, ask them to create more complex ones. For example, instead of two colors, make patterns with three.

3. Tell students that for their openings they will each create a pattern to present to the class. They may use the handout to draw a pattern, or they may use small objects or materials such as stickers, colored buttons, or cutouts. They may also use larger objects such as blocks by laying them out on a table, but they should have made a drawing of the pattern beforehand so that it can be quickly and accurately laid out. Their task during the opening is to describe the pattern and then ask, "Does anyone know what comes

next?" After calling on someone to respond, the presenter answers in a complete sentence by saying either "Yes, that is right" or "No, I'm sorry, that is not right. Does someone else know what comes next?" If nobody can answer, the presenter reveals how the pattern is completed.

4. Decide what your expectations will be for the written and visual parts of the assignment. Hand out the I Made a Pattern form and model how it should be completed. Students cut along the dotted line and glue the two strips together to make one long strip. They can use as many spaces as they need to make their pattern. Explain that students may create a pattern without using the template if they choose. For example, a student might choose to make a pattern using three-dimensional objects such as unifix cubes or toy animals.

5. Schedule class time for students to prepare their openings. Students complete their I Made a Pattern templates or use some other method of creating a pattern. Students who use objects (such as cubes or toy animals) that cannot be affixed to the template should draw examples of their patterns for this part of the assignment and then show or create the pattern with objects during the presentation. Preparation time will vary depending on your expectations and the readiness of your students. In general, this project should require no more than about one hour of class time prior to students making their presentations. This time is typically spread over several days. Some of this work may be done as a homework assignment.

6. Communicate with parents about the upcoming opening to inform them about the theme being covered and the requirements of students when making an opening. Ask them to practice with their children at home. (See pages 60–63 for parent letters to adapt.)

7. As needed, model part or all of an "I Made a Pattern" opening for the class. Demonstrate how to present the information in sequence ("This is the pattern I made. It goes triangle, circle, square, triangle, circle, square, triangle, circle . . . Can anyone tell me what comes next?").

8. *Optional:* Have students who finish their projects early create an "I Made a Pattern" sign or a large version of a pattern to serve as a backdrop to the opening presentations.

9. Make copies of the assessment form on page 206. Complete a form for each student after he or she has presented an opening.

10. Proceed with "I Made a Pattern" openings as you have planned them. Have students write their names on the board before they introduce themselves to the class. As necessary, prompt children to fulfill the key elements of the opening as they make their presentations.

Ideas for Extending or Modifying the Opening

1. Have students make bead necklaces or bracelets that can be used to demonstrate patterns.

2. Give students a set of objects and challenge them to create unique patterns that are different from everybody else's, even though they are all using the same objects. For example, a set of three shapes, each of which may be any of three colors (such as blue, yellow, and red triangles, squares, and circles), offers many pattern possibilities.

3. Display student-made patterns on the wall following their openings.

4. Go on a "pattern treasure hunt" in and around the school. Have students identify patterns that they can see in the building, such as the lighting arrangement in the ceiling or the tiles in the hallway or even the days on a calendar.

Classroom Differentiation Example: Mrs. O'Conner

Strategies: multiple intelligences, choice-as-motivator

Mrs. O'Conner's class is preparing to do "I Made a Pattern" openings. Mrs. O'Conner decided to incorporate multiple intelligences into the process by letting students choose from four different general ways of creating patterns and presenting them to the audience. She believed that students will naturally choose to use their strongest intelligence if given an opportunity to do so. Here are the choices she gave and the ways some of her students chose to make their patterns:

Art Project Patterns (visual/spatial option)

- James decided to draw pictures of his pattern, using shapes and colors.
- Lynette organized groups of colored beads into a pattern.

Move-Your-Body Patterns (bodily/kinesthetic)

- Dalia acted out a pattern with hops and twirls.
- Kim's preference was to use hand motions to show a pattern.

Shapes and Numbers Patterns (logical/mathematical)

- Ethan used geometric shapes to create a pattern.
- Sylvia formed a pattern with a sequence of numbers.

Sing It, Clap It, Tap a Beat! (musical/rhythmic)

- Madison chose to create a pattern by clapping her hands and stomping her feet.
- Jerome made up a song with a pattern of simple words.

I Made a Pattern

Name: _____ **Date:** _____

Cut along the dotted line and glue the two strips together to make one long strip.

1	2	3	4	Glue this rectangle under rectangle # 5 after cutting along the dotted line to make one long strip for your pattern.
5	6	7	8	9

Example:

I Understand Food Chains

Content Focus: Life Science
Topic and Assignment

Materials

 Whiteboard or easel and marker; or chalkboard and chalk

 Scissors

 Glue

This project focuses on ecosystems. Students are asked to develop a food chain by choosing one animal from each of several groups and showing on a flow chart which animals would eat other animals. Each student presents the food chain he or she creates to the class as an opening.

During this project students will:

- Sign in on a whiteboard, chalkboard, or easel to demonstrate writing skills.

- Understand that every animal needs food to live.

- Discover that some animals eat other animals.

- Learn what a food chain is.

- Create a food chain.

- Write a definition of a food chain.

- Present an opening in which they show and explain a food chain.

Student Handouts

- What Animals Eat
- I Understand Food Chains

Content Standards*

1. All students should develop abilities necessary to do scientific inquiry:

   - Ask a question about objects, organisms, and events in the environment; communicate investigations and explanations.

2. All students should develop an understanding of organisms and their environment:

   - All animals depend on plants. Some animals eat plants for food. Other animals eat animals that eat the plants.

Ideas for Introducing the Opening

- Talk with students about what animals eat. See if they can tell you what specific animals such as lions, antelopes, wolves, and rabbits eat.

- Draw or otherwise create a three-link food chain example such as grass, antelope, lion, to show students.

Project Steps

1. Introduce the project by discussing with students the fact that all animals need food. Help them understand that some animals eat plants and some animals eat other animals. Explain what a food chain is.

2. Give students the What Animals Eat handout. Explain that they will choose one animal from each group, and show how those animals make a food chain.

3. Decide what your expectations will be for the written and visual parts of the assignment. Give students the I Understand Food Chains handout. Have them put the animals they chose in the correct places to form a food chain. This can be done with drawings, words, or cutout pictures from the What Animals Eat handout. The handout will serve as the students' final written report and visual aid unless you choose to require them to create more elaborate or extensive written pieces and visual materials.

4. Schedule class time for students to prepare and present their openings. Preparation time will vary depending on your expectations and the readiness of your students. In general, this project should require no more than about one hour of class time prior to students making their presentations. This time is typically spread over several days.

5. Communicate with parents about the upcoming opening to inform them about the theme being covered and the requirements of students when making an opening. Ask

* Reprinted with permission from "National Science Education Standards" © 1995, by the National Academy of Sciences, Courtesy of the National Academies Press, Washington, D.C.

them to practice with their children at home. (See pages 60–63 for parent letters to adapt.)

6. As needed, model part or all of an "I Understand Food Chains" opening for the class. ("Here is a food chain that I made. It shows that sunlight goes to grass, grass is eaten by grasshoppers, grasshoppers . . .")

7. *Optional:* Have students who finish their projects early create an "I Understand Food Chains" sign to serve as a backdrop to the opening presentations. Or students could create several colorful paper chains to hang around the podium or music stand where students stand to give an opening.

8. Make copies of the assessment form on page 206. Complete a form for each student after he or she has presented an opening.

9. Proceed with "I Understand Food Chains" openings as you have planned them. Have students write their names on the board before they introduce themselves to the class. As necessary, prompt children to fulfill the key elements of the opening as they make their presentations.

Ideas for Extending or Modifying the Opening

1. Have students create simple food chains that include themselves. This opening might be titled "How I Get Energy from the Sun." For example: Sun —> green beans —> me; or, sun —> grass —> cow —> me. You might want to ask students to describe the form of the food they eat at the end. A student can get energy from a cow by eating cheese or by eating a hamburger.

2. Assign students a predator and have them make a food chain that ends with that animal. For example, a student is given an owl as the end of a food chain. The student finds out that owls eat mice, and that mice eat seeds from plants. So the food chain that this student presents is: sun —> seeds —> mouse —> owl.

3. Extend the idea of food chains to simple food webs. Give each student an animal, and instead of having the student trace a food chain, ask him or her to connect as many different food sources as possible to that animal. In an opening, the student would say "My animal is a hawk. A hawk eats mice, small birds, frogs, and snakes." From there you can have a discussion about what the other animals eat. You can even talk about the fact that snakes also eat mice, and mice and many small birds eat seeds. This is how food webs are formed.

4. Ask if any students have pets. What do they need? What do students do to take care of their pets? What about themselves? What are their basic needs? If you don't get responses you are looking for, ask questions about what would happen if pets (or people) *didn't* have certain things such as water, food, warmth, and protection (or safety). Explain that food chains provide something very basic to life. Ask if students can tell what that is.

Classroom Differentiation Example: Mr. Lopez

Strategies: choice-as-motivator, flexible grouping, kids teaching kids, scaffolding

Mr. Lopez has decided to have students work with partners as they prepare "I Understand Food Chains" openings. His idea is to pair struggling students with advanced students. These pairs will work together to select predators and develop food chains and then practice with each other before giving their openings to the class.

Juanita and Chen are paired together. Chen often has difficulty with learning activities, but he benefits greatly from seeing things modeled by his peers. Juanita grasps concepts quickly and is a wonderful model for Chen. Under Juanita's influence, Chen has completed a food chain and is excited about it. Juanita has also completed a food chain and has gone beyond the assignment by seeing how her food chain is connected to Chen's. She intends to show the class what she has discovered about the relationships between the animals in her chain and those in Chen's.

Melissa and Rudy are paired together. These two are neither struggling nor advanced, but since Mr. Lopez's class is a continuum of learners, some pairs do not differ much in their readiness to learn. However, by working together, both Melissa and Rudy have added a level of quality to their openings that would not have been possible otherwise.

Daniel and Latrice have proven to be what Mr. Lopez calls a dysfunctional partnership. The two are simply not able to be productive when they are together. As a result, Mr. Lopez has added a third person to their group: himself. He calls this scaffold "Mr. Lopez's Solution," which means that Daniel and Latrice should expect him to join them often during the project.

What Animals Eat

Name: _____ **Date:** _____

Start with the sun. Choose one living thing from each group to make a food chain.

	Group 1	Group 2	Group 3	Group 4
	plant leaves	grasshopper	frog	hawk
Sun	plant fruits	cricket	toad	snake
	plant seeds	caterpillar	lizard	fox

I Understand Food Chains

Name: _____ **Date:** _____

This is my food chain.

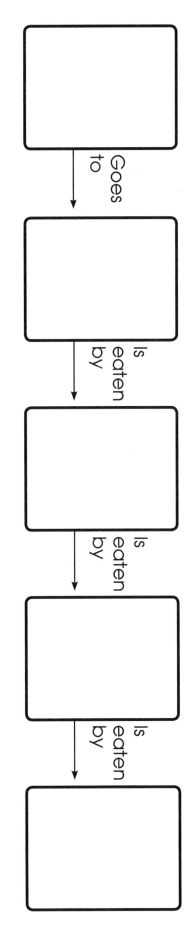

Goes to →

Is eaten by →

Is eaten by →

Is eaten by →

How would you describe to someone what a food chain is?

Write this in your own words.

_____

_____

_____

Middle Elementary Openings

- These Objects Are Classified

- Alien Broadcast System

- Local Hero of the Year

- This Place Is a Zoo

- The Shape Hunter

These Objects Are Classified

Content Focus: Classification

Topic and Assignment

Materials

 A different set of five objects for each set of partners to classify

 Poster board or art paper for the visual aid

An important part of elementary science instruction is helping students to sort and classify objects by identifying their attributes. The ability to distinguish the similarities and differences among objects is a key element of scientific investigation. For this project, students work in pairs, assuming the role of scientific investigators whose job is to document and present the attributes and properties of a variety of objects to demonstrate how they can be classified.

During this project partners will:

- Receive a set of five objects to classify.

- Analyze the objects and identify attributes that can be used for classification.

- Complete a classification chart for the five objects.

- Write a report to explain how the objects have been classified: what is the same for all five objects and what is different among them.

- Present an opening titled "These Objects Are Classified."

Student Handouts

- Assignment Sheet: These Objects Are Classified

- Instructions for Making an Opening: These Objects Are Classified

- Object Classification Chart

- Poster Model: These Objects Are Classified

Note: While these forms provide all the materials students need to complete a "These Objects Are Classified" opening, the CD-ROM included with this book contains a more detailed poster-making project that may be of interest for this and other openings.

Content Standards*

1. All students should develop abilities necessary to do scientific inquiry and understandings about scientific inquiry:

   - *Ask a question about objects, organisms, and events in the environment; plan and conduct a simple investigation, communicate investigations and explanations.*

* Reprinted with permission from "National Science Education Standards" © 1995, by the National Academy of Sciences, courtesy of the National Academies Press, Washington, D.C.

2. All students should develop an understanding of properties of objects and materials.

Idea for Introducing the Opening

Prepare a set of five objects to discuss as a class. "What is an attribute and what attributes do our five objects have? Do any of the objects share the same attribute? How are they different?" (See project step 6.)

Project Steps

1. Introduce the project scenario to the students: *You are a scientist who has been asked to classify a set of objects. You will work with a partner to describe your system for classifying the objects in a presentation to your fellow scientists.*

2. Divide the class into pairs by using a flexible grouping strategy: randomly, by student choice, by compatability, heterogenously, or homogenously (see pages 15–16).

3. Give each partner group a set of five objects to classify. Put the objects in a bag or box so they can be kept together. This will require some initial work, because the ideal is for every partner group to have a different set of objects, and you need to be sure that each set of five has at least two common attributes that students can identify. However, the object sets may be used again each year so that once they are assembled, this work does not have to be repeated. You do not need to physically keep the bags of objects on shelves in your room from year-to-year. Just keep a list of the object sets to make it easy to assemble the bags when you are ready to do this opening project again. (The difficult part is thinking of what to include in each set.)

4. Think about how this project can be differentiated for students who struggle and for advanced learners. For struggling learners, objects can be grouped together that have easily discerned similarities and differences.

Suggestions for Object Sets

Extra large yellow sticky note Large yellow sticky note Medium blue sticky note Small blue sticky note Extra small blue sticky note	Wooden pencil Toothpick Ink pen Mechanical pencil Finishing nail	Green marker Green ink pen Green lead pencil Green crayon Green mechanical pencil
Yellow notebook paper Yellow small note card Yellow large note card Yellow small sticky note Yellow large sticky note	Short, thick wood screw Long, skinny wood screw Short, thick bolt Short, skinny bolt Long, skinny bolt	Large green glass marble Small green glass marble Large blue glass marble Small blue glass marble Small red glass marble
Blue plastic triangle Blue plastic circle Blue plastic square Blue plastic diamond Blue plastic oval	Long steel screw Medium steel screw Short steel screw Long brass screw Short brass screw	Square of fine sand paper Square of medium sand paper Square of course sand paper Square of poster board Square of cardboard
Large red plastic triangle Small red plastic triangle Small red metal triangle Large red wood triangle Large red metal triangle	Small steel washer Medium steel washer Large steel washer Small plastic washer Large plastic washer	Small button Medium button Large button Small washer Large washer
Large square of aluminum foil Small square of aluminum foil Large metal paper clip Small metal paper clip Copper wire	Small nail Small paper clip Large paper clip Small screw Large screw	Small green plastic cube Large green plastic cube Small red plastic cube Large red plastic cube Small blue plastic cube

For more advanced learners, objects can be grouped that have less obvious common traits. You can provide challenge where needed and support where needed simply by the way you assign objects. This can be almost invisible to the students and yet powerful in its effect by addressing everyone's readiness to learn and need for challenge.

5. Give students the These Objects Are Classified assignment sheet. Explain that each set of partners will identify two attributes that are the same for all five objects and two attributes that are the same for some of the objects but not all five. For example, if the objects are five shapes—triangle, square, rectangle, circle, and oval—partners might find that all five objects are made of plastic and all of them are smooth (common attributes). Attributes that are the same for some of the objects (but not all) might be: three are big and two are small, and two are red and three are blue.

6. Talk with students about what attributes are, and give them plenty of examples so that they understand how to identify the attributes of their objects. Present the class with a variety of objects and have students share ideas about their attributes. Hand out a copy of the Object Classification Chart to each student. Make a transparency of the chart, too, and fill it in as a class activity so students can see how it is done. Here are some categories of attributes that you might cover with your students:

  - Texture (rough, smooth)
  - Flexibility (rigid, stiff, firm, flexible, bendable, strong)
  - Hardness (hard, soft)
  - Size (big, medium, small, long, short, wide, narrow)
  - Smell (pleasant, unpleasant; specific characteristics, for example "smells like lemon" or "smells like chocolate")
  - Density (sink, float)
  - Weight (heavy, light)
  - Color (any common colors)
  - Magnetic properties (attracted to a magnet or not)
  - Electricity conductor (yes or no)
  - Shape (triangle, square, rectangle, circle, oval)
  - Material (plastic, metal, wood, stone, glass, leather, cloth)
  - Parts of objects (anything that is a specific, identifiable part of an object: wings, wheels, stems, roots, text, buttons, teeth, knobs, and so forth)
  - Additional traits that can be observed (shiny, dull, sharp, thin, thick, transparent, opaque, straight edges, curved edges, pointy, striped, solid, hollow, and so forth)

7. Decide what your expectations will be for the visual and written parts of the assignment. There are at least three options for the visual aid that students will produce:

  - Allow students to use the Object Classification Chart as the visual aid.
  - Have students create a poster-sized replica of the Object Classification Chart.
  - Have students create a poster based on the Poster Model handout.

8. Give students the Instructions for Making an Opening handout. This provides the basic requirements of the opening and offers a good way to review with students what your expectations are and what they need to do to prepare for their presentations.

9. Communicate with parents about the upcoming opening to inform them about the theme being covered and the requirements of students when making an opening. A good way to do this is to send the Instructions for Making an Opening handout home with students. (Also see pages 60–63 for parent letters to adapt.) Ask them to practice with their children at home.

10. As needed, model part or all of a "These Objects Are Classified" opening for the class. Demonstrate how to present the information

("Our five objects are a big paper clip, a little paper clip, a strip of tin foil, some copper wire, and a piece of window screen. Here are two attributes that are the same for all five objects. . . ."). Partners are expected to present their five objects and tell two attributes that are the same for all of them and two more that are the same for some of them. Point out that both partners in the pair will be expected to introduce themselves and to deliver part of the opening. Partners will need to figure out how they will divide up the presentation: will they take turns talking throughout the opening or have one do the first half and the other the last half of the presentation?

11. Schedule class time for students to prepare and present their openings. Preparation time will vary depending on your expectations, the amount of prep work you assign as homework, and the readiness of your students. In general, this project should require no more than about two hours of class time prior to students making their presentations. This time is typically spread over several days.

12. *Optional:* Have students who finish their projects early create a "These Objects Are Classfied" sign to serve as a backdrop to the opening presentations. Alternatively, students could create a poster that has two questions on it: "How are they the same? How are they different?"

13. Make copies of the assessment form on page 207. Complete a form for each student after he or she has presented an opening.

14. Proceed with "These Objects Are Classified" openings as you have planned them. As necessary, prompt children to fulfill the key elements of the opening as they make their presentations.

Ideas for Extending or Modifying the Opening

1. Place increased emphasis on the visual aid that students use with their openings. Work with students to think of ways to create graphic organizers to illustrate how the five objects might be classified. An example organizer is provided at the end of the project that you may use as a model to help students create a poster. Note that this model could be carried even further, and some students will likely recognize this fact and want to show every classification possibility on their organizers.

2. Have each partner group join another partner group after doing their openings and combine their objects to form sets of ten. They can look for new attributes that are common to all ten objects or figure out which of the attributes already identified by each group fit some or all of the other group's objects.

3. At the end of each opening, unveil an object of your own and ask the presenters to tell which attributes from their chart can be identified in the new object. You may choose to have this be a class undertaking, in which case you might say, "Now that you know what the attributes of John and Leanne's objects are, look at this object I have brought in. Think about this for a minute and see if you can find any of the attributes they have listed on their chart in this new object."

4. Display a list of all the attributes students identify for their objects, adding newly presented attributes to the exhibit following each opening. After adding the new attributes, ask the class to identify attributes from the whole exhibit that can be found in the objects just presented. If you list all the attributes horizontally along a wall, you can list the objects beneath their attributes. Each object will be listed multiple times, depending on how many attributes can be identified for it.

5. Organize a large set of objects on a table and let students choose from it any five objects to use for their opening presentation. Or, allow more advanced learners this option while still assigning objects to students who struggle. If students choose their own objects there is an increased potential for ending up with objects that do not share many obvious attributes. Be sure to guide students to choose five objects that have some things in common rather than making five random selections. Challenge your advanced learners

to look for unusual shared attributes that are not immediately apparent.

6. Use this opening in conjunction with the starter opening titled "What Is the Same? What Is Different?" on page 42. Begin with the starter opening to introduce students to the concept of objects and their attributes.

For this starter opening, they observe two objects and report to the class on one thing that is the same about the two objects, and one thing that is different about them. After everyone has done a starter opening, introduce the "These Objects Are Classified" opening and have students take classifying objects to a deeper level.

Classroom Differentiation Example: Mr. Vandenberg

Strategies: flexible grouping, scaffolding, tiering

Mr. Vandenberg has decided to pair advanced learners together, on-target learners together, and struggling learners together. This will let him provide challenge where appropriate while directly supporting students who need help to complete the opening. He has carefully assembled a set of five objects for each pair to match their readiness for the project. He has also developed several challenge options for partners who are able to go beyond the basic assignment.

Angelica and Tariq are paired together because they both perform at an advanced level. They discover that their five objects are not very similar, and therefore the assignment is not easy for them: it requires quite a bit of thinking. As a challenge option, they have decided to join Leah and Ogden and combine objects. This new group of four now analyzes ten objects to identify some of their shared attributes.

Charlie and Latisha are on-target learners. The five objects given to them match their readiness for the project. Working together, they complete the project with time left to choose a challenge option. They have decided to identify three additional objects from Mr. Vandenberg's "Extra Objects Table" that share attributes with at least some of the original five.

Michelle and Lee are struggling learners. They are working with five objects for which Mr. Vandenberg believes they will be able to identify common attributes. They may not have time for a challenge option, but with Mr. Vandenberg's help, they will be able to successfully complete the basic assignment and better understand the concept of classification.

These Objects Are Classified

Name: _____ **Date:** _____

You are a scientist and a classification expert. You have been asked to think about ways to classify a set of objects. You will work with a partner to describe how you classified the objects in a presentation to your fellow scientists.

1. Record your five objects on the lines below:

Object 1: _____

Object 2: _____

Object 3: _____

Object 4: _____

Object 5: _____

2. Record two attributes that you can find in all five objects:

Attribute 1: _____

_____

_____

Attribute 2: _____

_____

_____

Continued ➡

These Objects Are Classified (continued)

3. Record two more attributes that you can find in some of the objects, but not all of them:

Attribute 3: _____

_____

_____

Objects it is found in: _____

_____

_____

Attribute 4: _____

_____

_____

Objects it is found in: _____

_____

_____

4. Write a report about the objects and their attributes.

5. Make a visual aid that you can show during your opening (you may be allowed to use the Object Classification Chart or the Poster Model handout as your visual aid).

6. Give an opening about the objects and their attributes to the class.

These Objects Are Classified

Name: _____ **Date:** _____

The Parts of an Opening:

Written Report (Write a report about the classification system)

★ Find information about each object by carefully observing it and talking with your partner about what you see.

★ Write down what you want to say about your objects and their attributes.

★ Use your best handwriting skills.

★ You may have your report with you when you present your opening.

Visual Aid (Make a visual aid that shows your objects and their attributes)

★ Clearly show or explain what the attributes of the objects are and which attributes are shared by at least some of the objects.

★ You may use the Object Classification Chart or the Poster Model to help you design a poster.

Oral Presentation (Talk to the class about how you and your partner have classified your objects)

★ Stand straight and tall.

★ Look at people in the audience while you talk.

★ Speak clearly and be sure everyone can hear you.

★ Show your visual aid to the audience when you present.

Questions and Answers (Ask if there are any questions)

★ Answer questions from the audience about your objects.

★ It's okay to say "I don't know" if you don't know an answer.

Continued ➡

These Objects Are Classified (continued)

Hints for a Successful Opening:

★ Look at your objects carefully before you identify their attributes. Make your opening more interesting by choosing attributes that other people might not think of.

★ Practice! Practice! Practice! Practice your opening with a parent several times. Focus on the four Oral Presentation points listed in "The Parts of an Opening."

Here is an example of what partners named Sasha and Karin said in their "These Objects Are Classified" opening:

Sasha and Karin's Opening

Sasha: "Good morning. My name is Sasha."

Karin: "My name is Karin, and we have an opening for you. Our opening is about classifying objects."

Sasha: "We have classified five objects. Our objects are: a penny, a key ring, a washer, a pie pan, and a pickle jar lid. All five objects are made of metal. They are all also the shape of a circle. In our classification system, all five objects are circles made of metal."

Karin: "Some of our objects have attributes that the others don't have. Look at our visual aid. As you can see, the key ring and washer have holes in the middle, while the penny, pie pan, and pickle jar lid are solid circles. The key ring, washer, pie pan, and pickle jar lid are all attracted to a magnet, but the penny isn't."

Sasha: "Thank you for listening. Are there any questions?"

Object Classification Chart

Name: _____ **Date:** _____

1. You have five objects. Write the name of each object in a box in the left column of the Classification Table (page 2 of this handout).

2. Think of an attribute that all five objects have and write it in the box at the top of the Classification Table labeled "Attribute 1."

3. Think of another attribute that all five objects have and write it in the box at the top labeled "Attribute 2."

4. Think of an attribute that only some of the objects have and write it in the box labeled "Attribute 3."

5. Think of another attribute that only some of the objects have and write it in the box labeled "Attribute 4."

6. Write "yes" or "no" in each box below each attribute to tell if the object has the attribute or not.

7. Fill in the bottom row with the number of objects that have each attribute.

8. Complete the sentence at the bottom of the chart.

Object Classification Chart (continued)

	All 5 objects Attribute 1:	All 5 objects Attribute 2:	Some objects Attribute 3:	Some objects Attribute 4:
Object 1:				
Object 2:				
Object 3:				
Object 4:				
Object 5:				
Number of objects that have this attribute:				

In our classification system, all five objects have the following attributes:

_____

_____ .

These Objects Are Classified

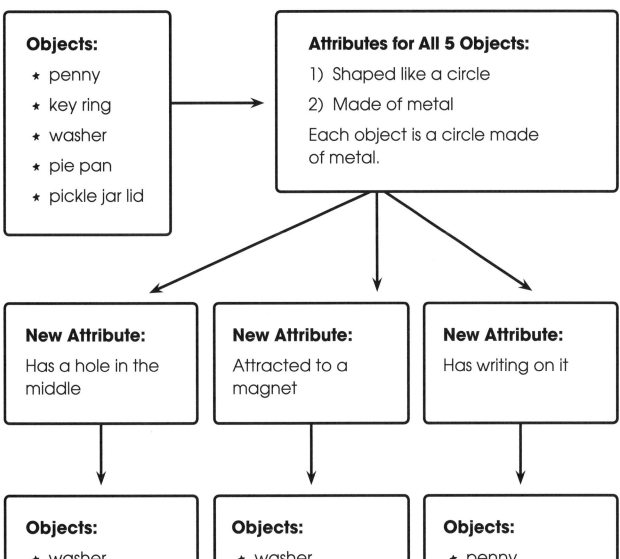

Objects:
* ★ penny
* ★ key ring
* ★ washer
* ★ pie pan
* ★ pickle jar lid

Attributes for All 5 Objects:

1) Shaped like a circle

2) Made of metal

Each object is a circle made of metal.

New Attribute:

Has a hole in the middle

New Attribute:

Attracted to a magnet

New Attribute:

Has writing on it

Objects:
* ★ washer
* ★ key ring

Each object is a circle made of metal with a hole in the middle.

Objects:
* ★ washer
* ★ key ring
* ★ pie pan
* ★ pickle jar lid

Each object is a circle made of metal that is attracted to a magnet.

Objects:
* ★ penny
* ★ pie pan
* ★ pickle jar lid

Each object is a circle made of metal that has writing on it.

Alien Broadcast System

Content Focus: Any Content Area

Topic and Assignment

Young students are captivated by the idea of communicating with intelligent beings from outer space. This project provides a fun way to ask: If you actually could communicate with curious aliens who wanted to know more about us, what would you tell them?

For this project, students assume the role of scientists who have received a message from an advanced civilization on a distant planet requesting information about life on Earth. They have decided to reply to this request by making presentations on topics that aliens would likely find interesting, and then laser-streaming the presentations back to the planet. They call these interstellar presentations the "Alien Broadcast System." The scientists work together to develop a list of topics and conduct research before making presentations to their alien "colleagues."

You can use this project to tie into a specific curriculum area that you are studying (maybe the aliens have a particular interest in plant or animal life, weather, government, customs and traditions, family life, or even mathematics). Or you can give your students free reign to choose any topic that interests them and that they want to share with the aliens.

The project also is designed to help kids think about doing research and writing short, factual reports based on what they discover.

During this project students will:

- Participate in a class discussion to create a list of interesting topics.

- Choose a topic for their presentations.

- Conduct research to find information about the topic.

- Write a report that describes and explains the topic.

Materials

 Resources for conducting research

 Drawing paper or poster board for visual aids

 Drawing and coloring materials for making visual aids

- Create a visual aid with information about the topic.

- Present an opening titled "Alien Broadcast System."

Student Handouts

- Assignment Sheet: Alien Broadcast System

- Instructions for Making an Opening: Alien Broadcast System

- Visual Transmission Planner: Alien Broadcast System

Note: *While these forms provide all the materials students need to complete an "Alien Broadcast System" opening, the CD-ROM included with this book contains a more detailed poster-making project that may be of interest for this and other openings.*

Content Standards

This project can address standards in any core content area, depending upon your chosen topics.

Idea for Introducing the Opening

Show students an interesting container in which you have already placed a written message that you received from aliens. "Dear Earthlings, we are friendly life forms from the Spectacula Galaxy and we are curious about . . ."

Project Steps

1. Decide on a topic focus area before introducing the openings assignment to students.

2. Introduce the project scenario to the students: *In this opening, you will pretend to be a scientist who has received a message from aliens, or beings that are not from Earth. These aliens want information about life on Earth. You and your fellow scientists will make presentations to send back to them through the Alien Broadcast System.*

3. Hand out the Alien Broadcast System assignment sheet and read through it with the

class. Discuss any requirements that might be unclear to students.

4. Have students record the content focus area on their assignment sheets. For example, the focus area might be "Animals of Earth."

5. Explain to students that as scientists, they will choose topics related to the focus area, find information, write reports, and create visual aids to be used in presentations to their alien colleagues.

6. Conduct a class discussion to make a list of possible topics for students to choose from. Narrow the conversation to the focus area you want to cover with the project. For example, you might decide to focus on "What Is a Community?" and ask students to think of as many topics as possible that are related to the concept of community.

7. Decide what your expectations will be for the visual and written parts of the assignment. Give students the Instructions for Making an Opening handout and the Visual Transmission Planner. These provide the basic requirements of the opening and offer a good way to review with students what your expectations are and what they need to do to prepare for their presentations. Explain what elements you expect them to include on their Visual Transmission Planner. Students should use the planner as a rough draft; then create their final visual on a new piece of paper or poster board.

8. Communicate with parents about the upcoming opening to inform them about the theme being covered and the requirements of students when making an opening. A good way to do this is to send the Instructions for Making an Opening handout home with students. (Also see pages 60–63 for parent letters to adapt.) Ask them to practice with their children at home.

9. As needed, model part or all of an "Alien Broadcast System" opening for the class. Demonstrate how to present the information ("Hello, alien scientists, and welcome to the Alien Broadcast System. You wanted to know more about communities. Well, here is some information for you . . ."). Each student is expected to present information

about his or her topic in a way that would help an alien understand it. The handouts will help students prepare for the opening presentation.

10. Schedule class time for students to prepare and present their openings. Preparation time will vary depending on your expectations, the amount of prep work you assign as homework, and the readiness of your students. In general, this project should require no more than about two hours of class time prior to students making their presentations. This time is typically spread over several days.

11. *Optional:* Have students who are done early create an "Alien Broadcast System" sign to serve as a backdrop to the opening presentations. Or, students could create a poster showing a setting from the other galaxy with an alien in it. This could be positioned to represent a television screen during the "live" broadcast of each student's opening.

12. Make copies of the assessment form on page 207. Complete a form for each student after he or she has presented an opening.

13. Proceed with "Alien Broadcast System" openings as you have planned them. As necessary, prompt children to fulfill the key elements of the opening as they make their presentations.

Ideas for Extending or Modifying the Opening

1. Make video recordings of students presenting their openings, and create an Alien Broadcast System digital video.

2. Have students use word processing for their reports and scan or take digital photographs of their visual aids to make the project completely digital. They may project their reports and visual aids onto a screen during their presentation.

3. Develop a list of questions from the aliens before the project begins so that students can choose specific topics to work with. For example:

    ▪ We would like to know what "adaptations" are. They seem to have something to do with survival.

- Because our knowledge of Earth is quite limited, we are curious to know more about what kinds of animals you have on Earth; how are they classified?

- Is it true that animals on your planet eat other animals? Does this have something to do with "food webs"?

- Could you please explain to us what an ecosystem is?

4. Focus the project on vocabulary. Have students concentrate on teaching the aliens the meaning and proper use of words from the curriculum. Each student would be responsible for one word. For example, instead of just using the word *community* in a presentation, a student's task would be to define it.

5. Cut a rectangular hole in a large piece of cardboard (such as a refrigerator box) to represent a computer screen, and have students present through the hole, as if the class were the alien scientists watching the transmission streaming in from Earth.

Classroom Differentiation Example: Ms. Garcia

Strategies: scaffolding, tiering, choice-as-motivator

Ms. Garcia is using the "Alien Broadcast System" opening project to help her students review and teach each other about science standards that have recently been covered. Each student will focus on a standard he or she clearly understands. Ms. Garcia will meet with students to help them choose topics.

To ensure accuracy and quality, students must complete the basic requirements of the project and show them to Ms. Garcia before the openings are presented. Students who are ready to go after their basics-first meeting with Ms. Garcia may extend their projects in a variety of ways.

Ms. Garcia has developed a list of science concepts that many students in the class seem to have difficulty with, and she has reserved these topics to offer as choices for students who are going to extend their projects. Sothy's basics-first meeting with Ms. Garcia went well. His overall mastery of science qualifies him to focus on any topic, so he has chosen to add an explanation of the water cycle to his opening presentation.

Jeanine struggled with several standards, but one of the things she understood well was the concept of erosion caused by rainfall. This is the topic she and Ms. Garcia agreed would be a good one for her to focus on. At her basics-first meeting, Ms. Garcia found several minor but important points that needed to be clarified and improved before she presented, so Jeanine spent extra time on those things.

Alien Broadcast System

Name: _____ **Date:** _____

You are a scientist who has received a message from outer space. Alien scientists on a distant planet have asked you to tell them about life on Earth. You and other scientists have decided to make presentations about topics that the aliens want to know about. You will send your presentations back to the planet over the Alien Broadcast System. Read the assignment below to get ready for your presentation.

The alien scientists have asked you to focus on this area:

_____

_____

_____

1. Choose a topic for the report.

Topic: _____

_____

2. Conduct research about your topic.

3. Think about what you have learned from your research and write three important facts that you want to be sure to include in your report.

Fact: _____

_____

_____

Continued ➡

Alien Broadcast System (continued)

Fact: _____

_____

_____

Fact: _____

_____

_____

4. Write a report to tell about your topic. Use the three facts above along with other information that you have found.

5. Use the Visual Transmission Planner to show what your visual aid will look like. Be sure to include information from your research so that it goes along with the report.

Alien Broadcast System

Name: _____ **Date:** _____

The Parts of an Opening:

Written Report (Write a report about the topic)

★ Find information by researching the topic.

★ Write facts from your research about the topic the way you want to present them.

★ Use your best handwriting skills.

★ You may have your report with you when you present your opening.

Visual Aid (Show the class information about the topic)

★ Put one or two interesting facts from your research about the topic on the visual.

Oral Presentation (Present to the class as if you were talking to alien scientists)

★ Stand straight and tall.

★ Look at people in the audience while you talk.

★ Tell about what you learned from your research.

★ Speak clearly and be sure everyone can hear you.

★ Explain what your visual aid shows about the topic.

Questions and Answers (Ask if there are any questions at the end of your opening)

★ Answer questions about the topic from the audience.

★ It's okay to say "I don't know" if you don't know an answer.

Continued ➡

Alien Broadcast System (continued)

Hints for a Successful Opening:

★ Find plenty of interesting facts about the topic. The more interesting the facts are, the more interesting your opening will be.

★ Practice! Practice! Practice! Practice your opening with a parent several times. Focus on the five Oral Presentation points listed in "The Parts of an Opening."

★ As you present your opening, imagine that you really are speaking to a group of alien scientists. If you are excited about your presentation, the people you talk to will be, too.

Here is an example of what a student named D'Metria said in her "Alien Broadcast System" opening about weather:

D'Metria's Opening

"Good morning. My name is D'Metria and I have an opening for you. Hello alien scientists, and welcome to the Alien Broadcast System! You have asked us to tell you about weather. Weather means things like wind, temperature, clouds, and rain. My topic is rain. Rain falls more in some places than in others. My drawing shows that when water in the ocean or lakes evaporates, it goes up in the air and makes clouds. When the water drops in the clouds get big enough, they fall back down to the ground. That is called rain. We need rain for plants to grow. Thank you for listening. Are there any questions?"

Alien Broadcast System

Name: _____ **Date:** _____

Sketch a plan for your visual transmission in the space below. Once you have a plan you like, make a large poster on poster paper.

Hello Out There!

Local Hero of the Year

Content Focus: Community
Topic and Assignment

Children often hear the term *hero* applied to people around them. The soldier who returns home from overseas is a hero. The police officer who prevents a crime or captures a criminal is a hero. The student who helps someone else in a dangerous situation is a hero. Even the athlete who makes a spectacular play at the end of a game is a hero. More broadly, everyday heroes do things like volunteer to help others, take care of a sick friend or relative, teach kids, coach sports teams, and serve as role models. A student's own parent or family member could be a hero.

For this project, students assume the role of committee members who nominate people for the community's annual Local Hero of the Year award.

During this project students will:

- Identify a local person who could be considered a hero.

- Decide how to describe this person to an audience.

- Develop an explanation of why this person is a hero.

- Write a report about the person being nominated as a hero.

- Create a cereal box cover with information about the hero.

- Present an opening titled "Local Hero of the Year."

Materials

Poster board or art paper for the visual part of the opening

Drawing and coloring materials for making visual aids

Student Handouts

- Assignment Sheet: Local Hero of the Year

- Instructions for Making an Opening: Local Hero of the Year

- Cereal Box Planner: Local Hero of the Year

Note: While these forms provide all the materials students need to complete a "Local Hero of the Year" opening, the CD-ROM included with this book contains a more detailed poster-making project that may be of interest for this and other openings.

Content Standards*

1. Recognize and interpret how the "common good" can be strengthened through various forms of citizen action.

2. Identify and describe the influence of perception, attitudes, values, and beliefs on personal identity.

Idea for Introducing the Opening

To help students visualize a format for an illustration and report about their topic, discuss with them stories of ordinary heroes that you have collected from your local newspaper or from news websites. Generate a list of criteria or qualities that heroes have.

Project Steps

1. Introduce the project scenario to the students: *You are a member of a community group that is going to give someone a Local Hero of the Year award. Your job is to choose somebody to suggest for the award and make a presentation to explain who the person is and why he or she deserves the award.*

2. Hand out the Local Hero of the Year assignment sheet and read through it with the class. Discuss any requirements that might be unclear to students.

3. Have a discussion about heroes. What makes a person a hero? Help students understand that while a hero can be a person who does something spectacular in an emergency or difficult situation, heroes are also people who care about others, work hard to contribute to their community, help kids, respond in times of need, and so forth. Based on these criteria, ask students to name some heroes that they know. Be prepared to offer several examples to show that a hero does not have

Expectations of Excellence: Curriculum Standards for Social Studies are from the National Council for the Social Studies (NCSS).

to have extraordinary powers or perform superhuman tasks. There are heroes all around us, and it is important for students to understand this concept before moving ahead with this project. This conversation will lay the groundwork for students to identify people around them who could be considered the Local Hero of the Year.

4. Decide what your expectations will be for the visual and written parts of the assignment. Give students the Instructions for Making an Opening handout and the Cereal Box Planner handout. These provide the basic requirements of the opening and offer a good way to review with students what your expectations are and what they need to do to prepare for their presentations. Explain what elements you expect them to include on their Cereal Box Planner. Students should use the planner as a rough draft; then create their final visual on a new piece of paper or poster board.

5. Communicate with parents about the upcoming opening to inform them about the theme being covered and the requirements of students when making an opening. A good way to do this is to send home the Instructions for Making an Opening handout with students. (Also see pages 60–63 for parent letters to adapt.) Ask them to practice with their children at home.

6. Have each student identify one local person to nominate for the Local Hero of the Year award. You may provide some suggestions and information for students to choose from, and parents may play a role in helping students identify someone, but it is ultimately the students' responsibility to decide who to nominate. Students should be ready to choose a hero within a day or two of having this discussion.

7. As needed, model part or all of a "Local Hero of the Year" opening for the class. Demonstrate how to present the information ("The person I think should be Hero of the Year is . . ."). Each student is expected to present information about who the person is and why he or she deserves to be the Local Hero of the Year.

8. Schedule class time for students to prepare and present their openings. Preparation time will vary depending on your expectations, the amount of prep work you assign as homework, and the readiness of your students. In general, this project should require no more than about two hours of class time prior to students making their presentations. This time is typically spread over several days.

9. *Optional:* Have students who finish their projects early create a "Local Hero of the Year" sign for students to stand next to while they do an opening. You also can have students create a "You Too Can Be a Hero!" poster that shows the silhouette of a student (with a hole to insert the student's face) and lists the criteria for a hero that the class came up with.

10. Make copies of the assessment form on page 207. Complete a form for each student after he or she has presented an opening.

11. Proceed with "Local Hero of the Year" openings as you have planned them. As necessary, prompt children to fulfill the key elements of the opening as they make their presentations.

Ideas for Extending or Modifying the Opening

1. Create a "Heroes" wall in the classroom, and after each opening put the student's cereal box cover on the wall to make a collage of hero nominees.

2. Set up a bulletin board as a "Hero of the Day" display and post the cereal box cover of the student or students who presented openings that day.

3. Have students bring in empty cereal boxes. Cut out each student's Cereal Box Planner template and paste it onto a box to create a cereal box hero.

4. At the conclusion of all of the presentations, have the class vote on an actual Hero of the Year. Send the winner an award certificate signed by everyone in the class along with an explanation of the project and the name of the student who nominated the winner.

5. Extend the project to include heroes from around the state, nation, or world.

Classroom Differentiation Example: Mrs. Larson

Strategies: reflection cards, scaffolding, multiple intelligences

Mrs. Larson wants her class do two openings this year. "Local Hero of the Year" is the first one. After presenting, Mrs. Larson intends to have students complete a reflection card on which they tell her two things they did well and one thing that could be improved (two "glows" and one "grow"). Mrs. Larson will use the students' feedback, along with her own assessments, to make decisions about how to differentiate the next opening for each student.

Oscar says on his reflection card that he did well in writing the report and answering questions. He says that the visual aid was hardest for him. Mrs. Larson agrees with this assessment, and plans to provide some scaffolded help for him on the next opening.

Marie indicates that her two "glows" are making the visual and talking to the audience, but she needs to "grow" on the written report. Again, Mrs. Larson agrees and begins thinking about how to help Marie with her "grow" area on the next opening.

Dominique is an interesting case. He insists that he did not do well on the visual aid. Mrs. Larson disagrees. This difference leads to a short conference, during which Mrs. Larson comes to understand that Dominique is very artistic and self-critical. He doesn't compare himself to others, but to his own idea of what he is capable of doing. After talking, the two agree that Dominique should continue being the judge of his own artistic production, but for the openings Mrs. Larson should help him with his speaking skills.

After analyzing the reflection cards, Mrs. Larson realizes that through this intrapersonal activity, her students are actually telling her about their multiple intelligence preferences. Since every opening emphasizes at least four of the eight most commonly recognized intelligences (verbal/linguistic, visual/spatial, bodily/kinesthetic, and interpersonal), she decides that she should look at future openings from a multiple intelligences perspective by recognizing where students' strengths and weaknesses are.

Local Hero of the Year

Name: _____ **Date:** _____

Some people from the community are planning to give a Local Hero of the Year award. You have been asked to name somebody you think should get this award. Read the assignment below to get ready for your presentation.

1. Choose a person who you think should be named Local Hero of the Year. Talk with your family, your teacher, neighbors, friends, and anyone else who might be able to help you make this decision.

The person I think should be Hero of the Year is:

_____

_____

2. Find information about the person by reading or talking to other people.

3. Write down three facts that you will tell the group about this person. For example, how old the person is, where he or she went to school, what job the person has, and so forth.

Fact: _____

_____

_____

Fact: _____

_____

_____

Continued ➡

Local Hero of the Year (continued)

Fact:_____

_____

_____

4. Write down why you think this person is a hero. What did he or she do?

_____

_____

_____

_____

_____

_____

_____

_____

5. Write a report about the hero.

6. Use the Cereal Box Planner to design a visual aid that you can show during your opening, then use that plan to make your final visual aid.

7. Give an opening about the hero to the class.

Local Hero of the Year

Name: _____ **Date:** _____

The Parts of an Opening:

Written Report (Write a report about the hero)

★ Find information by researching the person.

★ Write facts from your research about the person the way you want to present them.

★ Use your best handwriting skills.

★ You may have your report with you when you present your opening.

Visual Aid (Make a cereal box cover to show the audience why the person is a hero)

★ Put one or two interesting facts from your research about the person on the cereal box.

Oral Presentation (Talk to the class about the hero)

★ Stand straight and tall.

★ Look at people in the audience while you talk.

★ Tell about what you learned from your research.

★ Speak clearly and be sure everyone can hear you.

★ Explain what your visual aid shows about the person who you think is a hero.

Questions and Answers (Ask if there are any questions at the end of your opening)

★ Answer questions about the person from the audience.

★ It's okay to say "I don't know" if you don't know an answer.

Continued ➡

Local Hero of the Year (continued)

Hints for a Successful Opening:

★ Find plenty of interesting facts about the person. The more interesting the facts are, the more interesting your opening will be.

★ Practice! Practice! Practice! Practice your opening with a parent several times. Focus on the five Oral Presentation points listed in "The Parts of an Opening."

★ Choose a person you really want to learn about. If you are excited about your presentation, the people you talk to will be, too.

Here is an example of what a student named Joshua said in his "Local Hero of the Year" opening:

Joshua's Opening

"Good morning. My name is Joshua and I have an opening for you. My opening is called Local Hero of the Year. The person I think should be Hero of the Year is Samantha Rodrick. Samantha is a 5th-grade student at Summit School. She has two brothers and lives on Darwin Street. Last summer Samantha was at the community pool when she saw her brother Douglas lying on the bottom of the pool. On my cereal box I have some drawings that show what she did next. Samantha screamed for help and then jumped into the pool and swam down to Douglas. She grabbed hold of Douglas's ankle and started pulling him up. Then some adults came and got him out. They helped him breathe again and he was all right. I think that Samantha saved her brother's life. Thank you for listening. Are there any questions?"

Local Hero of the Year

Name: _____ **Date:** _____

Sketch a plan for your cereal box cover in the space below. Once you have a plan you like, make a large poster of your cereal box cover on poster paper.

Local
Hero

This Place Is a Zoo

Content Focus: Zoology
Topic and Assignment

Materials

 Reference materials for conducting research on animals and habitats

 Poster board or art paper for the visual part of the opening

 Drawing and coloring materials for making visual aids

Every year millions of people visit zoos and aquariums to marvel at the variety of animals that roam the earth. Almost every child loves to learn about animals, and many children dream of having careers that are related to animals. For this project, students assume the role of wildlife experts who develop and present educational lectures about animals being exhibited to the public in a zoo or aquarium.

During this project students will:

- Focus on one type of natural habitat.

- Study an animal that lives in that habitat.

- Conduct research on the animal.

- Write a report about the animal.

- Create a zoo sign with information about the animal.

- Present an opening titled "This Place Is a Zoo."

Student Handouts

- Assignment Sheet: This Place Is a Zoo

- Instructions for Making an Opening: This Place Is a Zoo

- Zoo Sign Planner

Note: While these forms provide all the materials students need to complete a "This Place Is a Zoo" opening, the CD-ROM included with this book contains a more detailed poster-making project that may be of interest for this and other openings.

Content Standard*

All students should develop understanding of the characteristics of organisms, life cycles of organisms, and organisms and their environments.

Idea for Introducing the Opening

Introduce the opening project dressed in a zoo docent vest and hat or wearing a button that says "Welcome to Our Zoo."

Project Steps

1. Introduce the project scenario to the students: *You are a wildlife expert who works for a zoo (or aquarium). Your job is to help zoo visitors learn more about the animals they see by making presentations that provide lots of interesting information.*

2. Hand out the This Place Is a Zoo assignment sheet and read through it with the class. Discuss any requirements that might be unfamiliar to them.

3. Explain to students that the zoo where they work is organized by natural habitats; for example, all of the desert animal exhibits in the zoo are grouped in an area called "Animals of the Desert." Let each student choose a zoo habitat area from the list below:

   - Jungle or rain forest
   - Polar region
   - Plains/grasslands
   - Freshwater lake or river
   - Forest or woods
   - Desert
   - Mountain
   - Ocean
   - Swamp or pond
   - Seashore

* Reprinted with permission from "National Science Education Standards" © 1995, by the National Academy of Sciences, courtesy of the National Academies Press, Washington, D.C.

4. Each student becomes an "expert" on one species of wildlife found in his or her chosen habitat. Students can choose which animal they'd like to study. Direct students to resource materials to discover what animals live in the habitat they've selected.

5. Provide class time for students to learn about habitats and choose animals to study.

6. Decide what your expectations will be for the visual and written parts of the assignment. Give students the Instructions for Making an Opening handout and the Zoo Sign Planner handout. These provide the basic requirements of the opening and offer a good way to review with students what your expectations are and what they need to do to prepare for their presentations. Explain what elements you expect them to include on their sign. Students should use the planner as a rough draft; then create their final visual on a new piece of paper or poster board.

7. Communicate with parents about the upcoming opening to inform them about the theme being covered and the requirements of students when making an opening. A good way to do this is to send the Instructions for Making an Opening handout home with students. (Also see pages 60–63 for parent letters to adapt.) Ask them to practice with their children at home.

8. As needed, model part or all of a "This Place Is a Zoo" opening for the class. Demonstrate how to present the information ("My opening is called This Place Is a Zoo. I am an expert on . . ."). Each student is expected to present information about the animal's natural habitat and other interesting facts discovered through research.

9. Schedule class time for students to prepare and present their openings. Preparation time will vary depending on your expectations, the amount of prep work you assign as homework, and the readiness of your students. In general, this project should require no more than about two hours of class time prior to students making their presentations. This time is typically spread over several days.

10. *Optional:* Have students who finish their projects early create a "This Place Is a Zoo" sign to serve as a backdrop for the opening presentations. Alternatively, students could create a small zoo setting with stuffed animals.

11. Make copies of the assessment form on page 207. Complete a form for each student after he or she has presented an opening.

12. Proceed with "This Place Is a Zoo" openings as you have planned them. As necessary, prompt children to fulfill the key elements of the opening as they make their presentations.

Ideas for Extending or Modifying the Opening

1. Add a classification component to the project. This can be as simple as having students tell what class their animals belong to (insect, fish, amphibian, reptile, bird, mammal, and so forth), or it could extend to the four main characteristics that place an animal in its class:

   - body covering (external skeleton; wet/slimy scales; moist skin; dry scales; feathers; hair or fur)

   - breathing system (body openings; gills only; gills and lungs; lungs only)

   - heating system (cold-blooded; warm-blooded)

   - reproduction (thin, moist eggs; leathery eggs; hard brittle eggs; born alive)

2. Add a diet component to the project by having students identify their animals as herbivores, omnivores, or carnivores. You might also ask them to discover through research what their animals eat and what eats their animals.

3. Add an adaptations component to the project. Ask students to identify adaptations that help their animals get food, protect themselves from predators, or help them survive in their natural habitat. To do this, students would describe a body part ("the bison has flat teeth") and tell what it does for the animal ("flat teeth allow the bison to grind tough grass before swallowing it").

4. Add a food chain component to the project. Ask students to show and explain how their animals fit into simple food chains that begin with the sun and end with a top predator. A typical four-part food chain looks like this: sun —> plant —> plant eater —> meat eater.

5. Add a geography component to the project. Give students an outline map of the world and have them color in the areas where their animals live in their natural habitats, or where they lived at one time if they are now endangered.

6. Put the focus on a single habitat and have all of the students focus on animals that live there. For example, the theme of the openings could be "Animals of the Rain Forest." In this case, each student would choose a rain forest animal to do an opening on. This approach can allow for discussions of the relationships, similarities, and differences among the animals students have studied, since they live in the same environment.

Classroom Differentiation Example: Mr. Jacobson

Strategies: resident expert, choice-as-motivator, scaffolding, tiering

Mr. Jacobson plans to use "This Place Is a Zoo" openings as a way to create a class full of resident experts, each of whom knows about one specific animal. This expertise will be useful during an upcoming unit on animals. Every student will have specialized knowledge that can be called upon later.

Mr. Jacobson has also decided to differentiate the project in other ways. Students can choose their own topics, but they are limited to those for which there is plenty of resource material at an appropriate reading level. He has also built in several challenge options for students once they have demonstrated that they have completed the basic assignment.

Cory is a struggling reader. Mr. Jacobson has created a library of resources that are all within his reading range. Cory's habitat is the ocean, and he has chosen to be a resident expert on bottlenose dolphins.

Holly is a grade-level reader and therefore has access to more resources than Cory. She has chosen the polar region as her habitat and has decided to be an expert on the emperor penguin. Because Holly works quickly, she finishes the basic assignment ahead of most other students. She has chosen to add an "adaptations" challenge option to her opening.

Neidra is an advanced reader and has no limits on the resources she may use. Her habitat is the desert and she is becoming an expert on rattlesnakes. Neidra often becomes so focused on the details of a task that she continues to work on it even when more work is not necessary. This tendency to perfectionism can prevent her from moving beyond the basic assignment and adding to the depth of what she is doing. Mr. Jacobson knows that Neidra sometimes over-performs on simple tasks, and so he reassures her that her work is more than acceptable and encourages her to add an interesting challenge option to her project.

This Place Is a Zoo

Name: _____ **Date:** _____

You are a wildlife expert who works for a zoo. Your job is to help visitors learn about the animals they see. Read the assignment below to get ready for your presentation.

1. Choose a habitat you want to study:

* ★ jungle or rain forest
* ★ forest or woods
* ★ ocean
* ★ polar region
* ★ desert
* ★ swamp or pond
* ★ plains or grasslands
* ★ mountain
* ★ seashore
* ★ freshwater lake or river

I will study this habitat: _____

2. Research the habitat and choose an animal that lives there.

I will study this animal: _____

3. Conduct research about your animal to find information that you can use in your opening. Think about what you have learned from your research and write five facts about the animal to share with your audience. Record the facts here:

Fact: _____

_____

_____

Continued ➡

This Place Is a Zoo (continued)

Fact:_____

_____

_____

Fact:_____

_____

_____

Fact:_____

_____

_____

Fact:_____

_____

_____

4. Write a report about the animal. Use your five facts along with other information you have found.

5. Use the Zoo Sign Planner to design a visual aid that you can show during your opening, then make your final visual aid. Be sure to include information from your research so that it goes along with the report.

6. Present an opening about the animal to the class.

This Place Is a Zoo

Name: _____ **Date:** _____

The Parts of an Opening:

Written Report (Write a report about the animal)

★ Find information by researching the topic.

★ Write facts from your research about the animal the way you want to present them.

★ Use your best handwriting skills.

★ You may have your report with you when you present your opening.

Visual Aid (Make a "Meet the Animals" poster to show your animal to the audience)

★ Put a drawing or picture of the animal on the poster.

★ Put one or two interesting facts from your research about the animal on the poster.

Oral Presentation (Talk to the class about the animal)

★ Stand straight and tall.

★ Look at people in the audience while you talk.

★ Tell about what you learned from your research.

★ Speak clearly and be sure everyone can hear you.

★ Explain what your visual aid shows about your animal.

Questions and Answers (Ask if there are any questions at the end of your opening)

★ Answer questions about the animal from the audience.

★ It's okay to say "I don't know" if you don't know an answer.

Continued ➡

This Place Is a Zoo (continued)

Hints for a Successful Opening:

★ Find plenty of interesting facts about the animal. The more interesting the facts are, the more interesting your opening will be.

★ Practice! Practice! Practice! Practice your opening with a parent several times. Focus on the five Oral Presentation points listed in "The Parts of an Opening."

★ Choose an animal you really want to learn about. If you are excited about your presentation, the people you talk to will be, too.

Here is an example of what a student named Lisa said in her "This Place Is a Zoo" opening:

Lisa's Opening

"Good morning. My name is Lisa and I have an opening for you. Welcome to the zoo! I am an expert on the American bison. You can see what a bison looks like in this picture on my poster. American bison are huge. They can weigh up to 2,000 pounds! A long time ago, Native Americans depended on bison for food, clothes, and tools. Then people began to hunt them a lot for their skins to sell for clothes and rugs. Millions of bison were killed in the 1800s. On my poster is a picture from back then of a man sitting on top of a pile of bison skulls. The pile is 40 feet high. Today bison live in zoos, in big parks like Yellowstone National Park, and on private ranches. Thank you for listening. Are there any questions?"

Zoo Sign Planner

Name: _____ **Date:** _____

Sketch a plan for your zoo sign in the space below. Once you have a plan you like, make a large poster of your sign on poster paper.

MEET THE
ANIMALS!

The Shape Hunter

Content Focus: Geometrical Shapes

Topic and Assignment

The physical world of human beings is made up of shapes. Everywhere you look you can see how people have combined simple shapes to make complex things. Students in the middle elementary grades should be able to identify a variety of simple shapes by name and describe the attributes of those shapes. A second grader should be able to identify a shape as a triangle and explain why it is a triangle. A third-grade student should be able to tell what kind of triangle it is (equilateral, isosceles, scalene, right, acute, obtuse, and so forth).

For this project, students assume the role of "shape hunters." They are given pictures to examine carefully, looking for embedded shapes. Then they present their findings to the class, pointing out the shapes they have found and describing the attributes of each shape they identify.

During this project students will:

- Choose (or be assigned) a picture that contains familiar shapes.

- Examine the picture to identify at least three shapes that they recognize.

- Write a brief report telling what the shapes are and giving the attributes of each.

- Present an opening titled "The Shape Hunter."

Materials

Pictures containing shapes (laminated—see project steps)

Dry (whiteboard) markers

Poster board or art paper for visual aids (optional—see Ideas for Extending or Modifying the Opening)

Student Handouts

- Assignment Sheet: The Shape Hunter

- Instructions for Making an Opening: The Shape Hunter

- Shapes Chart (optional)

Note: While these forms provide all the materials students need to complete a "Shape Hunter" opening, the CD-ROM included with this book contains a more detailed poster-making project that may be of interest for this and other openings.

Content Standards*

1. Analyze characteristics and properties of two- and three-dimensional geometric shapes and develop mathematical arguments about geometric relationships:

   - *Recognize, name, build, draw, compare, and sort two- and three-dimensional shapes; describe attributes and parts of two- and three-dimensional shapes.*

2. Use visualization, spatial reasoning, and geometric modeling to solve problems:

   - *Recognize geometric shapes and structures in the environment and specify their location.*

Idea for Introducing the Opening

Discuss what it means to observe our surroundings. Demonstrate with binoculars, a magnifying glass, a microscope, a camera, and so forth. Point out that the easiest way to observe is with our bare eyes.

Project Steps

1. Locate pictures that show a variety of simple shapes with which your students are familiar. These may be pictures from magazines, newspapers, websites, curriculum materials, or your own photographs. This will require some work the first time you do the project, but the pictures can be used year after year, so the work is only done once. You should have a minimum of one picture for every student in the class.

2. Laminate the pictures so that students can mark on them with dry-erase markers. Laminating will allow the pictures to be used multiple times.

---

* *Principles and Standards for School Mathematics* are listed with the permission of the National Council of Teachers of Mathematics (NCTM). NCTM does not endorse the content or validity of these alignments.

3. Introduce the project scenario to students: *You are "shape hunters" whose jobs are to find and describe shapes hidden in pictures.*

4. Hand out the Shape Hunter assignment sheet and read through it with the class. Discuss any requirements that might be unclear to students. A Shapes Chart is provided as an optional handout for use with this opening assignment.

5. Give each student a picture on which to base this opening. You may allow students to choose their own pictures, or you might want to assign pictures to students as a way of differentiating by readiness by giving students with advanced understanding of shapes more complex pictures.

6. Explain to students that as shape hunters, they are expected to find three different shapes in their picture, outline the shapes with markers, and then present the pictures to the class and show everybody the shapes they have discovered.

7. Decide what your expectations will be for the written part of the assignment. Give students the Instructions for Making an Opening handout. This provides the basic requirements of the opening and offers a good way to review with students what your expectations are and what they need to do to prepare for their presentations. The example is based on what a third grader might present, so if your students are younger, be sure to explain what kind of information you expect about the shapes they find.

8. Communicate with parents about the upcoming opening to inform them about the theme being covered and the requirements of students when making an opening. A good way to do this is to send the Instructions for Making an Opening handout home with students. (Also see pages 60–63 for parent letters to adapt.) Ask them to practice with their children at home.

9. As needed, model part or all of "The Shape Hunter" opening for the class. Demonstrate how to present the information ("I am a shape hunter, and here is the picture I looked at to find shapes . . .").

10. Schedule class time for students to prepare and present their openings. Preparation time will vary depending on your expectations, the amount of prep work you assign as homework, and the readiness of your students. In general, this project should require no more than about two hours of class time prior to students making their presentations. This time is typically spread over several days.

11. *Optional:* Students who are finished with their projects early can create a "Shape Hunter" sign to serve as a backdrop to the opening presentations. Alternatively, students could create an artistic display of shapes.

12. Make copies of the assessment form on page 207. Complete a form for each student after he or she has presented an opening.

13. Proceed with "The Shape Hunter" openings as you have planned them. As necessary, prompt children to fulfill the key elements of the opening as they make their presentations.

Ideas for Extending or Modifying the Opening

1. Have students find their own pictures to use with their presentations. You will need to involve parents more if you do this, to help them understand what needs to be in the picture to make it useful for "The Shape Hunter" opening.

2. Require that students draw the shapes in their picture on a small poster and label the shapes. This way they are actually re-creating the shapes. Additionally, they could cut out the shapes and hold them up during the opening.

3. This project offers a good opportunity to differentiate for advanced learners by assigning them more complex pictures to work with. For struggling learners, simple pictures that contain straightforward, easily identifiable shapes are sufficient to reach the goals of the opening. By offering varying degrees of challenge you can let each student operate at his or her comfort level without significantly changing the basic assignment for anyone.

4. Incorporate three-dimensional figures into the project (these are not on the Shapes Chart). You can use pictures that have solid figures in them, such as boxes, balls, cans, and so forth, or you can provide actual

objects for students to present that include cylinders, cones, rectangular prisms, pyramids, and spheres. Either way, students still show three figures that they have found and describe their attributes.

5. Find posters or other large-format pictures to use for the project, to give students larger visual aids that are more easily seen by the audience.

6. Take digital photographs of the pictures you find and project them on a screen for students to reference as they make their presentations. They can use a pointer to outline the shapes on the screen as they talk about them.

7. Go on a "shape walk" with the class. Walk around the school (inside and outside) and have students point out shapes in their environment. Take pictures of the shapes and bring them back into the classroom for students to use in their presentations.

8. Have students make drawings of houses, playground equipment, toys, buildings, bridges, or other structures and build into them geometric shapes that they can present to their classmates.

Classroom Differentiation Example: Ms. Gaborski

Strategies: scaffolding, flexible grouping, anchor activities

Ms. Gaborski has assigned each student a partner to work with while preparing for the "Shape Hunter" opening. The student pairs are mixed-ability: struggling learners are paired with more advanced learners. Resources are matched to student skill levels, meaning that struggling learners receive basic, uncomplicated pictures while advanced learners work with more challenging graphics. After everyone has done this opening, Ms. Gaborski plans to offer the same project as an anchor activity so that advanced students can be paired together.

Gina and Latisha are partners. Latisha has no difficulty with shapes and should do very well with the project. Gina will need support to do well. The two girls work together to identify shapes in their assigned pictures and then practice giving their openings to each other before presenting on their own to the class.

Brian and Felipe are partners. Brian is an advanced math student, but Felipe is new to the class and has expressed a reluctance to even do an opening. Ms. Gaborski wants Felipe to do well, and so she intentionally paired him with Brian, whom she feels can help him with the math and also with the important process of getting ready for an opening.

After finishing the openings, Ms. Gaborski offers the project again as an anchor activity for students who complete work ahead of others. Brian and Gina often get done with things early. They have decided to be partners to do an advanced version of the project by identifying shapes in a set of complex pictures.

The Shape Hunter

Name: _____ **Date:** _____

You are a shape hunter who has been asked to find three shapes in a picture and make a presentation to your class. Your job is to outline each shape with a different colored dry erase marker, show the shapes to the class, and tell how you know what each shape is. If you find more than three shapes, you may write them at the bottom of the page.

1. The first shape I found is: _____

It looks like this:

I know it's this shape because: _____

_____

2. The second shape I found is: _____

It looks like this:

I know it's this shape because: _____

_____

Continued ➡

The Shape Hunter (continued)

3. The third shape I found is: _____

It looks like this:

I know it's this shape because: _____

_____

4. Here are other shapes I found in the picture:

★ _____

★ _____

★ _____

★ _____

The Shape Hunter

Name: _____ **Date:** _____

The Parts of an Opening:

Written Report (Write a report about the shapes)

* ★ Identify shapes in your picture.
* ★ Write about each shape. Tell how you know what it is.
* ★ Use your best handwriting skills.
* ★ You may have your report with you when you present your opening.

Visual Aid (Use your picture as your visual aid)

* ★ Find shapes in the picture and trace them with a dry erase marker.

Oral Presentation (Talk to the class about the shapes you found)

* ★ Stand straight and tall.
* ★ Look at people in the audience while you talk.
* ★ Speak clearly and be sure everyone can hear you.
* ★ Show the shapes you have found in the picture while you talk about them.

Questions and Answers (Ask if there are any questions at the end of your opening)

* ★ Answer questions about the topic from the audience.
* ★ It's okay to say "I don't know" if you don't know an answer.

Continued ➡

The Shape Hunter (continued)

Hints for a Successful Opening:

★ Make a game of looking for shapes at home with your family, just for fun. Look at pictures or things around your house or neighborhood, and say, "I see a shape; this is the shape I see."

★ Practice! Practice! Practice! Practice your opening with a parent several times. Focus on the four Oral Presentation points listed in "The Parts of an Opening."

Here is an example of what a student named Yim said in his "The Shape Hunter" opening:

Yim's Opening

"Good morning. My name is Yim and I have an opening for you. My opening is about shapes that I found in a picture. This is a picture of a building with a fence and gate in front of it. The first shape I found is an isosceles triangle. You can see it here in this fence. I traced it in red. I know it is an isosceles triangle because it has three sides and two of them are the same length. The second shape I found is a circle, here in the gate. I traced the circle in blue. I know it is a circle because every point on it is the same distance from the center. The third shape I found is a trapezoid. You can see it in the building. I traced it in black. I know it is a trapezoid because it has four sides and two of the sides are parallel but the other two sides are not. Thank you for listening. Are there any questions?"

Shapes Chart

Name: _____ **Date:** _____

Use the shapes and descriptions below to help you complete this project.

Name	Shape	Description
Line	←————————→	A line is a set of points that go on forever in both directions.
Ray	•————————→	A ray starts at a point and goes on forever in one direction.
Line Segment	•————————•	A line segment is part of a line and has two end points.
Intersecting Lines	✕	Intersecting lines cross each other at one point. The two lines share one point.
Parallel Lines	←————→ ←————→	Parallel lines go in the same direction and never cross.
Circle	◯	A circle is a shape in which all of the points are the same distance from a point in the middle called the center.
Equilateral Triangle	△	All triangles have three sides. An equilateral triangle is one in which all three sides are the same length.
Isosceles Triangle	△	All triangles have three sides. An isosceles triangle is one in which at least two of the sides are the same length.

Continued ➡

Shapes Chart (continued)

Name	Shape	Description
Scalene Triangle		All triangles have three sides. A scalene triangle is one in which none of the sides are the same length.
Right Triangle		All triangles have three sides. A right triangle is one in which one of the angles is a right angle. A right angle is 90°.
Rectangle		A rectangle is a quadrilateral. It has four right angles and opposite sides are the same length.
Square		A square is a quadrilateral. It has four right angles and all four sides are the same length. A square is also a rectangle.
Parallelogram		A parallelogram is a quadrilateral. It has opposite sides that are parallel and opposite sides that are the same length.
Rhombus		A rhombus is a quadrilateral. It has opposite sides that are parallel and all of its sides are the same length.
Trapezoid		A trapezoid is a quadrilateral. It has two sides that are parallel, but the other two sides are not parallel.

Upper Elementary Openings

- The Naturalist

- Buying the Car of My Dreams

- It's Written in the Stars

- Family Ties to History

- Featured Expert Series

The Naturalist

Content Focus: Animals in an Ecosystem

Topic and Assignment

It is important for students to understand and appreciate the variety and complexity of life that coexists in ecosystems. Learning about animals in an ecosystem like a pond provides insights into the relationships and interdependence among living things in general.

For this project, students take on the role of naturalists who specialize in the animal life of a specific ecosystem. Each naturalist is an expert on one creature that lives in the ecosystem and must prepare a presentation on the animal for his or her colleagues and create an educational sign for a nature center exhibit.

During this project students will:

- Learn about a specific ecosystem.

- Study an animal that lives in that ecosystem.

- Identify at least three focus areas related to the animal.

- Write a report about the animal, with emphasis on the three focus areas.

- Create an educational sign with information about one of the focus areas for a nature center exhibit.

- Present an opening titled "The Naturalist."

Student Handouts

- Assignment Sheet: The Naturalist

- Instructions for Making an Opening: The Naturalist

- Life in a Pond (optional student guidelines for studying a pond ecosystem)

- Educational Sign Planner: The Naturalist

Note: *While these forms provide all the materials students need to complete "The Naturalist" opening, the CD-ROM included with this book contains a more detailed poster-making project that may be of interest for this and other openings.*

Materials

 Reference materials on the ecosystem being studied

 Reference materials on individual animals

 Poster board and other visual aid materials

Content Standard*

All students should develop understanding of the characteristics of organisms, life cycles of organisms, and organisms and environments.

Idea for Introducing the Opening

Discuss how scientists always start their research with a question. Have a large photo of a toad, for example, to have the class look at. "What questions could we ask about this toad?" Have the class think of everything they might want to know about the toad, such as "Why is it that color?" and "What does it eat?"

Project Steps

1. Identify an ecosystem to be the basis for the project. An example student handout, Life in a Pond (see pages 143–144), may be used to help students choose animals to study if you decide to focus the project on a pond ecosystem (see project step 5).

   The ideal situation is to study an ecosystem that you can visit locally, so a field trip could be included in the project. Check with local nature centers to see if this can be arranged, and also to find out if a real naturalist is available to collaborate with you on the project. A nature center is an excellent resource from which to get reference materials and lists of animals that inhabit the ecosystem. If you do organize a field trip, be sure students have chosen their animals beforehand. Students will gain a great deal more from the experience if they can collect information about their own animals while visiting the nature center. As part of the research process, students then know which exhibits and displays to concentrate on, and can ask targeted questions related to their own topics.

2. Introduce the project scenario to the students: *You are a naturalist who is an expert on an animal that lives in an ecosystem that you and your colleagues are studying. You have developed a presentation about the animal to share with your fellow naturalists that includes an educational sign showing one aspect of the animal for a nature center exhibit.*

3. Hand out the Naturalist assignment sheet and read through it with the students. Discuss any concepts that might be unfamiliar to them.

4. Explain to the class that everyone will study an animal from a single ecosystem. Spend some time discussing the general characteristics or attributes of the ecosystem you have chosen for the project. For example, if you're focusing on ponds, this discussion revolves around the question "What is a pond?"

5. Have each student choose an animal to study. If you are studying ponds, use the Life in a Pond handout to help students make their choices.

   If you use the Life in a Pond handout, it is important to realize that there are usually multiple species of each type of animal (and plant) listed. For example, "frogs" is listed as one type of animal, but there are many species of frogs from which to choose. Be sure students choose species that are native to your region.

   If you're focusing on a different ecosystem, try to identify enough animals to allow each student's opening to be unique. There are enough options and choices within the structure of the project to ensure variety even if two or more students choose the same animal, so it is not a problem if the list of animals is smaller than the number of students in the class. More important is that plenty of information be available about each of the animals on the list.

6. Instruct each student to select at least three focus areas from the list provided on the assignment sheet. The focus areas determine what information will be presented during the opening.

7. Differentiate this project by gently guiding struggling students toward animals and focus areas that have plenty of information, or information written at an appropriate reading level, in order to increase the likelihood of a successful opening. Encourage advanced learners to select animals and focus areas that are more challenging, either because they require more research or because the concepts are more complex or less defined.

---

8. Decide what your expectations will be for the written and visual parts of the assignment. Give students the Instructions for Making an Opening handout. This provides the basic requirements of the opening and offers a good way to review with students what your expectations are and what they need to do to prepare for their presentations.

9. Give students the Educational Sign Planner handout and discuss the visual aid requirement with the class. Each student will choose one of his or her three focus areas and create an educational sign that presents information about just that aspect of the animal for a nature center exhibit. Explain what elements you expect students to include on their signs. Students should use the planner as a rough draft and create their final visual on a new piece of paper or poster board. You also may want to give students the option of creating a model or multimedia program, or of using other media instead of a poster for their visual aid. The requirement is that it provides information about the identified focus area and is incorporated smoothly into the oral presentation.

10. Communicate with parents about the upcoming opening to inform them about the theme being covered and the requirements of students when making an opening. A good way to do this is to send the Instructions for Making an Opening handout home with students. (Also see pages 60–63 for parent letters to adapt.) Ask them to practice with their children at home.

11. As needed, model part or all of "The Naturalist" opening for the class. Demonstrate how to present the information ("We are studying ponds, and I am an expert on . . ."). Each student is expected to present information about the three focus areas chosen for the animal.

12. Schedule time for students to prepare and present their openings. Preparation time will vary depending on your expectations, the amount of prep work you assign as homework, and the readiness of your students. In general, this project should require no more than about four hours of class time prior to

students making their presentations. This time is typically spread over several days.

13. *Optional:* Have students who finish their projects early create a "The Naturalist" sign to serve as a backdrop to the opening presentations. Students could also create a large "Nature Center" sign to hang in the presentation area and/or create a nature center name tag to wear while they give an opening.

14. Make copies of the assessment form on page 208. Complete the form for each student after he or she has presented an opening.

15. Proceed with "The Naturalist" openings as you have planned them. As necessary, prompt children to fulfill the key elements of the opening as they make their presentations.

Ideas for Extending or Modifying the Opening

1. Expand the topics to include plants. Students might be allowed to choose a plant *or* an animal, or they might be required to choose a plant *and* an animal.

2. Have students join a partner, based on their animals' (and/or plants') natural relationships. For example, two students might become a pair if their animals have a predator-prey relationship. Or a pair might form if their animals have a competitive relationship (compete for the same food), or a mutually helpful (symbiotic) relationship, or a harmful (parasite-host) relationship. Schedule partners to give their openings back-to-back, and then present together about the relationship that exists between their animals.

3. Create a food web on a wall of the room as the openings are presented. After each opening, put a picture or the name of the animal on the wall and connect it with colored yarn with each animal that it eats and each animal that eats it. Put arrowheads at the end of the yarn to indicate which animal is doing the eating (the arrows point in the direction that energy flows). Include plants in the food web whenever a plant-eating animal is added.

4. Divide the class in half and do openings on two different ecosystems. Spend discussion

time comparing and contrasting them (What is the same? What is different? Why are certain animals found in one but not the other? Why might some animals be found in both?).

5. Give students "human impact" scenarios and have them predict the effect they would have on the ecosystem they are studying. For example, tell them that agricultural runoff (insecticides and fertilizers) during a torrential spring rain has killed nearly all of the tadpoles in their pond ecology. What impact does this have on the pond? Or tell them that someone has released into the pond several foreign fish that reproduce rapidly and eat algae. Nothing in the ecosystem will eat the new fish. What impact does this have on the pond?

6. Have students (or the class) make a word finder game using the terms from their openings.

Classroom Differentiation Example: Ms. Flores

Strategies: scaffolding, multiple intelligences

Ms. Flores has a collection of reference materials that are written at different levels of complexity and reading difficulty, which she is using to scaffold "The Naturalist" openings for her students. She will require students to choose topics that are aligned with their interests and supported by appropriate resources.

Ms. Flores is also using multiple intelligences. Openings always emphasize the verbal/linguistic (word smart) intelligence, and the naturalist intelligence is built in. Additionally, students may develop a visual aid that is compatible with one of these intelligences: visual/spatial (picture smart), logical/mathematical (number smart), or bodily/kinesthetic (body smart).

Kyle struggles with reading but he is a strong artist. Ms. Flores has given him a list of topics to choose from that have plenty of accessible information. He has chosen to use his drawing skills to produce a visual aid.

Monsurat is an on-target reader and therefore has a wider range of topics available to her than Kyle. She enjoys performing for others and has developed an educational skit that she wants to record on video to use as her visual aid.

Tyra is an advanced reader. Ms. Flores has pushed her to choose one of several topics that will stretch her reading and research skills, and she has accepted the challenge. Tyra is a logical/mathematical thinker. She has chosen to create a chart and graph to show information about her topic.

The Naturalist

Name: _____ Date: _____

You are a naturalist who knows all about ecosystems. You are an expert on an animal that lives in an ecosystem that you and your colleagues are studying, and you have been asked to share your knowledge about that animal. You plan to make a presentation about the animal to your fellow naturalists. Read the assignment below to prepare for this presentation.

My team of naturalists is studying this ecosystem: _____

I am an expert on this animal: _____

1. Choose three focus areas to include in the presentation, and put a check in the "Focus" column next to each one. Then choose one of those three focus areas to highlight in your visual aid, and put a check in the "Visual" column next to it.

Visual	Focus	Focus Area Choices
		Predator/prey relationships (what does it eat and what eats it?)
		Food chain (where does it fit in a line from the sun to a top predator?)
		Survival through winter (how does the species make it through the winter?)
		Adaptations (what special body structures and features help it survive?)
		Camouflage (how does it hide from predators and/or prey?)
		Transport (how does it move from one place to another?)
		Young (what do they look like; how do they behave; how are they cared for?)
		Behavior (what does it do to survive; what are some unusual behaviors?)
		Life cycle (what phases/stages are involved in its life from beginning to end?)

Continued ➡

The Naturalist (continued)

Visual	Focus	Focus Area Choices
		Body covering (what is it covered with and why is this important?)
		Body heating system (how does it stay warm?)
		Digestive system (how does it take food in and process it?)
		Circulatory system (what kind of heart does it have; how is blood circulated?)
		Respiratory system (how does it take in oxygen and get rid of carbon dioxide?)
		Reproductive system (how are young born?)
		Skeletal system (what kind of body structure does it have?)
		Muscular system (how does it move its body parts?)
		Nervous system (what kind of brain and nerves does it have?)
		Excretory system (how does it get rid of body wastes?)
		Endocrine system (what does this system do for the animal?)

2. Conduct research and write a report about the animal. Emphasize the three focus areas you have chosen.

3. Create an educational sign for a nature center exhibit about your animal to use during your opening. The visual aid should provide clear, detailed information about one focus area that you have identified.

4. Present an opening about the animal to your fellow naturalists.

The Naturalist

Name: _____ **Date:** _____

The Parts of an Opening:

Written Report (Compose a report from your research information)

* ★ Conduct research to find information about your animal. Look for facts that are interesting, accurate, and clearly connected to the three focus areas you have chosen. If your teacher has asked you to follow certain research guidelines, be sure you follow them correctly.
* ★ Write in the "voice" of a naturalist.
* ★ Write about the three focus areas you have identified.
* ★ Include plenty of accurate, carefully developed information about the animal.
* ★ Use your best handwriting or word processing skills.
* ★ You may have your report with you when you present your opening.

Visual Aid (Create a poster to show the class information about your animal)

* ★ Produce an educational sign about your animal that is clearly related to one focus area for the nature center exhibit.
* ★ Organize information so that it can be easily explained and understood.
* ★ Plan the opening so there is a natural place to talk about the visual aid.

Oral Presentation (Present your information to your naturalist "colleagues")

* ★ Use good posture at all times.
* ★ Have regular eye contact with various people in your audience.
* ★ Speak clearly and be sure everyone can hear you.
* ★ Speak as if you really are a naturalist who is talking to his or her colleagues.
* ★ Refer smoothly and naturally to your visual aid at least once during the opening.

Questions and Answers

* ★ Answer questions about your animal from the audience.
* ★ It's okay to say "I don't know" if you don't know an answer.

Continued ➡

The Naturalist (continued)

Hints for a Successful Opening:

★ Do a thorough and complete job of conducting research. Your opening is only as good as the information you present. Find appropriate facts that are clearly related to the focus areas you have chosen.

★ Take the scenario for the project seriously, and work to build the "voice" of a naturalist into your written report and oral presentation. In other words, try to write—and talk—like a naturalist would. It will make your opening more fun and more authentic.

★ Practice! Practice! Practice! Practice your opening with a parent or friends. Focus on the five Oral Presentation points listed in "The Parts of an Opening."

Here are examples of how a student might present various parts of this opening:

Introduction

"Good morning. My name is Ingrid and I have an opening for you. As naturalists, we are all interested in pond ecosystems, and I am an expert on the northern leopard frog. My presentation today will be about these three focus areas . . ."

Focus Area

"One of the focus areas that I am interested in is frog adaptations. The leopard frog has a mottled dark green or brown back and a white underbelly. From above, a predator has difficulty seeing the frog's dark back against the dark bottom of the pond, and from below a predator sees white against a bright sky."

Connection to the Visual Aid

"I have shown the life cycle of a frog on my poster. All frogs begin life as an egg that is laid in water. As you can see, the eggs must be in water because they don't have strong shells and will dehydrate if they are not always moist. When they emerge as tadpoles, I've shown how they breathe with gills. Here you can see the metamorphosis they go through as they change from tadpoles into frogs. After this change, they begin breathing with lungs. Amphibians are the only class of vertebrates that breathe with gills and lungs at some point in their lives."

Ending

"Thank you for listening to my report on leopard frogs. Are there any questions?"

Life in a Pond

Name: _____ **Date:** _____

You are a naturalist who will make a presentation to a group of fellow naturalists about pond ecology. Below is a list of animals and plants that can be found in a pond. Examine the list and follow your lead naturalist's directions to choose a topic for your presentation.

Pond Animals	Pond Plants
Worms	Algae
Earthworms	Moss
Leeches	Vascular Plants
Crustaceans	Ferns
Crayfish	Cattails
Insects	Pondweeds
Mayflies	Naiads
Dragonflies and Damselflies	Water Plantains
True Bugs (e.g., Water Striders)	Sedges
Beetles	Rushes
Mosquitoes	Arums
Horse Flies	Duckweeds
Moths	Water Lilies
Mollusks	Trees
Snails	Shrubs
Clams	Vines
Fish	
Suckers	
Carp	

Continued ➡

Life in a Pond (continued)

Pond Animals	Pond Plants
Sunfish	
Bluegill	
Bullheads	
Amphibians	
Salamanders	
Frogs	
Toads	
Reptiles	
Turtles	
Snakes	
Birds	
Geese	
Ducks	
Herons	
Killdeer	
Kingfishers	
Hawks	
Perching Birds (sparrows, etc.)	
Mammals	
Raccoons	
Muskrats	
Beavers	
Mice/Voles	
Bats	

The Naturalist

Name: _____ **Date:** _____

Sketch a plan for your poster in the space below. Once you have a plan you like, make a large poster on poster board or paper.

```
NATURE CENTER
    EXHIBIT
```

Buying the Car of My Dreams

Content Focus: Consumer Math
Topic and Assignment

Who couldn't use an introduction to consumer math? Give your students a look at what it costs to drive off in the car of their dreams. In this project, students imagine they are old enough to drive and have decided to buy a new car. A wealthy relative has agreed to finance the car by lending students the money to buy whatever car they wish. The students have agreed to repay the loan, with interest, in annual payments of $4,800. They will continue paying $4,800 a year until the loan is paid off. In exchange for the loan, the rich relative has stipulated that the students make a presentation to tell what they have learned about buying a car. This seems like a simple request, and the students readily agree to it.

During this project students will:

- Identify a new car to "buy."

- Conduct research to determine the cost of the car.

- Conduct research to determine the interest to be applied to the loan.

- Complete worksheets to organize data for a presentation.

- Write a report about the car and the repayment process.

- Create a visual aid with information about the car and the repayment process.

- Present an opening titled "Buying the Car of My Dreams."

Student Handouts

- Assignment Sheet: Buying the Car of My Dreams

- Instructions for Making an Opening: Buying the Car of My Dreams

- Researching Principal and Interest

- Figuring the First Year's Costs

- Loan Payment Chart

- Graphing Interest

Note: While these forms provide all the materials students need to complete a "Buying the Car of My Dreams" opening, the CD-ROM included with this book contains a more detailed poster-making project that may be of interest for this and other openings.

Content Standards*

1. Analyze change in various contexts:

   - *Investigate how a change in one variable relates to a change in a second variable; identify and describe situations with constant or varying rates of change and compare them.*

2. Communicate their mathematical thinking coherently and clearly to peers, teachers, and others.

3. Create and use representations to organize, record, and communicate mathematical ideas.

4. Recognize and apply mathematics in contexts outside of mathematics.

5. Use mathematical models to represent and understand quantitative relationships:

   - *Model problem situations with objects and use representations such as graphs, tables, and equations to draw conclusions.*

Idea for Introducing the Opening

Discuss the importance of making smart decisions about things you buy—that it costs money to borrow money. "If you borrow $100 at 10 percent interest a year, how much interest would you owe at the end of one year?" Use play money to lay this out for students to see.

* *Principles and Standards for School Mathematics* are listed with the permission of the National Council of Teachers of Mathematics (NCTM). NCTM does not endorse the content or validity of these alignments.

Project Steps

1. Introduce the project scenario: *You have just turned 18 and want to buy yourself a new car. A rich relative has agreed to buy you any car you want, with the understanding that you will repay the loan with interest. The interest rate will be 1 percent lower than the best interest rate you can find in your town or on the Internet. The agreement is that you will give your relative $4,800 once a year until the loan is repaid, and that you will make a presentation to others to tell what you have learned about buying a car.*

   This project is designed to use annual payments based on the interest owed for twelve months, rather than recalculating interest payments each month. Students will understand the relationships between principal and interest without having to do nearly so many repetitive calculations.

2. Hand out the Buying the Car of My Dreams assignment sheet and read through it with the students. Discuss the concepts of *principal* and *interest*. The entire project is based on their understanding of the equation **P** x **R** x **T** = **I** (**P**rincipal x **R**ate of interest x **T**ime = **I**nterest owed), so it is critical that this equation be carefully explained before proceeding.

3. Help students identify a car to buy. Bring in newspaper advertising, automotive magazines, and dealers' brochures for them to browse through and find cars that interest them. If computers are available, let them explore websites like Kelly Blue Book (www.kbb.com) or Edmunds (www.edmunds.com). Ask them to talk with parents, relatives, and friends about new cars.

   There is an upper limit to what students can spend on their car. If the annual interest they'd owe is $4,800 or more, students won't be able to repay any principal on the loan. Discuss this with students and determine the upper limit in class.

   Choose a sample interest rate that is somewhat higher than the one students will actually discover through research, and use the equation **$4,800 ÷ R = Principal** to demonstrate how to determine the price at which the annual payment becomes nothing but interest. For example, if the rate of interest (**R**) is 8 percent, then the equation is $4,800 ÷ .08 = $60,000. This means that if

   a student buys a car that costs $60,000 at 8 percent interest, every penny of the annual $4,800 payment will be interest and nothing will ever be paid on the principal.

   Remember that the interest rate students will pay on their loan is 1 percent less than the lowest rate they can find through research. They should see clearly that it is to their benefit to discover the lowest rate possible. You may want to help students find interest rates at bank or credit union websites, car dealership websites or advertisements, or elsewhere. Do not allow the interest rate students pay fall below 1 percent. In other words, in the unlikely event that students find a loan institution that offers car loans at a rate of 1 percent or lower, tell them that their relative is not willing to give the loan at no interest at all and therefore will charge 1 percent.

4. Give students the Researching Principal and Interest worksheet. This is where students prepare to use the equation **P x R x T = I** by recording price information about their chosen cars and determining what interest rate will be used. Collect the completed worksheets to be sure they were done correctly. Put your initials in the box under "Teacher Check Point" to indicate that the student is permitted to continue to the next stage of the project.

5. Give students the Figuring the First Year's Costs worksheet. This is where students go through the step-by-step process of calculating what part of the first payment is interest and what part is principal. They also calculate monthly savings information and what the new principal will be after making the first annual payment. Collect the completed worksheets and put your initials in the box under "Teacher Check Point" to indicate that the student is permitted to continue to the next stage of the project.

6. Give students the Loan Payment Chart worksheet. They will now calculate their payment plan for each year until the car loan is paid off, following the same process used for figuring the first year's costs. Be sure that students understand that the new principal recorded at the bottom of each column is the amount they will enter at the top of the next

column. Also, remind students to transfer data they've already calculated for year one into the first column before beginning year two. Again, put your initials in the box under "Teacher Check Point" to indicate that the student is allowed to continue.

7. Give students the Graphing Interest worksheet. Here they will make a bar graph to show how much of the total payment each year is interest, and how much is principal. This graph is a key part of the visual aid that will be used during the opening.

8. Decide what your expectations will be for the visual and written parts of the assignment. Give students the Instructions for Making an Opening handout. This provides the basic requirements of the opening and offers a good way to review with students what your expectations are and what they need to do to prepare for their presentations.

9. Discuss the visual aid requirement with the class. Each student will show the car he or she has decided to buy, and include the bar graph to show the relationship between interest and principal for each annual payment. The visual aid will likely be a poster, but students may also choose to use other media. Regardless, the visual aid should provide information about the car and how it is financed.

10. Communicate with parents about the upcoming opening to inform them about the theme being covered and the requirements of students when making an opening. A good way to do this is to send the Instructions for Making an Opening handout home with students. (Also see pages 60–63 for parent letters to adapt.) Ask them to practice with their children at home.

11. As needed, model part or all of a "Buying the Car of My Dreams" opening for the class. Demonstrate how to present the information ("The car I have decided to buy for myself is . . ."). Each student is expected to present information about the car and explain the relationship between principal and interest payments that will have to be made each year to pay for it. The handout provides a template for the presentation.

12. Schedule time for students to prepare and present their openings. Preparation time will vary depending on your expectations, the amount of prep work you assign as homework, and the readiness of your students. In general, this project should require no more than about four hours of class time prior to students making their presentations. This time is typically spread over several days.

13. *Optional:* Have students who finish their projects early create a "Buying the Car of My Dreams" sign to serve as a backdrop to the opening presentations. Students could also create a bank sign or bank office setting where students would stand to give an opening.

14. Make copies of the assessment form on page 208. Complete the form for each student after he or she has presented an opening.

15. Proceed with "Buying the Car of My Dreams" openings as you have planned them. As necessary, prompt children to fulfill the key elements of the opening as they make their presentations.

Ideas for Extending or Modifying the Opening

1. Change the amount of the annual payment. You can decrease it to limit the car choices students can make (focus the selections on less expensive models), or you can increase it to let students choose high-end luxury and sports cars.

2. Eliminate the specified annual payment and instead let each student decide what the annual payment should be for the chosen car. This approach allows students to buy any car imaginable, so you could get students buying exotic luxury cars with annual payments of $20,000 for a period of twenty years.

3. Add an insurance component. After choosing their cars, have students collaborate with parents to contact insurance agents or check online to discover what the annual insurance costs for the car would be.

4. Give students a set number of years to repay their relatives and have them find the best car possible that can be paid off in that amount of time. For example, what is

the best (or most expensive) car that can be bought with $4,800 annual payments at 7 percent interest over a 5-year period?

5. Add a gas mileage/fuel cost component to the project. Suggest a monthly driving distance allotment, such as 1,200 miles, and have students use the car's estimated city and/or highway mileage along with a current gas price to calculate the cost of fuel for the car each year. Challenge advanced learners by having the price of gas increase by a certain percent each year. For example, use the price of gas at a local filling station as the starting point, then tell students that the price will increase by 5 percent each year over the period of the loan.

6. Have students create a line graph to show the relationship between principal and interest over time. Have them put both lines on the same graph, using different colors, and explain the trends they observe.

7. Integrate technology into the project by having students use spreadsheets to record data and generate graphs.

Classroom Differentiation Example: Mr. Norquist

Strategies: scaffolding, multiple intelligences, tiering, anchor activity

Mr. Norquist plans to use "Buying the Car of My Dreams" as a way of giving the logical/mathematical learners in his class a chance to shine. He has built scaffolding into the assignment to provide immediate support when students struggle, and he has designed challenge options for motivated students. In addition, he has developed an anchor activity based on the project so that students who like the project can carry the idea further later in the year when they have time available.

Lucinda generally does well with tasks that utilize her verbal/linguistic strength, but the emphasis that this project places on graphing, charting, and calculating has thrown her for a loop. By monitoring student work through built-in "check points," Mr. Norquist provides support for Lucinda and others who struggle with various aspects of preparing for the opening.

Gerald loves cars and dreams of having his own some day. Being allowed to choose a favorite make and model has motivated him to include insurance, license, and gas mileage costs as challenge options to his project. He wants to get an idea of what the real cost of owning his car would be.

Malik often completes tasks ahead of everyone else, so Mr. Norquist offers anchor activities for him (and others) to work on when time is available. After the class has completed the "Buying the Car of My Dreams" opening, Malik is looking forward to working on the anchor activity version later in the year. For that, he will take a fanciful look at buying a very expensive sports car.

Buying the Car of My Dreams

Name: _____ **Date:** _____

You have just turned 18 and want to buy yourself a new car. A rich relative has agreed to buy you any car you want (the car of your dreams!) and pay for it completely right now, with the understanding that you will repay the loan, with interest.

* ★ Your relative will charge you 1% less than the best interest rate you can find in town or on the Internet.

* ★ Your relative also insists that in exchange for this help, you must agree to present what you learn about buying a car to an audience, and you have agreed to do this.

* ★ After studying your finances and thinking about how much money you can make in a year, you've determined that you can spend $4,800 a year on your car loan.

* ★ You will put a regular monthly payment of $400 into a savings account each month and then make one $4,800 payment to your relative every 12 months.

* ★ You will continue making annual (once per year) $4,800 payments until the car is paid for, no matter how long it takes.

This project helps you see what it costs to buy a car. Real-world auto financing is a bit more complex, but understanding the costs of borrowing money is the first step in making sound financial decisions.

For this project, you will research how much your car costs and what interest rate you will pay, and then calculate how long it will take you to pay off your loan. Four handouts will help you do your research and calculations.

When you borrow money, you need to understand two important terms: **principal** and **interest.** When you ask a bank or credit union (or relative) for a loan, you ask for the amount that you need to make the purchase. This is called the principal. Banks and credit unions, however, don't lend money for free. They earn income by charging people for the money being borrowed. Interest is the money they charge you for borrowing. The interest you pay is calculated as a percentage of what you owe. You and your relative have agreed to use an annual percentage rate (APR), which is calculated once a year. For example, if you borrow $1,000 at a 10% APR, you will owe $1,100 at the end of one year. Here's how to figure this out:

Continued ➡

Buying the Car of My Dreams (continued)

P x R x T = I
Principal x **R**ate of interest x **T**ime (in years) = **I**nterest owed

$1,000 (**P**) x 10% per year (**R**) x 1 year (**T**) = $100 (**I**)

The total amount you owe on the loan at the end of the year is principal plus interest:
Principal + **I**nterest = **T**otal owed
$1,000 (**P**) + $100 (**I**) = $1,100 (**T**)

Assignment Summary:

1. Use the four handouts provided to do your research and complete your calculations.

★ Researching Principal and Interest

★ Figuring the First Year's Costs

★ Loan Payment Chart

★ Graphing Interest

2. Write a report about the car financing process in the style of a magazine article with information and advice about buying a car.

3. Create a visual aid for your opening that

★ gives information about your car

★ provides a bar graph that shows the relationship between principal and interest for each annual payment

4. Give your oral presentation to the class. Include information about your car, the financing process, and what you learned about borrowing money.

Buying the Car of My Dreams

Name: _____ Date: _____

The Parts of an Opening:

Written Report (Compose a report from your research information)

★ Conduct research to find information about your choice of car and interest rates. Look for a car that you would really like to own, and look for the best (lowest!) interest rate you can find.

★ Write in the "voice" of a first-time car buyer who is writing to other car buyers.

★ Describe the car and give your reasons for choosing it.

★ Tell what you have learned about **principal** and **interest.** What do these terms mean? What should a person buying a car know about principal and interest before making the purchase?

★ Use your best handwriting or word processing skills.

★ You may have your report with you when you present your opening.

Visual Aid (Make a poster to show the class information about your car)

★ Provide information about how the car looks and operates (why you chose it).

★ Provide information about paying for the car (bar graph of principal and interest).

★ Organize information so that it can be easily explained and understood.

★ Plan the opening so there is a natural place to talk about the visual aid.

Oral Presentation (Present your information to other car buyers)

★ Use good posture at all times.

★ Have regular eye contact with various people in your audience.

★ Speak clearly and be sure everyone can hear you.

★ Speak as if you really are a young adult who is talking to peers about buying a car.

★ Refer smoothly and naturally to your visual aid at least once during the opening.

Questions and Answers

★ Answer questions from the audience about your car.

★ It's okay to say "I don't know" if you don't know an answer.

Continued ➡

Buying the Car of My Dreams (continued)

Hints for a Successful Opening:

★ Do a thorough and complete job of conducting research. Your opening is only as good as the information you present. Find accurate information about the car you've chosen and interest rates on which to base your presentation.

★ Provide solid reasons for choosing this particular car. Give details about special features, styling, performance, and so forth.

★ Take the scenario for the project seriously, and work to build the "voice" of a young adult into your written report and oral presentation. In other words, try to write—and talk— like a person who is 18 years old and has an opportunity to purchase his or her first car. It will make your opening more fun and more authentic.

★ Practice! Practice! Practice! Practice your opening with a parent or friends. Focus on the five Oral Presentation points listed in "The Parts of an Opening."

Here are examples of how a student might present various parts of this opening:

Introduction

"Good morning. My name is David and I have an opening for you. It's great to see all of these new car buyers in the same room! Let me tell you about the car of my dreams . . ."

Car Features, Principal and Interest

"This car has a lot of really exciting features. One feature I insisted on when I was choosing a car was that it had to be a convertible. This car has a hard roof that automatically folds into the trunk. Something else I love about my new car is . . ."

"My new car is kind of expensive. I found a good interest rate at Community Bank, but even after subtracting 1% from that rate, it is still going to take a long time to pay for it. Here are some important things I learned about principal and interest . . ."

Connection to the Visual Aid

"My poster shows a picture of my car with the top down and one with the top up. You also can see from my poster that I will be spending quite a bit of money to own this car. Here is what my graph shows about principal and interest . . ."

Ending

"Thank you for listening to my opening. Are there any questions?"

Researching Principal and Interest

Name: _____ Date: _____

1. Decide what kind of new car you want to buy and find the best price available. You can look in many places to find out how much the car of your dreams will cost. You can call or visit a car dealership, compare auto prices on the Internet, or check in newspapers, magazines, or reference books. Ask your parents for help if you need to.

   Use the chart below to calculate your total principal.

Car Data		Where Did You Get Your Data?
Make, model, and color:		
Base Price	$	
Major Extras/Options		
1.	$	
2.	$	
3.	$	
Total Car Price	$	
Sales Tax	$	
License Plates	$	
Total Principal	$	

Continued ➡

Researching Principal and Interest (continued)

2. What's the best car loan interest rate you can find? You may be able to find bank and credit union interest rates in the local newspaper, or you can call lenders and ask for their lowest new car loan interest rates. You can also go to sites on the Internet. Check at least three sources because interest rates can vary.

Lender	Annual Rate	Where Did You Get Your Data?

Subtract 1% from the best interest rate you found and record it below. This is the interest rate you will pay on the loan from your relative:

Best Interest Rate _____ % − 1% = _____ % (Interest Rate on Loan)

3. Calculate the interest for the first year of your car loan.

$$\underset{\text{Principal}}{\underline{\hspace{3cm}}} X \underset{\text{Rate}}{\underline{\hspace{3cm}}} X \underset{\text{Time}}{\underline{\frac{1 \text{ year}}{}}} = \underset{\text{Interest (1st year)}}{\underline{\hspace{3cm}}}$$

Teacher Check Point

4. Stop here and have your work checked; when the box has been initialed, you may continue.

☐ OK to Continue

Figuring the First Year's Costs

Name: _____ **Date:** _____

1. Perform the necessary calculations to complete the chart below for the first year of your loan.

   Year: 1

Principal owed at the end of this year:	
Annual percentage rate (APR):	
Total annual (yearly) payment:	$4,800.00
Amount of annual payment that is interest:	
Amount of annual payment that is principal:	
Total amount put into savings each month:	$400.00
Amount of monthly savings that is interest (annual interest divided by 12):	
Amount of monthly savings that is principal (annual principal divided by 12):	
New principal after making the year 1 payment:	

Teacher Check Point

2. Stop here and have your work checked; when the box has been initialed, you may continue.

 OK to Continue

Loan Payment Chart

Name: _____ **Date:** _____

1. Fill out a column on the chart below for each year until you completely repay your car loan. You will have to complete more than one chart if it takes more than five years to pay for the car. Be sure to use the data from the "Figuring the First Year's Costs" chart in the first column.

	Year:	Year:	Year:	Year:	Year:
Principal owed at the end of this year:					
Annual interest rate:					
Total annual payment:	4,800.00	4,800.00	4,800.00	4,800.00	4,800.00
Amount of annual payment that is interest:					
Amount of annual payment that is principal:					
Total amount put into savings each month:	400.00	400.00	400.00	400.00	400.00
Amount of monthly savings that is interest:					
Amount of monthly savings that is principal:					
New principal after annual payment:					

2. How much will you eventually pay for your car? $ _____

Teacher Check Point

3. Stop here and have your work checked; when the box has been initialed, you may continue.

 OK to Continue

Graphing Interest

Name: _____ **Date:** _____

1. Make a bar graph to show the interest payments you will make at the end of each year. Your completed graph will show how much of each $4,800 annual payment went to interest, and how much went to principal. It will also show how long it will take to pay for the car, and how much money you will spend on interest over the life of the loan.

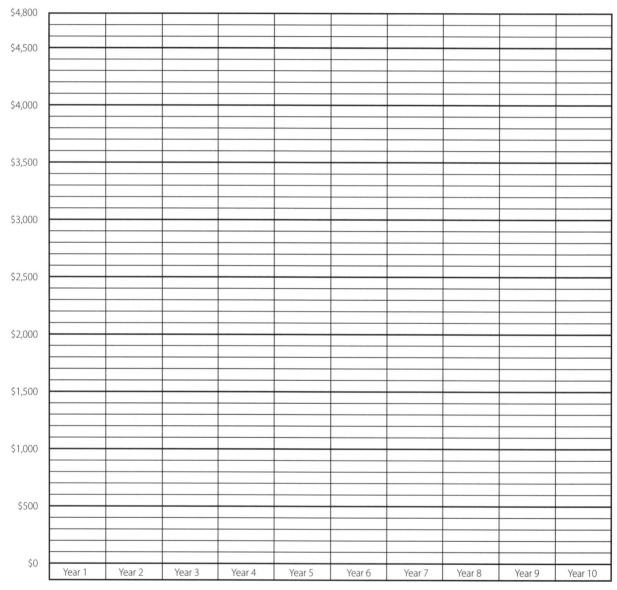

Teacher Check Point

2. Stop here and have your work checked.
When the box has been initialed, you may continue.

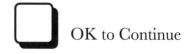

OK to Continue

It's Written in the Stars

Content Focus: Astronomy
Topic and Assignment

People around the world and throughout the ages have watched and wondered about the stars and other celestial bodies. Over the centuries, their questions and observations have shaped the science of astronomy. The discoveries of astronomers have profoundly changed how people think about our planet, the solar system, and the mystifying universe.

For this project, students assume the role of young astronomers who work at a local planetarium. They have been asked to develop and present a plan for a display that could be used in the planetarium. The purpose of the display is to teach the public about some aspect of astronomy. Their task is to convince the planetarium's board of directors that the display they are proposing is worth including in a new exhibit.

During this project students will:

- Choose a topic from the area of astronomy about which to become an "expert."

- Conduct research about the topic.

- Develop an idea for an exhibit that could be used to teach people about the topic.

- Write a report that explains what the exhibit teaches.

- Create a visual aid that shows what the exhibit will look like or include.

- Present an opening titled "It's Written in the Stars."

Student Handouts

- Assignment Sheet: It's Written in the Stars

- Instructions for Making an Opening: It's Written in the Stars

- Display Planner

Materials

Reference materials related to astronomy

Poster board and other visual aid materials

Note: *While these forms provide all the materials students need to complete an "It's Written in the Stars" opening, the CD-ROM included with this book contains a more detailed poster-making project that may be of interest for this and other openings.*

Content Standard*

All students should develop an understanding of Earth in the solar system.

Idea for Introducing the Opening

Hold a class discussion to think of astronomy topics. Use a helpful website such as www.nasa.gov. Try to cover most of the topic areas from the It's Written in the Stars assignment sheet.

Project Steps

1. Introduce students to the project scenario: *You are a young astronomer who works at the local planetarium. The chief curator has made plans to add a major new exhibit to the planetarium that will be titled* It's Written in the Stars: The Never-Ending Quest for Understanding. *You have been asked to propose a display that you think should be included in the exhibit. You will develop a presentation for the planetarium's board of directors in which you will describe your idea and explain how information will be presented and what visitors will learn from the display.*

2. Hand out the It's Written in the Stars assignment sheet and go over it with the students. Discuss any concepts or expectations that might be unfamiliar to them. It's important for you at this time to clarify what topics are available for students to focus on. You may decide to leave it wide open and allow students to choose any topics that are related to astronomy. Or, you might want to narrow the options to topics that are aligned with your grade's science standards. The assignment sheet includes a list of potential topics. You may use the list as it is, add to the list,

---

* Reprinted with permission from "National Science Education Standards" © 1995, by the National Academy of Sciences, courtesy of the National Academies Press, Washington, D.C.

remove unapproved topics from the list, or create a new list.

3. Decide what your expectations will be for the visual and written parts of the assignment. Guide students through the process of planning their openings. A student's plan involves answering three primary questions:

   - **What topic will I study?** Each student should end up with a unique topic so there are no duplicate presentations. Students will record their topics on the assignment sheet.

   - **What key idea or concept will I focus on?** It is important to help students keep this project clearly focused and manageable by insisting that they choose one main idea or concept as the central focus of the displays they are proposing. Other information may be included, but the primary purpose of each display proposal should be to explain, describe, illustrate, or demonstrate one aspect of the topic. The assignment sheet provides a place to record the key idea or concept, and also requires each student to identify three specific things that planetarium visitors will learn from his or her display.

   - **What will my display look like?** This project asks students to develop an idea for a display that could be included in a planetarium exhibit. They have to describe what the display would look like and what it would teach, using a poster and an oral presentation. So, for example, a student whose topic is comets might propose a display that is designed to help people understand the concept of a comet's tail being the result of solar wind. In the proposed display, visitors would first view a model of a comet that shows what it most likely consists of, and then they would view a holographic representation of a comet traveling in an elliptical orbit with its tail always pointing away from the sun. Computers would allow a viewer to watch the comet from a number of perspectives, including from the surface of the comet and the

surface of the sun. Students will use the display plan template to help develop their ideas.

4. Hand out the Display Planner and discuss it. Explain to the class that the purpose of the project is for them to describe a *plan* for a display. In other words, the poster they create is not actually a museum display item. Rather, it is a blueprint or design for what a display would look like. The oral presentation is a way of explaining how the proposed display depicts or conveys factual information and will help people understand concepts related to astronomy. This way, students can come up with grand ideas that would be impossible for them to actually construct but that would be workable ideas in a real museum setting. Students should use the planner as a rough draft, then create their final visual on a new piece of paper or poster board.

5. Be sure to provide plenty of resource materials for students to use for research. Here are two websites that will be very helpful with this project:

   - Windows to the Universe from the University of Michigan: www.windows.ucar.edu

   - NASA's official website: www.nasa.gov

6. Differentiate this project by gently guiding struggling students toward topics that have plenty of information, or information written at an appropriate reading level, in order to increase the likelihood of a successful opening. You can encourage advanced learners to select topics that are more challenging, either because they require more research or because the concepts are more complex or less defined.

7. Collect the completed assignment sheets and display planners to check that students have followed directions and are ready to develop and present their openings.

8. Give students the Instructions for Making an Opening handout. This provides the basic requirements of the opening and offers a good way to review with students what your expectations are and what they need to do to prepare for their presentations.

9. Communicate with parents about the upcoming opening to inform them about the theme being covered and the requirements of students when making an opening. A good way to do this is to send the Instructions for Making an Opening handout home with students. (Also see pages 60–63 for parent letters to adapt.) Ask them to practice with their children at home.

10. As needed, model part or all of an "It's Written in the Stars" opening for the class. Demonstrate how to present information ("I would like to propose a new display in our planetarium. My proposal is focused on . . ."). Each student is expected to present a plan for a display in the planetarium. The handout provides a template for the presentation.

11. Schedule time for students to prepare and present their openings. Preparation time will vary depending on your expectations, the amount of prep work you assign as homework, and the readiness of your students. In general, this project should require no more than about four hours of class time prior to students making their presentations. This time is typically spread over several days.

12. *Optional:* Have students who finish their projects early create an "It's Written in the Stars" sign to serve as a backdrop to the opening presentations. Students could also create a presentation setting filled with astronomy topics or images as a backdrop for the openings.

13. Make copies of the assessment form on page 208. Complete the form for each student after he or she has presented an opening.

14. Proceed with "It's Written in the Stars" openings as you have planned them. As necessary, prompt children to fulfill the key elements of the opening as they make their presentations.

Ideas for Extending or Modifying the Opening

1. Change the content focus of the project. Here are some examples:

   - It's Written in the Bones: study paleontology.
   - It's Written in the Sky: study meteorology.
   - It's Written in the Cells: study cell biology.
   - It's Written in the Rocks: study geology and the rock cycle.
   - It's Written in the Genes: study genetics and heredity.

2. Create a "museum" in your classroom by collecting and displaying student posters on a wall after each opening.

3. Allow students to work on related topics in pairs, and either make their opening presentations together or one after the other. For example, two students could collaborate on the topic of asteroids, with one student focusing on "what is an asteroid?" and the other focusing on "when asteroids hit Earth."

4. Build a technology component into the project. Students can make multimedia presentations to show their ideas for displays and to provide current information in the form of images and information taken from the Internet.

5. Choose one broad topic and have everyone in the class focus on a different idea or concept related to it. For example, if the topic is the sun, students can study concepts such as sunspots, solar flares, solar wind, the speed of light, the birth of stars, the death of stars, the northern lights, the orbits of planets, solar energy, day and night on Earth, seasons, solar eclipses, seasons on Earth, and so forth.

Classroom Differentiation Example: Mr. Mehta

Strategies: choice-as-motivator, tiering

Mr. Mehta organizes "It's Written in the Stars" so that students work with self-selected partners to choose topics, conduct research, and practice presentations. Each partner will focus on a different aspect of the topic, and both will present their openings on the same day. To determine the order of presentations, partners' names are drawn out of a bowl. The first pair drawn will present first and also have first choice of topic. Mr. Mehta has built "challenge options" into the project. Any student may choose to add a challenge option, even if his or her partner decides not to do one.

James and Adam are best friends. They share an interest in space and are glad that the International Space Station is still available when it's their turn to select a topic. Both partners have chosen to complete the basic project without taking on a challenge option.

Jason and Celeste are not close friends but they are serious students. They chose each other because they wanted to be paired with someone who would work hard and focus on quality. Their topic is "Seasons on Earth." Each partner has chosen a challenge option to include in the final presentation.

Juanita and Gabrielle chose each other as partners but now they are both unhappy with that decision. Mr. Mehta has met with them to iron out their differences and help them move forward with the project. After some negotiating, they have agreed to work on a topic called "A Closer Look at Mars." Juanita likes the topic and has already chosen a challenge option to add to her presentation. Gabrielle is fine with Mars as a topic and is working to complete the basics of the assignment.

It's Written in the Stars

Name: _____ Date: _____

You are an astronomer who works at the local planetarium. The chief curator has made plans to add a major new exhibit to the planetarium that will be titled *It's Written in the Stars: The Never-Ending Quest for Understanding.* You have been asked to propose a display that you think should be included in the exhibit. You will develop a presentation for the planetarium's board of directors in which you will describe your idea and explain how information will be presented. You will also explain what visitors will learn from the display.

1. Conduct research about an idea or concept related to your topic.

2. Write a report, focusing on specific things that planetarium visitors will learn from your display.

3. Create a visual aid (poster) to show what the display you are proposing will look like and what it will teach visitors. Use the Display Planner handout to develop a plan for the poster.

4. Give an opening about your proposed display to the planetarium directors.

Topic Choice List		
Distances in space	Temperatures in space	How stars are born
Space exploration	The Big Bang theory	How stars die
International Space Station	The solar system	The inner planets
The Hubble space telescope	Black holes	The outer planets
Telescopes through the ages	Asteroids	A closer look at Mars
Myths, stories, and beliefs	Meteors	Earth's path through space
Comets	Gravity	Seasons on Earth
The sun	The northern lights	Motion in the night sky
The moon	Galaxies	Other:
The sun and the moon	Constellations	Other:

Continued ➡

It's Written in the Stars (continued)

My topic for the display proposal will be: _____

I will focus my display proposal on this idea or concept: _____

Here are three specific things that planetarium visitors will learn from my display:

★ _____

★ _____

★ _____

Instructions for the Display Planner

An important part of this project is the poster you create to show your ideas for a planetarium display. Make a drawing of your poster ideas on the Display Planner handout. Keep these things in mind as you develop your plan:

1. The purpose of the poster is to show your plan for the display.

★ What materials, models, equipment, or special effects will be included?

★ How will the display be organized and arranged?

★ How will information be provided to visitors (signs, audio recordings, video, interactive media, hands-on experiences, simulations, and so forth)?

2. The poster should show clearly how the display will present the three things you want planetarium visitors to learn when they see it.

3. The poster is not just a drawing. It should include written explanations, enlarged sketches and diagrams, and anything else you can think of to make clear what the display will look like and what it will offer to visitors.

4. You don't need to be a great artist! If you are more comfortable using simple sketches and mostly words to explain what the display will look like, that's okay.

It's Written in the Stars

Name: _____ **Date:** _____

The Parts of an Opening:

Written Report (Compose a report from your research information)

★ Conduct research to find information about your astronomy topic. Look for facts that are interesting, accurate, and clearly connected to the idea or concept you have chosen to focus on. If your teacher has asked you to follow certain research guidelines, be sure you follow them correctly.

★ Write in the "voice" of an astronomer who is proposing an idea for a display.

★ Write about the display and the three main things visitors will learn.

★ Include plenty of accurate, carefully developed information about the topic.

★ Use your best handwriting or word processing skills.

★ You may have your report with you when you present your opening.

Visual Aid (Make a poster to show your plan for a planetarium display)

★ Produce a poster that describes what will be included in the display.

★ Organize information so that it can be easily explained and understood.

★ Plan the opening so there is a natural place to talk about the visual aid.

Oral Presentation (Present your proposal to the planetarium's board of directors)

★ Use good posture at all times.

★ Have regular eye contact with various people in your audience.

★ Speak clearly and be sure everyone can hear you.

★ Speak in the voice of an astronomer who is talking to his or her board of directors.

★ Refer smoothly and naturally to your visual aid at least once during the opening.

Questions and Answers

★ Answer questions about your proposal from the audience.

★ It's okay to say "I don't know" if you don't know an answer.

Continued ➡

It's Written in the Stars (continued)

Hints for a Successful Opening:

★ Do a thorough and complete job of conducting research. Your opening is only as good as the information you present. Find appropriate facts that are clearly related to the idea or concept you have chosen to focus on.

★ Take the scenario for the project seriously, and work to build into your written report and oral presentation the "voice" of an astronomer who is serious about designing a display for the planetarium exhibit. In other words, try to write and talk like an astronomer in this situation would. It will make your opening more fun and more authentic.

★ Practice! Practice! Practice! Practice your opening with a parent or friends. Focus on the five Oral Presentation points listed in "The Parts of an Opening."

Here are examples of how a student might present various parts of this opening:

Introduction

"Good morning. My name is Robert and I have an opening for you. I'm proposing a display that I think would be a valuable addition to the planetarium. My topic is gravity, and I will focus on the difference between mass and weight. . . ."

Things Visitors Will Learn

"One area in my display will demonstrate how objects have different weights on different planets. Visitors will get to lift objects to see the differences. For example, one object will be a softball. On Mars, things weigh about one-third as much as they do on Earth, so the softball for Mars will be made of plastic that weighs one-third as much as a real softball. On Jupiter, it will weigh about 2.3 times more, so the example will be made of much heavier material. Another area of my display will show . . ."

Connection to the Visual Aid

"You can see how I have organized the areas of my display. Look at the entrance. Here, visitors can step on a scale and see how much they would weigh on each planet and a few other places in the galaxy. As they move into the next section . . ."

Ending

"Thank you for listening to my proposal for a display in our planetarium's new exhibit. Are there any questions?"

Display Planner

Name: _____ **Date:** _____

Sketch a plan for your poster in the space below. Once you have a plan you like, make a large poster on poster paper.

It's Written in the Stars

Family Ties to History

Content Focus: Historical Events from Years of Family Significance

Topic and Assignment

A great way to help build students' interest and excitement about history is to have them make personal connections to events from the past. Children are often engaged by the idea that important things were happening at the same time that people they know were living their everyday lives. For this project, students assume the role of "timeline historians." Their task is to discover and report on local, national, and international events that happened in the year they were born, the year one of their parents was their age, and the year one of their grandparents was their age.

During this project students will:

- Identify an event that happened during the year they were born.

- Identify an event that happened when a parent was their age.

- Identify an event that happened when a grandparent was their age.

- Write a report that describes each of the three events.

- Develop a visual aid (Family Ties Timeline Event Template) for each event.

- Present an opening titled "Family Ties to History."

- Attach the templates to a "Family Ties" timeline.

Materials

Reference materials related to the events being studied

Drawing and other visual aid materials

Student Handouts

- Assignment Sheet: Family Ties to History

- Instructions for Making an Opening: Family Ties to History

- Family Ties Timeline Event Template

- Family Ties Timeline Event Template (Completion Guidelines)

Content Standards*

1. Relate personal changes to social, cultural, and historical contexts.

2. Describe personal connections to place—as associated with community, nation, and world.

3. Analyze examples of conflict, cooperation, and interdependence among groups, societies, and nations.

4. Demonstrate an ability to use correctly vocabulary associated with time such as past, present, future, and long ago; read and construct simple timelines; identify examples of change; and recognize examples of cause and effect.

Idea for Introducing the Opening

Show the class old photos of your own family members when they were young (grandparent, parent, and you). Talk about some of the events that happened in the world during the time periods in which the photos were taken.

Project Steps

1. Choose a wall space in the room, hallway, gym, or other area as a place to construct a timeline for the project. The timeline will cover a span of years from the time students' grandparents were their age up to the year in which students were born. The end of the timeline that represents the year students were born will have a template from every student in the class mounted around it. This means that the wall space you choose needs to have enough room available to cluster twenty-five or so visual aid templates around that end of the timeline. The rest of the templates will be more spread out because of the variance in ages of parents and grandparents.

---

* *Expectations of Excellence: Curriculum Standards for Social Studies* are from the National Council for the Social Studies (NCSS).

2. Set a date at the beginning of the project for each student to report to you the year when one parent and one grandparent was his or her age. This information will help you gather resources and plan the timeline. The beginning of the timeline will be the year when the oldest grandparent was the age of the students, and the end will be the year the youngest student in the class was born. The number of years in between will tell you what kind of scale you should use for the timeline. For example, if your available wall space is 25 feet long, and the span between the oldest grandparent and youngest student is 50 years, then the scale for the timeline should be $\frac{1}{2}$ foot = 1 year.

3. Introduce the project scenario to the students: *You are a timeline historian who is investigating events to be presented to your fellow historians and then placed on a "Family Ties" timeline. The events are to be directly connected to 1) the year you were born, 2) the year in which one of your parents was your age, and 3) the year in which one of your grandparents was your age.*

4. Hand out the Family Ties to History assignment sheet and read through it with the class. Discuss any requirements that might be unclear to students. If any students are raised by someone other than a parent, tell them they can use another family adult.

5. Explain that each student will need to choose one parent and one grandparent, and find out in what year each person was the same age as the student is now. This is a matter of adding the student's age to the year in which the parent and the grandparent were born. There is a place on the assignment sheet for students to record these years.

6. Have a class discussion of events and topics from the year the students were born. This will be the same year for most of the students in an upper elementary classroom. Knowing what year this is, you can have resources available for students to find events and make a list. Every student will need to find a unique topic from that year to focus on, so it is important to develop a list with enough options for everyone to choose something different.

7. Choosing events or topics from the time when a parent and grandparent were the age of the student is a more individualized undertaking. Each student will likely be working with different years, although there will probably be some overlap. Encourage students to talk with their parents and grandparents about things from their life when they were this age that might be interesting to learn about. You can make good use of websites such as the following to help students find engaging topics and events:

   - Historycentral.com: www.historycentral.com/20th/index.html

   - Infoplease: www.infoplease.com/yearbyyear.html

   - Fact Monster: www.factmonster.com/yearbyyear.html

8. The assignment sheet asks students to record two events from the year one of their parents was their age and two events from the year one of their grandparents was their age. They are told to turn in the assignment sheet to get your approval for the events they identify. If both events are appropriate, they may pursue either one for the project. There is a place next to each event for you to check "OK" to indicate that it may be used.

9. Decide what your expectations will be for the visual and written parts of the assignment. Hand out one of each timeline template (blank and completion guidelines) and explain what elements you expect students to include on their visuals. For this opening, students will use three blank templates to plan a graphic for each of the three events they will talk about; then they will create their final timeline visuals on three additional blank Timeline Templates. Students do not create large posters because their final visuals must be small enough to display on a wall timeline.

10. Discuss with students the use of the Family Ties Timeline Event Template as both a visual aid for the opening presentation and as a display to be included with the timeline. During the opening, each student will refer to the three templates he or she has created. Then those templates will be attached in the correct places along the timeline to represent each student's family ties to history.

11. Give students the Instructions for Making an Opening handout. This provides the basic requirements of the opening and offers a good way to review with students what your expectations are and what they need to do to prepare for their presentations.

12. Communicate with parents about the upcoming opening to inform them about the theme being covered and the requirements of students when making an opening. A good way to do this is to send the Instructions for Making an Opening handout home with students. (Also see pages 60–63 for parent letters to adapt.) Ask them to practice with their children at home. You may also ask them to discuss events from their youth with their child.

13. As needed, model all or part of a "Family Ties to History" opening for the class. Demonstrate how to present the information ("We are creating a timeline to show what has happened during our own lives, our parents' lives, and our grandparents' lives. I will start with my grandfather's life. Grandpa Holt was my age in the year . . ."). Each student is expected to present information about important or interesting events.

14. Schedule time for students to prepare and present their openings. Preparation time will vary depending on your expectations, the amount of prep work you assign as homework, and the readiness of your students. In general, this project should require no more than about four hours of class time prior to students making their presentations. This time is typically spread over several days.

15. *Optional:* Have students who finish their projects early create a "Family Ties to History" sign to serve as a backdrop to the opening presentations. Students could also create a collage of photos of classmates and family members.

16. Make copies of the assessment form on page 208. Complete the form for each student after he or she has presented an opening.

17. Proceed with "Family Ties to History" openings as you have planned them. As necessary, prompt children to fulfill the key elements of the opening as they make their presentations.

Ideas for Extending or Modifying the Opening

1. Add a current events component by having students include in their openings events that are happening in the world right now. This can either replace the event that happened the year in which the students were born or be in addition to that requirement.

2. Give students the option of going further back in history by reporting on an event that happened during the year that one of their great-grandparents was their age.

3. Include a technology requirement by having the class create an electronic timeline instead of a paper-based one on a wall. This can be done using a program such as Microsoft Excel (see www.microsoft.com/education/createtimeline.aspx for tips). A technology-based project might also include a multimedia presentation.

4. Have students study events that happened on specific dates—such as their birthday, a parent's birthday, and a grandparent's birthday—throughout history. In this case, the events would not necessarily have happened in the year of each person's birth, but on the same date in history. For example, if a mother's birthday is September 8, a student could choose to discuss the hurricane that hit Galveston, Texas, and killed 8,000 people on September 8, 1900; Louisiana Senator Huey P. Long being shot to death by Dr. Carl Austin Weiss on that date in 1935; the signing of the San Francisco Peace Treaty to officially end World War II hostilities with Japan on that date in 1951; or any other event he or she uncovers. Here are some websites that may be used to discover events that happened on specific dates:

- History.com: www.history.com/this-day-in-history

- Infoplease: www.infoplease.com/dayinhistory

- Fact Monster: www.factmonster.com/dayinhistory

5. Focus the project on just one event, such as "something that happened when one of my parents was my age." This will reduce the size of the timeline and allow students to create more detailed visual aids and conduct more in-depth research.

Classroom Differentiation Example: Mr. Tran

Strategies: scaffolding, tiering, choice-as-motivator, multiple intelligences

Mr. Tran has decided to conduct a "basics first" opening project. Each student must satisfactorily complete the basic assignment before he or she is allowed to move on to one of the challenge options that Mr. Tran has provided. He has built in scaffolding to support students through each step of the process. This means that students receive help where needed for such things as topic selection, finding resources, conducting research, writing the report, creating the visual, and preparing for the presentation.

Adrianna has little difficulty with the assignment, except that she has chosen fairly obscure topics for which there is not much information readily available. Mr. Tran has lent a helping hand in her search for useful resources. After having her work checked for quality, Adrianna has chosen as a challenge option to write an extended report in the form of a journal.

Javier has difficulty with the research process. Mr. Tran has arranged to meet with him occasionally to review what he has done and to provide help where needed. With this support, Javier is able to complete his project at an acceptable level of quality, and he chooses as a challenge option a drawing assignment that allows him to take advantage of his artistic skills.

Rachel is a struggling learner who needs extra support. Mr. Tran has placed her in a small group of students who need similar help, and they meet with him daily as they work on the project. Mr. Tran helps them with topic selection, research, writing, and preparing for the opening. Rachel does not have time for a challenge option, but she successfully completes the project.

Family Ties to History

Name: _____ **Date:** _____

You are a timeline historian who is investigating events to be placed on a special "Family Ties" timeline. The events are directly connected to 1) the year you were born, 2) the year in which one of your parents was your age, and 3) the year in which one of your grandparents was your age. Your job is to learn about interesting local, national, or international events, and make a presentation to an audience to explain something that happened during each of these important years in your family's history. Read the assignment below to prepare for this presentation.

Part 1: The Year You Were Born: _____

In a class discussion, develop a list of events that happened during the year that you and your classmates were born. You may be asked as a homework assignment to talk with a parent or other adult who can help you think of things to contribute to this discussion. You may identify events from any of the following categories:

* politics
* economics
* wars/conflicts
* entertainment/sports/leisure
* popular culture
* health/medicine
* environment
* transportation

* science/technology
* energy
* fashion
* natural disasters
* man-made disasters
* inventions/discoveries
* people in the news

Choose three events from the discussion that interest you most and record them below. When it is your turn to select a topic, choose one of these three events for your project.

Events from the Year I Was Born: Top Three Choices	
1	
2	
3	

Continued ➡

Family Ties to History (continued)

Part 2: The Year Your Parent Was Your Age: _____

You will likely be studying a different year from everyone else, so it is your responsibility to research the year and identify two events on your own and record them below. Your teacher will check the events you have written down to make sure at least one of them is appropriate for the assignment.

Events from the Year One of My Parents Was My Age	OK
1	
2	

Part 3: The Year Your Grandparent Was Your Age: _____

Again, this year will probably be different from anyone else in the class, so you will research the year, identify two events on your own, and record them below. Your teacher will check the events you have written down to make sure at least one is appropriate for the assignment.

Events from the Year One of My Grandparents Was My Age	OK
1	
2	

Assignment

1. Identify one event for each of the three years that you will present in your opening.

2. Conduct research and write a report about the events you have chosen.

3. Complete a "Family Ties Timeline Event Template" for each of the three years. The templates will be used as visual aids during the presentation and then exhibited on a timeline to provide information about something that happened during each year.

4. Give an opening about the three events to your fellow timeline historians.

Family Ties to History

Name: _____ **Date:** _____

The Parts of an Opening:

Written Report (Compose a report from your researched information)

★ Conduct research to find information about events from the year you were born, the year one of your parents was your age, and the year one of your grandparents was your age. Look for facts that are interesting, accurate, and clearly connected to the years you are focusing on. If your teacher has asked you to follow certain research guidelines, be sure you follow them correctly.

★ Write in the "voice" of a historian who is writing about events on a timeline.

★ Write about all three events you have identified.

★ Include plenty of accurate, carefully developed information about the events.

★ Use your best handwriting or word processing skills.

★ You may have your report with you when you present your opening.

Visual Aid (Make timeline templates to show information about the events)

★ Produce three timeline templates, one for each event that you are presenting.

★ Organize information so that it can be easily explained and understood.

★ Plan the opening so there is a natural place to talk about each template.

Oral Presentation (Present your proposal to your fellow historians)

★ Use good posture at all times.

★ Have regular eye contact with various people in your audience.

★ Speak clearly and be sure everyone can hear you.

★ Speak in the voice of a historian who is talking to his or her colleagues.

★ Refer smoothly and naturally to your visual aid at least once during the opening.

Questions and Answers

★ Answer questions about the events from the audience.

★ It's okay to say "I don't know" if you don't know an answer.

Continued ➡

Family Ties to History (continued)

Hints for a Successful Opening:

★ Do a thorough and complete job of conducting research. Your opening is only as good as the information you present. Find appropriate and interesting facts that help describe and explain the events you have chosen.

★ Take the scenario for the project seriously, and work to build the "voice" of a timeline historian into your written report and oral presentation. In other words, try to write and talk like a historian would. It will make your opening more fun and more authentic.

★ Practice! Practice! Practice! Practice your opening with a parent or friends. Focus on the five Oral Presentation points listed in "The Parts of an Opening."

Here are examples of how a student might present various parts of this opening:

Introduction

"Good morning. My name is Johan and I have an opening for you. My opening is called Family Ties to History. As timeline historians, we are all interested in when things happened and how they can be described. We are creating a timeline to show what has happened during our own lives, our parents' lives, and our grandparents' lives. My presentation today will be about events from these three years . . ."

The Three Years

Let's take a look at the year 1957, when my Grandpa Hendriks was my age. This was a fascinating year, as I found out when I interviewed my grandpa. He agrees with me that one of the most interesting events of that year was . . ."

Connection to the Three Visual Aids

"As you can see in my visual for the year I was born, this photograph that my dad took shows what the downtown streets looked like when they were flooded on July 12, and the graph beneath it shows the hour-by-hour amount of rainfall that fell over a 24-hour period . . ."

Ending

"Thank you for listening to my report on my family ties to history. Are there any questions?"

Family Ties Timeline
Event Template

Name: _____ **Date:** _____

_____

_____   _____   _____   _____

Family Ties Timeline Event Template (Completion Guidelines)

Name: _____ Date: _____

1. Write on the line how the year was determined.

For example:

"I was born in" or **"My mom was born in"** _____

2. Write the year in large numbers on the lines below:

_____ 2 _____ 0 _____ 0 _____ 1 _____

3. Put a picture of you, your parent, or your grandparent here. If a picture is not possible, make a drawing or write something about the person to help your audience know him or her better.

4. Write a summary of the event in one or two sentences.

5. Put a drawing or graphic in this space to help illustrate or explain something about the event.

Featured Expert Series

Content Focus: Any Content Area

Topic and Assignment

Television news magazine programs have been viewer favorites for years. The journalists who produce these shows report and interpret stories on many topics to help inform people about current or historical events and issues. Often, experts are used to give the stories authority and authenticity. For this project, students assume the role of "featured experts." They are allowed to choose any topic, within established guidelines, about which to develop their own expertise. Their task is to prepare a presentation for a television news magazine segment called "The Featured Expert Series." Each day a new expert is given an opportunity to share his or her knowledge with program viewers.

During this project students will:

- Choose a topic about which to become an "expert."

- Conduct research to gather information about the topic.

- Write a report about the topic.

- Develop a visual aid to help in the presentation of the topic.

- Present an opening titled "The Featured Expert Series."

Materials

 Reference materials related to the topics students are studying

 Poster board and materials to make visual aids

Student Handouts

- Assignment Sheet: Featured Expert Series

- Instructions for Making an Opening: Featured Expert Series

- Topic Selection Form: Featured Expert Series

- TV Magazine Visual Planner

Note: While these forms provide all the materials students need to complete a "Featured Expert Series" opening, the CD-ROM included with this book contains a more detailed poster-making project that may be of interest for this and other openings.

Content Standards

This project can address standards in any core content area, depending upon your chosen topics.

Idea for Introducing the Opening

Hold a class discussion about what makes someone an expert. Provide several examples of experts and their areas of expertise.

Project Steps

1. Before introducing the project to students, decide what guidelines or parameters you want to establish for topic selection. This project has the potential to be completely open-ended, giving students the ability to choose virtually any topic, or it can be very controlled and narrowly focused. Whatever way you choose to do it, prepare ahead of time so students can follow your directions. Here are several options you may choose from:

   - Allow students to choose any topic that meets your standards for classroom appropriateness. This would mean that students could focus on hobbies, personal interests, current events, local issues, or any number of other topics that may be meaningful or interesting to them.

   - Reduce the scope of choice to any topic that is connected to the current curriculum. This can be accomplished by telling students that they may choose any topic that has been covered in class or that they can find in one of their textbooks.

- Limit student choices to a single content area, and focus on that area only. For example, you might decide to have all of the openings be related to science. In this case, any science topic that aligns with your grade's science curriculum would be an acceptable topic choice.

- Narrow the range of topics even further by focusing on a single unit of study. For example, you might decide to have the project emphasize the Age of Exploration. Students would be restricted to choosing topics related to the history, economics, geography, biographies, and human drama of that time period.

- Focus the project on a single topic that has many possible angles, sub-topics, categories, or areas of interest. For example, have all of the openings be related to the sun. A few of the many possible choices that students could make are: sunspots, gravity, photosynthesis, seasons, global warming, phases of the moon, tides, myths and legends, solar wind, northern lights, birth of stars, and death of stars, just to name a few.

2. Introduce the project scenario to the students: *You are an expert on a topic that will be the focus of an upcoming broadcast of a popular television news magazine program. The program includes a segment called the "Featured Expert Series," and you have been invited to make a guest appearance to share your expertise. Your job is to develop an informative and interesting presentation that will help viewers understand the topic better.*

3. Decide what kind of "set" you want for these openings. The scenario places students in a television studio, where they provide expert insights and information about specific topics to a TV audience. You might want to have students sit at a table or in a more relaxed setting than is typical for other openings. You could also arrange for a moderator or interviewer to introduce the students and possibly ask questions or provide feedback. This could be another student, or you could play the role.

4. Hand out the Featured Expert Series assignment sheet and read through it with the class. Discuss any requirements that might be unclear to students. Clarify what topics are available for students to focus on. If you have decided to allow students to choose any topic related to the curriculum, you may use the Topic Selection Form (page 185) to help them identify topics. Otherwise, it is a good idea to conduct a class discussion to generate a list of acceptable topics from which students may choose. You might want to introduce the project and give students a homework assignment to identify possible topics to contribute in a discussion the following day.

5. Collect the students' topic choices and check for appropriateness and availability of information. If you use the Topic Selection Form, you can ask that it be turned in to receive your approval.

6. Decide what your expectations will be for the written and visual parts of the assignment. Give students the Instructions for Making an Opening handout and the TV Magazine Visual Planner. These provide the basic requirements of the opening and offer a good way to review with students what your expectations are and what they need to do to prepare for their presentations. Students should use the TV Magazine Visual Planner as a rough draft; then create their final visual on a new piece of paper or poster board.

7. Communicate with parents about the upcoming opening to inform them about the theme being covered and the requirements of students when making an opening. A good way to do this is to send the Instructions for Making an Opening handout home with students. (Also see pages 60–63 for parent letters to adapt.) Ask them to practice with their children at home.

8. As needed, model part or all of a "Featured Expert Series" opening for the class. Demonstrate how to present the information ("I am an expert on ___ and I have been asked to spend a few minutes to help you understand this topic. Let me begin by telling you . . ."). Each student is expected to present his or her topic as if talking to a television audience.

9. Schedule time for students to prepare and present their openings. Preparation time will vary depending on your expectations, the amount of prep work you assign as homework, and the readiness of your students. In general, this project should require no more than about four hours of class time prior to students making their presentations. This time is typically spread over several days.

10. *Optional:* Have students who finish their projects early create a "Featured Expert Series" sign to serve as a backdrop to the opening presentations. Students could also create a television studio setting in which to present their openings.

11. Make copies of the assessment form on page 208. Complete the form for each student after he or she has presented an opening.

12. Proceed with "Featured Expert Series" openings as you have planned them. As necessary, prompt children to fulfill the key elements of the opening as they make their presentations.

Ideas for Extending or Modifying the Opening

1. Make audio and/or video recordings of the openings. The presence of a video camera in the room gives the scenario authenticity. You might even create podcasts or videos of your students' work and post them to your classroom website. Be sure that you are within your district's policy guidelines before posting images of your students on the Web.

2. Implement a small group project that involves an anchorperson and two or three "experts" that the anchor can introduce and/or interview. The dynamics of the project will change when implemented in this way. Each small group can work together to conduct research and to identify logical connections among their topics that will make smooth transitions. They might decide to focus on related topics that complement each other or take a point/counterpoint approach to show two or more conflicting sides to a topic. This form of the project requires the creation of a script to provide an organizing structure for the presentation.

3. Incorporate a multimedia requirement into the project. For example, students can create video clips (they might interview parents or grandparents), show websites that provide relevant information, or produce slide shows that include maps, photographs, newspaper headlines, and quotes from famous people associated with events. The text, graphics, and sounds that students use would be what a viewing audience would see and hear if the presentation were actually being broadcast on television.

4. Design the project to be a culminating activity for the year, and invite parents to sit in the audience when their children present. In this case, student presentations should be directly connected to the curriculum and should reflect substantial learning that has taken place over the course of the year. In other words, students are demonstrating for their parents that they have learned at a deep and meaningful level.

5. Use the project to focus on current events. This works best if you intentionally and substantially discuss and debate current events for some time in class prior to initiating the project. Have students identify a range of topics and begin following them in newspapers and magazines. Cut out articles and put them on bulletin boards for students to see regularly. Current events is a viable focus only if students have enough background knowledge to understand basic cause and effect relationships, unless the topics are restricted to things like natural or man-made disasters and one-time occurrences. However, the best approach is to have each student choose a current event and then learn about background history to help explain how and why the event happened.

Classroom Differentiation Example: Ms. Kiley

Strategies: choice-as-motivator, multiple intelligences, flexible grouping

Ms. Kiley is excited about having her students do "Featured Expert Series" openings. She plans to differentiate the project in three ways. First, each student will choose a personally interesting topic that is connected to at least one content standard; the topic can come from any subject area, so long as it is directly related to the curriculum. Second, she has developed a number of options for the visual aid, and students may choose one that fits with their own type of multiple intelligence. Third, she is willing to let students work in pairs or small groups if they agree to align their topics and plan a cooperative/collaborative presentation.

Jacob prefers to work on his own. He is interested in chemistry and wants to become an expert on atoms and molecules. He has decided to use the multimedia visual aid option, so he is developing a presentation that includes computer graphics and video.

Janice will also work alone. She wants to be an expert on solving algebra equations. Janice will use the table-chart-graph option for her visual aid. Her goal is to identify and describe several kinds of equations and to systematically demonstrate a step-by-step procedure for solving certain kinds of equations.

Kwame, Zane, and Lisa have gotten permission to work together in a small group. They want to be experts on slavery and its impact on African-American families before the Civil War. Each student will focus on a different aspect of slavery and family. They will use the collage option for their visual aids, combining their own artwork with images from the Internet.

Featured Expert Series

Name: _____ **Date:** _____

You are an expert on a topic that will be the focus of an upcoming broadcast of a popular television news magazine program. The program includes a segment called the "Featured Expert Series," and you have been invited to make a guest appearance to share your expertise. Your job is to develop an informative and interesting presentation that will help viewers understand the topic better.

I am an expert on this topic: _____

1. Get approval from the TV program's executive producer (your teacher) to focus on the topic you have recorded above. Have you received approval to work with this topic?

    Yes _____   No _____

2. Conduct research to discover interesting information to share during your opening. In the space below, give a brief summary of the information you plan to present:

    _____

    _____

    _____

    _____

    _____

3. Write a report about the topic. Write in the "voice" of an expert who is sharing information with a television audience.

4. Use the TV Magazine Visual Planner to create a visual aid to go along with your opening. The visual aid should provide clear, detailed information about some part of the topic you are presenting.

5. Give an opening about the topic to the television audience.

Featured Expert Series

Name: _____ **Date:** _____

The Parts of an Opening:

Written Report (Compose a report from your research information)

★ Conduct research to find information about your chosen area of expertise. Look for facts that are interesting, accurate, and clearly connected to the topic you are focusing on. If your teacher has asked you to follow certain research guidelines, be sure you follow them correctly.

★ Write in the "voice" of an expert who is being featured on a TV news magazine program.

★ Write about the topic that you have identified as your area of expertise.

★ Include plenty of accurate, carefully developed information about your topic.

★ Use your best handwriting or word processing skills.

★ You may have your report with you when you present your opening.

Visual Aid (Make a poster to show information about your topic)

★ Produce a visual aid that is clearly related to the topic.

★ Organize information so that it can be easily explained and understood.

★ Plan the opening so there is a natural place to talk about the visual aid.

Oral Presentation (Present your proposal to a television audience)

★ Use good posture at all times.

★ Have regular eye contact with various people in your audience and camera if there is one.

★ Speak clearly and be sure everyone can hear you.

★ Speak in the voice of an expert who is talking to people watching a TV program.

★ Refer smoothly and naturally to your visual aid at least once during the opening.

Questions and Answers

★ Answer questions about your topic from the studio audience.

★ It's okay to say "I don't know" if you don't know an answer.

Continued ➡

Featured Expert Series (continued)

Hints for a Successful Opening:

★ Choose a topic that interests you personally. If you are going to take on the role of an expert, it is important that you choose a topic that is meaningful to you.

★ Do a thorough and complete job of conducting research. Your opening is only as good as the information you present. Find appropriate and interesting facts that are clearly related to the topic you have chosen.

★ Take the scenario for the project seriously and work to build the "voice" of an expert into your written report and oral presentation. In other words, try to write and talk like a television expert would. It will make your opening more fun and more authentic.

★ Practice! Practice! Practice! Practice your opening with a parent or friends. Focus on the five Oral Presentation points listed in "The Parts of an Opening."

Here are examples of how a student might present various parts of this opening:

Introduction

"Good morning. My name is Jocelyn and I have an opening for you. Thank you for inviting me to be a featured expert on this program. I'm here because I believe I have valuable information to share with you about the early days of our democracy . . ."

Providing Information About Topic

"I hope our viewers can understand what an important moment it was when men like Thomas Jefferson and John Hancock signed the Declaration of Independence. They had no idea what the result would be, but by signing they were committing treason against Great Britain, and they knew they could be hanged for it . . ."

Connection to the Visual Aid

"I have brought along a reproduction of the Declaration of Independence for the audience to see. The original handwritten document is on display at the National Archives in Washington, D.C. This picture was not taken of the original document. It is from an engraving that was made in 1823. I also have a map that shows which colony each person who signed the Declaration of Independence came from . . ."

Ending

"Thank you for tuning in to my discussion of the signing of the Declaration of Independence. Are there any questions from the studio audience?"

Featured Expert Series

Name: _____ **Date:** _____

This form is designed to help you choose a topic that is a part of your grade's standard core curriculum. You may choose any topic that has been covered in class or that you can find in one of your textbooks. After looking over the information on this page, fill out the bottom part and turn it in to your teacher to get approval for the topic you have chosen.

English/Language Arts Options

★ Choose a piece of literature and develop a presentation like a book report.

★ Choose an author you have studied this year.

★ Choose a piece of your own writing from a class assignment to share with the audience.

Mathematics Options

★ Demonstrate two different ways to solve a story problem taken from your book.

★ Explain a mathematics concept and show how the concept is applied in problem solving. For example, demonstrate the use of the distributive property or the area model for multiplying fractions or mixed numbers.

★ Explain where or how a math concept might be applied in a real-world situation.

Science Options

★ Demonstrate the procedure of an experiment that you have conducted or observed this year. Explain the results and conclusions.

★ Choose a topic or concept you have studied this year.

★ Identify a scientist and report on his or her discoveries, theories, or inventions.

Continued ➡

Featured Expert Series (continued)

Social Studies Options

* ★ Choose a person or event you have studied this year.
* ★ Choose a concept you have studied this year, such as supply and demand, push-pull immigration model, or checks and balances.
* ★ Describe a culture you have studied, or compare and contrast two cultures.

What content area will you focus on?

- ❏ English/Language Arts
- ❏ Science
- ❏ Mathematics
- ❏ Social Studies

Record a specific topic here: _____

I know this topic is part of our curriculum because:

- ❏ We covered it in class discussions or assignments.
- ❏ I found it in the textbook on page _____
- ❏ Other: _____

❏ Teacher Approval

TV Magazine Visual Planner

Name: _____ **Date:** _____

Sketch a plan for your poster in the space below. Once you have a plan you like, make a large poster on poster paper.

Featured Expert Series • Featured Expert Series • Featured Expert Series • Featured Expert Series

Additional Handouts

Student Preparation Materials

- Focus Wheel: 3 Writing Skills
- Focus Wheel: 3 Speaking Skills
- Focus Wheel: 3 Showing Skills
- Focus Wheel: 3 Answering Skills
- Standard Openings Format: Sign In
- Standard Openings Format: Introduce Yourself
- Standard Openings Format: Explain Your Topic
- Standard Openings Format: Present Your Information
- Standard Openings Format: Talk About Your Visual Aid
- Standard Openings Format: Conclude your Opening
- Standard Openings Format: Answer Questions
- Is My Opening Ready? (Early Elementary)
- Is My Opening Ready? (Middle Elementary)
- Is My Opening Ready? (Upper Elementary)
- Parent-Student Opening Agreement
- Challenge Option Request Form

Assessment Materials

- Starter Opening Feedback Form
- Opening Assessment (Early Elementary)
- Opening Assessment (Middle Elementary)
- Opening Assessment (Upper Elementary)
- Listening Assessment (Early Elementary)
- Listening Assessment (Middle Elementary)
- Listening Assessment (Upper Elementary)

Audience Feedback Materials

- Audience Feedback Participation Form
- Audience Feedback: Eye Contact
- Audience Feedback: Voice Projection
- Audience Feedback: Visual Materials
- Audience Feedback: Questions for the Presenter
- Audience Feedback: Central Idea

Teacher Tools

- Openings Planner
- Certificate of Achievement

Focus Wheel: 3 Writing Skills

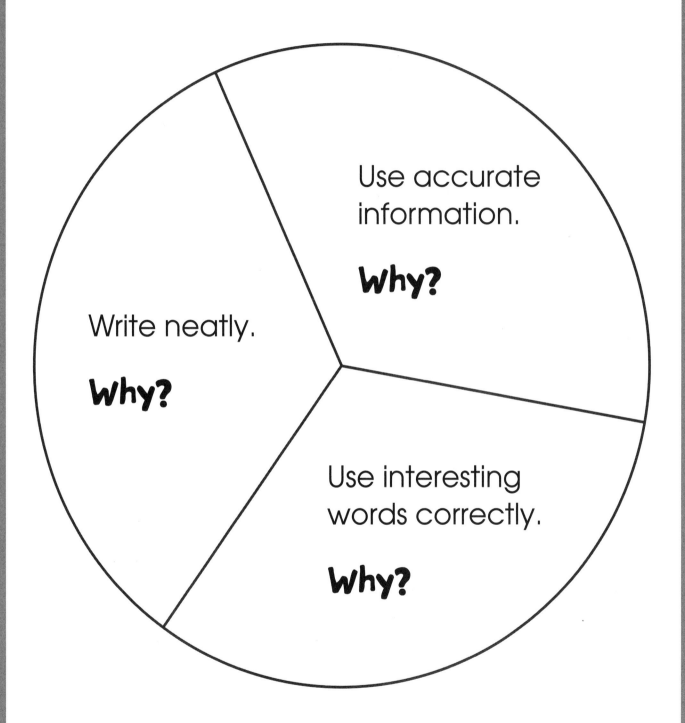

Use accurate information.

Why?

Write neatly.

Why?

Use interesting words correctly.

Why?

Focus Wheel: 3 Speaking Skills

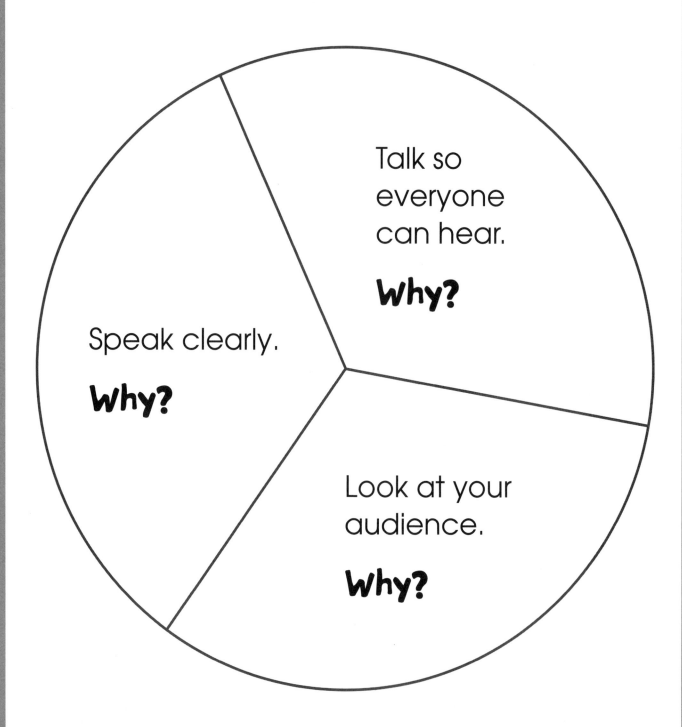

Talk so everyone can hear.

Why?

Speak clearly.

Why?

Look at your audience.

Why?

Focus Wheel: 3 Showing Skills

Include a picture or drawing on your poster.

Why?

Write a caption under each picture.

Why? What is a caption?

Think of ways to make your poster interesting.

How? Why?

Focus Wheel: 3 Answering Skills

It's OK to say you don't know the answer to a question.

Why?

Ask: "Does anyone have a question?"

Why?

Give your best answer based on what you know.

Why?

sign in

Standard Openings Format

Introduce yourself

From *Teaching Kids to Be Confident, Effective Communicators* by Phil Schlemmer, M.Ed., and Dori Schlemmer, copyright © 2011. Free Spirit Publishing Inc., Minneapolis, MN; 800-735-7323; www.freespirit.com. This page may be reproduced for individual, classroom, and small group work only. For all other uses, contact www.freespirit.com/company/permissions.cfm.

Explain your topic

Standard Openings Format

Present your information

From *Teaching Kids to Be Confident, Effective Communicators* by Phil Schlemmer, M.Ed., and Dori Schlemmer, copyright © 2011. Free Spirit Publishing Inc., Minneapolis, MN; 800-735-7323; www.freespirit.com. This page may be reproduced for individual, classroom, and small group work only. For all other uses, contact www.freespirit.com/company/permissions.cfm.

Talk about your visual aid

Standard Openings Format

Conclude your opening

Answer questions

Is My Opening Ready?

(Early Elementary)

Name: _____

Opening Topic: _____

	Yes	No
Do I know how to begin my opening?		
Do I know how to end my opening?		
Are my written materials ready?		
Are my visual materials ready?		
Have I practiced my opening?		
Am I ready to do my opening in front of my friends?		
Comments:		

Parent Signature: _____

Teacher Signature: _____

Student Signature: _____

Is My Opening Ready?

(Middle Elementary)

Name: _____

Opening Topic: _____

	Yes	No
Do I have a beginning for my opening?		
Do I have an ending for my opening?		
Are my written materials ready?		
Are my visual materials ready?		
Have I gathered enough information for my opening?		
Have I practiced my opening?		
Do I know my topic well enough to answer basic questions?		
Am I ready to do my opening in front of an audience?		
Comments:		

Parent Signature: _____

Teacher Signature: _____

Student Signature: _____

Is My Opening Ready?

(Upper Elementary)

Name: _____

Opening Topic: _____

	Yes	No
Have I chosen an appropriate focus for my opening?		
Do I have an interesting or "catchy" introduction for my opening?		
Do I have a clear ending or wrap-up for my opening?		
Are my written materials ready?		
Are my visual materials ready?		
Have I conducted enough research?		
Am I certain about the accuracy of all my information?		
Do all the points in my presentation relate to my topic?		
Have I practiced my opening?		
Am I ready to answer questions about my presentation?		
Do I feel well prepared?		
Comments:		

Parent Signature: _____

Teacher Signature: _____

Student Signature: _____

Parent-Student Opening Agreement

Student Agreement

I agree to do these things to the best of my ability:

1) Learn as much as I can about my topic.

2) Finish each part of the assignment sheet that my teacher has given me.

3) Spend time practicing my opening.

4) Be ready to do my opening when it is my turn.

Signature: _____

Date: _____

Parent Agreement

I have read my child's assignment sheet and understand what the expectations of an opening are. I will talk with my child about working hard to complete the requirements with quality, and I will spend time listening to my child practice his or her opening before it is due to be presented in class.

Signature: _____

Date: _____

Notes:

Challenge Option Request Form

Name: _____ **Date:** _____

A challenge option is a special feature that you would like to include in your opening in addition to the regular assignment. It may be a specific use of technology, working with another student to coordinate your presentations, bringing in an adult as a special resource, or something else—whatever you want to do to increase the interest or challenge of your assignment.

Name of Class Opening Project: _____

Your Topic: _____

Describe the challenge option you would like to add:

_____

_____

_____

_____

_____

_____

Teacher Approval: ❏ Yes   ❏ No   ❏ Maybe

Comment: _____

_____

Teacher Signature: _____ Date: _____

Parent Approval: ❏ Yes   ❏ No   ❏ Maybe

Comment: _____

_____

Parent Signature: _____ Date: _____

Starter Opening Feedback Form

Presenter's Name: Topic: Date:	Excellent!	Needs a Little Work	Not There Yet
1. Had a positive attitude about the starter opening.			
2. Began with a simple introduction of himself or herself.			
3. Told what the topic is.			
4. Had proper body posture.			
5. Had good eye contact with members of the audience.			
6. Spoke clearly in a voice that all could hear.			
7. Used proper vocabulary.			
8. Presented correct information.			
9. Ended with a clear, appropriate conclusion.			
10. Answered questions from the audience (optional).			
11.			
12.			
Comments:			
Glow 1:			
Glow 2:			
Grow:			

Opening Assessment

(Early Elementary)

Name: Date:	Yes!	Needs Work
Topic:		
Wrote his or her name on the board legibly, with the first letter capitalized and with proper letter formation.		
Willingly presented in front of the class (may have needed some coaxing).		
Gave the opening a beginning or introduction.		
Stood with good posture and used hands appropriately.		
Used a drawing or other visual aid to help with the presentation.		
Spoke loudly enough for good listeners to hear some of the time.		
Looked at someone in the audience at least once.		
Signaled the end of the opening by saying "Thank you for listening."		
Answered one question with some help or guidance.		
Showed confidence while presenting.		
Followed the assignment and completed all requirements.		
Comments:		

Opening Assessment

(Middle Elementary)

3 = Exceeds Expectations • **2** = Meets Expectations • **1** = Needs Work to Meet Expectations

Name:	Date:
Topic:	

Oral Presentation	Score
Gave the opening an appropriate beginning or introduction, including a clear statement of the opening's topic ("My opening is about . . .").	
Stood with good posture and used hands appropriately.	
Spoke loudly enough for good listeners to hear most of the time.	
Spoke clearly enough for good listeners to understand most of the time.	
Had eye contact with at least two different people in the audience.	
Presented correct information that made sense and was well organized.	
Presented enough information to cover the topic.	
Used correct vocabulary in most cases throughout the presentation.	
Gave the opening an ending so that the audience knew it was over.	
Showed confidence while presenting.	
Followed the assignment and completed all requirements.	
Visual Aid	**Score**
Created a visual aid that related to the opening in some way.	
The visual aid could be seen by most people in the audience.	
Used the visual aid to help with the presentation and told what it was or explained what it showed.	
Writing	**Score**
Wrote a report or story that had correct, easy-to-understand information.	
Used correct punctuation, capitalization, spelling, and grammar.	
Used complete sentences in most of the report or story.	
Question and Answer	**Score**
Gave a complete answer to at least two questions with little help or guidance.	
Comments:	

Opening Assessment

(Upper Elementary)

3 = Exceeds Expectations • **2** = Meets Expectations • **1** = Needs Work to Meet Expectations

Name:	Date:
Topic:	

Oral Presentation	Score
Gave the opening an interesting and inviting beginning.	
Had appropriate posture, body movement, and facial expressions throughout the opening.	
Spoke loudly and clearly enough for everyone to hear and understand.	
Spoke slowly and distinctly and used an expressive tone of voice most of the time.	
Had regular eye contact with a variety of people throughout the opening.	
Presented enough accurate, connected information to cover one aspect of the topic adequately.	
Used correct vocabulary and understood what all words meant.	
Ended the opening with a well-developed conclusion statement.	
Followed the assignment and completed all requirements.	
Visual Aid	**Score**
Created a drawing or other visual aid that was clearly related to the opening and provided correct information about the topic.	
The visual aid captured the attention and interest of the audience.	
Referred to the visual periodically during the opening to help present information.	
Writing	**Score**
Wrote a report or story that included accurate, clearly written information that was relevant to the presentation (few extraneous facts).	
Used correct punctuation, capitalization, spelling, and grammar.	
Produced correctly developed, clearly connected paragraphs.	
Developed a recognizable central idea with supporting details and examples.	
Chose appropriate vocabulary that contributed to the writing's effectiveness.	
Question and Answer	**Score**
Demonstrated understanding of the topic by giving complete, correct answers.	
Provided an accurate description of the opening's central idea when asked.	
Comments:	

Listening Assessment
(Early Elementary)

Name of Listener: Date: Name of Presenter:	Yes!	Needs Work
Used good listening manners (listened quietly without interrupting)		
Used appropriate body language (eye contact, nods, posture, facial expressions)		
Ignored distractions from others in the audience		
Provided positive feedback at the end of the opening (applauded, made positive comments, or asked good questions)		
Comments:		

Listening Assessment
(Early Elementary)

Name of Listener: Date: Name of Presenter:	Yes!	Needs Work
Used good listening manners (listened quietly without interrupting)		
Used appropriate body language (eye contact, nods, posture, facial expressions)		
Ignored distractions from others in the audience		
Provided positive feedback at the end of the opening (applauded, made positive comments, or asked good questions)		
Comments:		

Listening Assessment
(Middle Elementary)

3 = Exceeds Expectations • **2** = Meets Expectations • **1** = Needs Work to Meet Expectations

Name of Listener: Date:	Score
Name of Presenter:	
Demonstrated good listening manners (listened quietly without interrupting)	
Used appropriate body language (eye contact, nods, posture, facial expressions)	
Seemed interested in what was said (did not act bored)	
Ignored distractions from others in the audience or from the environment	
Showed patience by listening to the whole message without interrupting	
Provided positive feedback at the end of the opening (applauded, made positive comments, or asked good questions)	
Comments:	

Listening Assessment
(Middle Elementary)

3 = Exceeds Expectations • **2** = Meets Expectations • **1** = Needs Work to Meet Expectations

Name of Listener: Date:	Score
Name of Presenter:	
Demonstrated good listening manners (listened quietly without interrupting)	
Used appropriate body language (eye contact, nods, posture, facial expressions)	
Seemed interested in what was said (did not act bored)	
Ignored distractions from others in the audience or from the environment	
Showed patience by listening to the whole message without interrupting	
Provided positive feedback at the end of the opening (applauded, made positive comments, or asked good questions)	
Comments:	

Listening Assessment

(Upper Elementary)

3 = Exceeds Expectations • 2 = Meets Expectations • 1 = Needs Work to Meet Expectations	
Name of Listener: **Name of Presenter:** **Date:**	**Score**
Demonstrated good listening manners (listened quietly without interrupting)	
Used appropriate body language (eye contact, nods, posture, facial expressions)	
Seemed interested in what was said (did not act bored)	
Ignored or adjusted to peer and environmental distractions	
Showed patience by listening to the whole message without interrupting	
Asked clarifying questions to gain a better understanding or more information	
Participated in discussions about what was said	
Provided positive feedback at the end of the opening (applauded or made positive comments)	
Comments:	

Audience Feedback Participation Form

Put dates, checkmarks, or other symbols in the appropriate boxes to indicate that each student has contributed audience feedback during opening presentations.

Name	Eye Contact			Voice Projection			Visual Materials			Questions			Central Idea		

Eye Contact

Presenter:	Topic:
My Name:	Date:

Feedback on how well the presenter looked at me:

	I had good eye contact several times.
	I had some eye contact.
	I had almost no eye contact.

Feedback on how well the presenter looked at others in the room:

	The presenter looked regularly at different people.
	The presenter looked at some people once in a while.
	The presenter looked at almost nobody.

What I thought was good about this opening:

What I thought could be improved about this opening:

Voice Projection

Presenter:	Topic:
My Name:	Date:

Feedback about the presenter's voice projection:

	His or her voice was loud enough; I had no problem hearing.
	I could hear OK, but it was soft.
	I had trouble hearing; it was too soft most of the time.

Feedback about how well I could understand the presenter's words:

	His or her words were very clear; I had no problem understanding.
	I could understand most of what was said.
	The words were not very clear; it was hard to understand.

What I thought was good about this opening:

What I thought could be improved about this opening:

Visual Materials

Presenter:	Topic:
My Name:	Date:

Feedback about how well I could see the presenter's visual materials:

	All parts of the visual were large enough and were easy to see.
	I could see everything, but some parts should be larger or highlighted better.
	I had trouble seeing some things because they were too small or not highlighted.

Feedback about how well I could understand the presenter's visual materials:

	The information was very clear; I had no problem understanding.
	I could understand most of the information.
	The information was not very clear; it was hard to understand.

What I thought was good about this opening:

What I thought could be improved about this opening:

Questions for the Presenter

Presenter:	Topic:
My Name:	Date:

As you listen to the presenter, think of at least one question to ask during the Question/Answer time that is directly related to the topic. Write your question(s) here:

What I thought was good about this opening:

What I thought could be improved about this opening:

Central Idea

Presenter:	Topic:
My Name:	Date:

As you listen to the presenter, decide what you believe is the central idea of the opening. Your feedback to the presenter will be to explain why you think this is the central idea. Write the central idea here, along with your reasons for thinking so:

What I thought was good about this opening:

What I thought could be improved about this opening:

Openings Planner

Content Focus: _____

Content Standards (in addition to the six language arts strands):

Overview of opening:

Start openings on: _____ Finish openings on: _____

Written Report:	
Oral Presentation:	
Visual Aid:	

During this project students will:

Continued ➡

Openings Planner (continued)

Handouts:

Materials:

Use of Technology:

Resources:

Special Preparation:

Project Steps:

Notes:

Certificate of Achievement

OPENINGS

This certificate of achievement is awarded to:

_____

For successfully presenting an opening titled:

_____

_____
(date)

Congratulations! You are on your way to becoming a skilled communicator.

_____
Teacher

_____
Name of School

Recommended Resources

Building a School Website by Wanda Wigglebits (www.wigglebits.com). If you'd like to make a class or school website—for the Community Cam project or to show off any or all of your group's openings—this learn-as-you-go, hands-on Web project is a great way to go. Teachers and kids can do it together.

CASEL: Collaborative for Academic, Social, and Emotional Learning (www. casel.org). A leading advocate for establishing social-emotional learning (SEL) as an essential part of education. Their website provides basic guidelines for SEL, answers FAQs, and provides resources for educators.

Education World (www.educationworld.com). This website provides educators with lesson plans, professional development, and help integrating technology into the classroom. You can also access national education standards here.

Fact Monster (www.factmonster.com). Fact Monster is a kid-friendly website with basic information about lots of topics—a great resource for openings, particularly the information about years needed for "Family Ties to History."

Edutopia: Teaching Module— Project-Based Learning (www.edutopia.org/teaching-module-pbl). Among many other things, you will find in-depth, carefully organized coverage of essential questions regarding project-based learning. You will find a wealth of ideas, resources, and supporting research at this site. Emphasis is placed on the use of technology, but you don't need to be a technology wizard to make good use of the information provided. The only requirement is that you recognize the value of projects and be an advocate for kids and their learning needs.

"Howard Gardner, Multiple Intelligences and Education" (www.infed.org/thinkers/gardner.htm). An article providing detailed information about multiple intelligences, including other possible intelligences being considered.

Illinois Learning Standards for Social-Emotional Learning (SEL) (www.isbe.net/ils/social_emotional/standards.htm). Illinois is a leading state in developing SEL education goals, standards, and descriptors, and the Illinois State Board of Education offers their complete listing here.

Microsoft Education: Lesson Plans, Tutorials, and Education Resources (www.microsoft.com/education/default.mspx). This website provides resources for educators—including lesson plans and professional development—as well as for students, including templates for projects and presentations, student stories, and product tutorials. Type "timeline" into the search window to find a quick, easy way to use Microsoft Excel to make timelines (for example, for the "Family Ties to History" opening).

Weblogg-ed (weblogg-ed.com). Weblogg-ed is a website dedicated to discussions and reflections on the use of blogs, wikis, RSS, audiocasts, and other Web-related technologies in the K–12 realm, technologies that, as Will Richardson, the site administrator says, "are transforming classrooms around the world." If you want to keep up-to-date on discussions of technology in the classroom, or if you want to learn how other teachers are making classroom presentations more public via the World Wide Web, this is a great blog to follow. Click the "ed blogs" tab for links to hundreds of classroom, teacher, principal, education, brain research, and other education-related blogs.

Bibliography

Bar-On, R., Maree, J.G., and Elias, M.J. (eds.) (2007). *Educating People to Be Emotionally Intelligent.* Westport, CT: Praeger Publishers.

Bloom, B., (ed.) (1956). *Taxonomy of Educational Objectives, Handbook 1: Cognitive Domain.* Reading, MA: Addison Wesley.

Caine, R., Caine, G., Klimek, K., and McClintic, C. (2005). *12 Brain/Mind Learning Principles in Action.* Thousand Oaks, CA: Corwin Press.

Elias, M.J., and Arnold, H. (2006). *The Educator's Guide to Emotional Intelligence and Academic Achievement: Social-Emotional Learning in the Classroom.* Thousand Oaks, CA: Corwin Press.

Gardner, H. (1983). *Frames of Mind: The Theory of Multiple Intelligences.* New York: Basic Books.

Gardner, H. (2000). *Intelligences Reframed: Multiple Intelligences for the 21st Century.* New York: Basic Books.

Gregory, G., and Chapman, C. (2002). *Differentiated Instruction Strategies: One Size Doesn't Fit All.* Thousand Oaks, CA: Corwin Press.

Heacox, D. (2002). *Differentiating Instruction in the Regular Classroom.* Minneapolis: Free Spirit Publishing.

International Reading Association and the National Council of Teachers of English (1996). *Standards for the English Language Arts.* Newark, DE: International Reading Association; Urbana, IL: National Council of Teachers of English.

Jensen, E. (2003). *Tools for Engagement: Managing Emotional States for Learner Success.* San Diego, CA: The Brain Store.

Kingore, B. (2004). *Differentiation: Simplified, Realistic, and Effective: How to Challenge Advanced Potentials in Mixed-Ability Classrooms.* Austin, TX: Professional Associates Publishing.

National Center on Education and the Economy and the University of Pittsburgh (2001). *Speaking and Listening for Preschool through Third Grade.* Washington, DC: New Standards Speaking and Listening Committee; Peak Printers.

National Council for the Social Studies (1994). *Expectations of Excellence: Curriculum Standards for Social Studies.* Silver Spring, MD: NCSS Publications.

National Council of Teachers of Mathematics (2000). *Principles and Standards for School Mathematics.* Reston, VA: National Council of Teachers of Mathematics, Inc.

National Research Council (1996). "National Science Education Standards." Washington, DC: National Academy Press.

Neeld, E.C., and Cowan, G. (1986). *Writing.* Glenview, IL: Scott, Foresman.

Schlemmer, P. (1987). *Learning on Your Own* (A five-volume series). West Nyack, NY: Center for Applied Research in Education.

Sousa, D.A. (2005). *How the Brain Learns.* Thousand Oaks, CA: Corwin Press.

Tomlinson, C.A. (2001). *How to Differentiate Instruction in Mixed-Ability Classrooms.* Alexandria, VA: Association for Supervision and Curriculum Development.

Stiggins, R. (2001). *Student-Involved Classroom Assessment.* Upper Saddle River, NJ: Prentice Hall.

Tate, M. (2003). *Worksheets Don't Grow Dendrites.* Thousand Oaks, CA: Corwin Press.

Wiggins, G., and McTighe, J. (2005). *Understanding by Design.* Alexandria, VA: Association for Supervision and Curriculum Development.

Winebrenner, S. (2001). *Teaching Gifted Kids in the Regular Classroom: Strategies and Techniques Every Teacher Can Use to Meet the Academic Needs of the Gifted and Talented.* Minneapolis: Free Spirit Publishing.

Index

About the Authors

Phil Schlemmer, M.Ed., is currently curriculum director for Holland Public Schools in Holland, Michigan. He has been a teacher, administrator, writer, consultant, and curriculum designer since 1973, and during that time has written ten books. His main areas of expertise are differentiated instruction, project-based learning, and instructional innovation. Throughout his career he has focused his efforts on helping students become self-directed, lifelong learners.

Dori Schlemmer designed and developed specialized resource materials for students and staff and worked as the high school career resource technician for the Kentwood, Michigan, Public Schools. For over three decades, she collaborated with her husband Phil researching, writing books, and presenting workshops for educators. Until her death in May 2010, Dori lived with Phil in Kentwood, Michigan.

Teachers, Administrators, Librarians, Counselors, Youth Workers, and Social Workers
Help us create the resources you need to support the kids you serve.

Join the Free Spirit Advisory Board

In order to make our books and other products even more beneficial for children and teens, the Free Spirit Advisory Board provides valuable feedback on content, art, title concepts, and more. You can help us identify what educators need to help kids think for themselves, succeed in school and life, and make a difference in the world. Apply today! For more information, go to **www.freespirit.com/educators**.

More Great Books from Free Spirit

Differentiating Instruction in the Regular Classroom

How to Reach and Teach All Learners, Grades 3–12

by Diane Heacox, Ed.D.

176 pp.; softcover; Macintosh and Windows compatible CD-ROM; 8½" x 11", grades 3–12

Making Differentiation a Habit

How to Ensure Success in Academically Diverse Classrooms

by Diane Heacox, Ed.D.

198 pp.; softcover; Macintosh and Windows compatible CD-ROM; 8½" x 11", grades K–12

Advancing Differentiation

Thinking and Learning for the 21st Century

by Richard M. Cash, Ed.D., foreword by Diane Heacox, Ed.D.

208 pp.; softcover; Macintosh and Windows compatible CD-ROM; 8½" x 11", grades K–12

Teaching Beyond the Test

Differentiated Project-Based Learning in a Standards-Based Age, Grades 6 & Up

by Phil Schlemmer, M.Ed., and Dori Schlemmer

256 pp.; softcover; Macintosh and Windows compatible CD-ROM; 8½" x 11", grades 6 & up

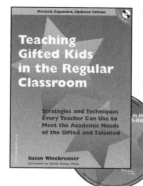

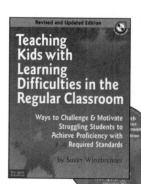